H. RIDER HAGGARD

A VOICE FROM THE INFINITE

H. RIDER HAGGARD

A VOICE FROM THE INFINITE

PETER BERRESFORD ELLIS

Routledge & Kegan Paul

LONDON AND HENLEY

First published in 1978
by Routledge & Kegan Paul Ltd
39 Store Street, London WC1E 7DD and
Broadway House, Newtown Road,
Henley-on-Thames, Oxon RG9 1EN
Photoset in 11 on 13 Garamond by
Kelly and Wright, Bradford-on-Avon, Wiltshire
and printed in Great Britain by
Lowe & Brydone Printers Ltd, Thetford, Norfolk
Plates printed by
Headley Brothers Ltd, Ashford, Kent

ISBN 0 7100 0026 X

S/T EA/TF

To my mother, Eva Daisy Ellis, who
introduced me to the works of
H. Rider Haggard. Dedicated with
love and affection.

CONTENTS

ILLUSTRATIONS

between pages 146 and 147

PREFACE

Because of the subtle change in its general usage, it should be explained that the word *romance* is used throughout this work to mean 'a fictitious narrative in prose or verse which passes beyond the limits of ordinary life'.

I have left the orthography of the Zulu language as Henry Rider Haggard wrote it although the modern accepted form of writing the language in Latin characters differs considerably. The difficulty arises from certain sounds in Zulu which are not used in European languages – mainly three tongue clicks, an imploded *b* and a voiceless fricative represented by *hl*. This makes Zulu phonetics difficult to render. So, for acceptibility for those familiar with Haggard's works, his spellings remain. For example: Cetywayo instead of the now standard form of Cetshwayo, pronounced Tsk-tsk-why-o; Chaka instead of Shaka, pronounced Oo-sha-ge; and Dingaan instead of Dingane, pronounced Di-nga-nyeh.

ACKNOWLEDGMENTS

I would like to express my gratitude to all the many people who have offered me advice and encouragement while I have been researching and writing this biography. In particular, I am indebted to Commander Mark Cheyne RN (Retd) of Ditchingham (Rider Haggard's grandson) and his wife, Nada, without whose generous help, advice and hospitality this book could not have been produced in its present form. I would especially like to acknowledge my indebtedness to them for much of the photographic material in this work.

Special thanks must go for the courteous help and advice of Roger Lancelyn Green who also gave me his unpublished biographical manuscript on Haggard (written in the late 1950s) entitled 'The Adventures of Rider Haggard'.

I would also like to thank A. P. Watt & Son and the National Trust as executors of the Kipling Estate for permission to quote from Kipling's letters to Haggard (Norfolk Record Office MSS. 4694 21/1–42 and 22/1–7) and A. P. Watt & Son and Mark Cheyne as executors of the Haggard Estate for permission to quote from the Haggard Diaries of 1914–25 (Norfolk Record Office MSS. 4694 1/1–22); to acknowledge the help of Michael Horniman of A. P. Watt & Son, Miss Jean M. Kennedy BA, County Archivist of the Norfolk Record Office and her assistant Paul Rutledge; John Gammons of John Murray Ltd; Piers Haggard; Maria V. Soteriades, who helped me with my American researches; and Charles E. Carley of San Francisco for his expertise on Haggard films. Acknowledgment is also due to the Boydell Press and Waveney Publications for permission to quote from *The Cloak That I Left* by Lilias Rider Haggard and to Morton Cohen for permission to quote from his two studies – *Rider Haggard: His Life and Works* and *Rudyard Kipling to Rider Haggard: The Record of a Friendship*.

A special debt of thanks is due to the late Frank Vernon Lay, specialist bookseller and Haggard enthusiast, who not only helped me with items of Haggardiana but was always on hand to give advice and encouragement. He sadly died before the fruition of his enthusiastic support.

Similarly, for advice and encouragement I am grateful to many friends, bibliophiles and Haggard collectors, in Britain, America and Australia.

Lastly an extra-special 'thank you' to Dorothea, my personal She-Who-Must-Be-Obeyed, not only for sharing me with Haggard over the past few years but also for aiding and abetting me in my researches especially on our memorable trip to Norfolk.

In making these acknowledgments, I hasten to add that all interpretations are my own and that any errors that may occur, with all opinions given in this work, are the responsibility of nobody but myself.

Peter Berresford Ellis

INTRODUCTION

> In that book is my philosophy . . . the Eternal
> War between Flesh and Spirit, the Eternal Loneliness
> and Search for Unity. . . .
> Rider Haggard to Rudyard Kipling, 1 August 1923,
> on his book *Wisdom's Daughter*.

A rather tattered manuscript found its way into the hands of the poet and critic William Ernest Henley during the early months of 1885. Henley, who was then editor of Cassell's *Magazine of Art*, was a reader for the firm's book publishing house and the manuscript had been given to him by the editor-in-chief, John Williams, for an assessment. The well-thumbed appearance of the manuscript indicated that it had already been read by a number of publishers and politely returned to the author as unsuitable. Henley, however, became fascinated by the tale, which was a romance set in Africa, and decided to show it to his friend, Andrew Lang, editor of the English edition of *Harper's Magazine*. Lang was very impressed.

On the recommendation of two such eminent men of letters, Cassells decided to offer the author a contract.

The author turned out to be a 29-year-old, newly qualified barrister named Henry Rider Haggard. The book was entitled *King Solomon's Mines* and it had taken Haggard six weeks to write during his spare time. When it was published it was heralded as 'The Most Amazing Story Ever Written'. The book has passed into literary history as a classic adventure story and has never been out of print since its first publication in September 1885.

Haggard's subsequent romances, among them another classic

tale, *She* (published in 1887), have enthralled generations of readers in many countries. By the time he died in 1925, Haggard had written forty-two romances, twelve serious, contemporary novels and ten works of non-fiction. In the year of his death only two of his works of fiction were out of print and in the next fifteen years less than half a dozen ceased to be available. There was sufficient demand for nearly all his novels to be reprinted between the two world wars and during the late 1940s and 1950s. No literary contemporary could boast such popularity. His works were highly regarded among fellow writers such as Robert Louis Stevenson, Andrew Lang, Rudyard Kipling, J. M. Barrie, Marie Corelli and W. E. Henley. Haggard also won the praise of subsequent generations of writers. Writers as diverse as D. H. Lawrence, C. S. Lewis, Henry Miller and Graham Greene have paid tribute to him as an influence. Both the Freudian Nándor Fodor and the Jungian Cornelia Brunner have found Haggard's fantasies worthy of study. Jung himself thought his work a serious contribution to psychology and considered the romance, *The World's Desire*, 'a remarkable expression of a truth about the human soul, an expression made still more clear in Haggard's later allegory *Wisdom's Daughter*'.[1]

While it is Haggard the writer who is known to posterity, Haggard was a man with many talents and ambitions which were equally as important to him as the literary one. There was the youthful Haggard – the imperial adventurer whose hand actually raised the Union Jack over Pretoria when Britain annexed the Transvaal Republic in 1877. There was the mature Haggard – Haggard the social reformer; Haggard the agricultural revolutionary whose ideas on rural England were in advance of their day: he sought changes in farming techniques with government action to help develop a system of small holdings with a co-operative management, enjoying protective tariff barriers against foreign competition. He even advocated nationalization of farm lands. His reforms were considered too radical by the Conservative Party, for whom he once stood as a parliamentary candidate, but were adopted in part, several years later, by the Liberal Party. There was also Haggard the public servant who served on several royal commissions considering such subjects as coast erosion and afforestation, the settlement of the poor of industrial England in the colonies and the state of the dominions, for which services he received knighthoods in 1912 and in 1919.

Haggard was a man seething with energy, a humane idealist whose idealism often brought him into conflict with the orthodoxy and prejudice of his time and class. He was a complex personality who stands apart from his literary contemporaries in his concern with the ambiguity of man's place and purpose in a universe characterized by chance and change. It was his exposition of the evolutionary idea and repudiation of the popular and arrogant notion of the 'white man's burden' which showed how Haggard despised the cultural exclusiveness which was part and parcel of the myth of the Victorian British Empire. His tales remain remarkably free from the racial prejudices to which many of his contemporaries succumbed.

When a boy, I was introduced to Haggard's books by my mother who often recommended authors and books to me and thus influenced my earliest forays into literature. I read *She* as a starting point and can even now remember cowering in bed, my electric torch shaking as, long past midnight, I had to finish that final scene of Ayesha's horrifying decay at the Pillar of Fire. Throughout my teenage I devoured practically every available Haggard romance. Then came early manhood during which I foolishly thought it was time to put away fantasy and romance as things of childhood. Haggard's novels became a pleasant memory of boyhood. Then, some years ago, while I was researching for a book in Ireland, in the Irish-speaking area of An Clochan in Connemara, I came across a turf-cutter, a *móinbhainteoir*, a man of middle age, sitting eating his lunch and reading a book with obvious enjoyment. The book was entitled *Croidhe na Cruinne*, Niall Ó Domhnaill's Irish rendering of *The Heart of the World* by Rider Haggard.[2]

The incident so struck me that some time later I picked up a Haggard romance and started to re-read it. I was pleasantly surprised. Like Andrew Lang I found that the 'eternal boy' was still with me. I enjoyed the tales as much as I had in my youth and, in my maturity, found greater enjoyment in the new depths which I had missed in my inexperienced boyhood. Once more I devoured Haggard's romances, his novels and his non-fiction work. I began to see why Haggard casts an ageless spell over his readers and became fascinated by the complexity of the man and his ideas.

There have been three biographical studies of Haggard, each one naturally displaying a degree of bias. This has led me to offer my own bias to the Haggard canon.

In 1912, thirteen years before his death, Haggard wrote an autobiography, *The Days of My Life*, which was then locked in the safe of Haggard's friend, the publisher Charles Longman, to be taken out and published after his death. Before publication in book form an abbreviated version was serialized in the *Strand Magazine* between April and October 1926. It had been arranged that this serialization should be prefaced by a note to the effect that the contents were abbreviated but, through an oversight, this note was omitted. Consequently, when the two-volume autobiography was published on 7 October 1926, in an edition of only 3000 copies, very few copies sold because the public thought this was simply another and more expensive edition of the *Strand Magazine*'s version.

The second biographical study, *The Cloak That I Left*, was published in 1951 and was written by Haggard's youngest daughter, Lilias Rider Haggard who, quite naturally, sees her father with the fairly uncritical eyes of an affectionate and loving daughter.

The third biography, *Rider Haggard: His Life and Works*, published in 1960, is by an American, Morton Cohen, who presents the thesis that Haggard was a failure in everything he did: not a total failure, of course, but a failure nevertheless. He sums up this lack of success with this passage:

> In public life, where Haggard wanted most to succeed, he
> was blocked by the exigencies of politics; in literature,
> where he might have triumphed without any outside

assistance, he was blocked by his own narrow view. Although he was exceptionally enterprising, he vacillated between the world of affairs and the world of literature, never fully accepted in the one, never completely comfortable in the other. And because the public issues which commanded his attention have been so submerged in the greater cataclysms of the twentieth century, his name has not been written large in his country's history and men do not esteem him for his selflessness, for service to Country and Empire, for devotion to justice, agricultural reform and social work, or for his schemes of colonial settlement.

Morton Cohen is particularly devastating when he comes to a critique of Haggard's literary style and, having made such criticism, he concludes:

> These weaknesses in Haggard's writing stand between him and immortality. And when we ask why they existed and why Haggard did so little to change, we find ample reasons. Had the boy been given an adequate schooling, had he been conditioned by a literary environment, had he been taught the refinements and graces of the English language, had he been steeped in the classics and grown conscious of his own shortcomings, had he not had to struggle so for financial independence, and above all had he been more secure psychologically, he might have woven his tales into a finer fabric.

I find it impossible to seriously accept that any weaknesses that occur in Haggard's literary style 'stand between him and immortality'. It is a fact that, over fifty years after his death, many of Haggard's works are still in print and are still avidly read around the world in numerous translations. What other word but 'immortal' can describe *She* and *King Solomon's Mines* which inspired over a dozen film versions, stage productions, radio serials, an opera and even a ballet? Several times they have been transcribed to comic-strip forms and printed as full-colour comic books, the most recent of which has appeared, even as I write, from Marvel Comics. Surely these two works alone have purchased the immortality that Morton Cohen would deny Haggard? It is true that there have been greater literary figures but there have been few finer storytellers.

In my quest for Haggard, one aspect of his work particularly fascinated me and that was his lack of racial prejudice and cultural exclusiveness which was so often a dominant factor in literature of the period. How did Haggard come to break out of the confines of his cultural upbringing and environment when he expressed himself in the literary medium and did he, in fact, break out of those confines in his personal life? Certainly, at times, he gave the appearance of a square peg in a round hole.

For example, although he stood as a parliamentary candidate for the Conservative Party in 1895, he afterwards wrote 'now I understand that I never was a real Tory'; he added that if he had won the seat in the House of Commons the party whip would have struck him off the list 'as a dangerous and undesirable individual who, refusing to swallow the shibboleth of his tribe with shut eyes, actually dared to think for himself'. When it came to politics Haggard felt that 'people generally remain in the political fold wherein they were born' and as his father had been a 'Tory to the backbone' then 'all his sons were brought up in that fossilised creed'. But if Haggard truly regarded Victorian Conservatism as a 'fossilised creed' he made no effort to join a political group more in keeping with his own personality although, in 1888 after a visit to the famous artist and exponent of socialism, William Morris, he wrote wistfully 'when I departed I rather wished that Fate had made me a Socialist also'. Haggard was too much an individualist in his ideas to be associated for any length of time with one political group. His advocacy of nationalization of farm lands in 1911 labelled him as 'a dangerous radical' by horrified Conservatives and Liberals. Yet, after the Russian Revolution and when it seemed, in 1919, Britain herself stood on the verge of revolution, Haggard joined Kipling in forming The Liberty League to fight against 'Bolshevism' and was also involved with such right-wing organizations as the Council of Public Morals and the National League for Promotion of Physical and Moral Race Regeneration. With Kipling, Haggard agreed 'the more advanced forms of Radicalism are a disease – not a set of ideas'.[3] Haggard was far from casting off all the values of his upbringing. In public life he did propound a belief in the British Empire. It was a naïve belief, an attitude reminiscent of the ideals put forward in a number of Victorian colonial adventure books and one that was contradicted by his own writings. Perhaps he was not even aware that the contradiction existed. His attitude to empire was always slightly vague, he believed that Britain, explicitly England, had a civilizing mission in the world by which the mantle of the British Empire would bring peace and prosperity to all the nations which it enfolded. But it was obvious that he disagreed with the then current patriotic belief that the 'sun would never set' on the empire. He demonstrated in his books that the British Empire was, to him, a thing of transience as had been all other empires since the dawn of time – Egypt, Persia, Greece and Rome among them. Above all, he believed that the British Empire was not possessed of an inalienable virtue.

When Haggard came up against a *genuine* imperialist, the man for whom empire spelled financial exploitation and profit, he was sickened. He recorded in his diary the event which occurred during a visit to South Africa in 1914: the diamond-mine magnate, Sir Abe Bailey, revealed that the Jameson military raid into the Transvaal had been planned by Cecil Rhodes in an attempt to create an insurrection in the Boer republic and give Britain an excuse for intervening and annexing the country. Britain had long had her eyes on the vast mineral wealth of the Transvaal. Haggard was shocked and said so. Bailey told him that he was being 'old fashioned'. Haggard indignantly asked what had been gained by the raid which was 'a wretched failure'. Bailey replied that, on the contrary, the raid was successful in that it provoked the Boers to retaliate and invade British territory in Natal which then led to the Second Boer War which Britain had won. Horrified, Haggard pointed out the number of lives which the war had cost. 'What matters?' said the magnate who was making millions out of the former Boer territories, 'lives are cheap.'[4] The empire of the British financiers and soldiers was not the empire of Haggard which was to bring financial benefit, peace and civilization to the new colonies. Allan Quatermain expresses his creator's view:

> Well, it is not a good world – nobody can say that it is save them who wilfully blind themselves to the facts. How can a world be good in which Money is the moving power, and Self-Interest the guiding star? The wonder is not that it is so bad but that there should be any good left in it.[5]

After visiting Zululand in 1914 and witnessing the condition of a once proud civilization who had suffered military defeat, and had its lands expropriated and settled by whites, Haggard wrote a moving appeal to the Rt Hon. Lewis Harcourt at the British Colonial Office. In his analysis of the mistakes being made by Britain in southern Africa he clearly foresaw the rise of the modern-day racist Republic of South Africa.

Though Haggard often wrote in the imperial milieu, especially with his African tales. Alan Sandison points out that 'the tensions of his art have no moral connection with the tensions of the imperial idea'.[6] Sandison demonstrates that in his works Haggard acknowledges that people are ever in a state of flux and change and he therefore wonders whether, in fact, events are predestined by some Providence. He seems to incline towards the theory that whatever design there is in nature has been inflicted by man, but he is also fascinated with the theory of order or design in the universe with its determination purely mechanical and with accident as its first cause. 'Process' and 'purpose' are seen by Sandison as the two words vital to an appraisal of Haggard's work.

> It can be shown clearly that Haggard's relationship to the imperial idea, as it emerged in the role assumed by the latter in his fiction, is dictated by an idea of nature rooted in his reaction to the evolutionary doctrine advanced by Charles Darwin.[7]

This awareness of the transiency of human civilization was central to Haggard's humanism and his humility. In endeavouring to grasp and understand differing cultures, whether of the Zulus or the primitive Bushman or, indeed, the civilization of ancient Egypt, Iceland or Mexico, there is no trace of racism or the familiar Victorian paternalism which contact with 'natives' usually elicited in the empire builders of the day. Haggard's perspective of life was much wider.

Through Allan Quatermain, Haggard frequently rebukes his fellow Englishmen for their facile assumption about the importance of their own nationality and civilization compared to the Africans. They may be different, he argues, but in no way superior. Also, in *Child of Storm*, Quartermain points out:

> We white people think we know everything; for instance,
> we think we understand human nature. And we do, as
> human nature appears to us, with all its trappings and its
> accessories seen dimly through the glass of our own
> conventions, leaving out those aspects of it which we have
> forgotten or do not think positive to mention.

Remembering the prejudices of the time, it is astonishing that Haggard lets his protagonists form varying emotional relationships with the 'natives'. The English hunter, Allan Quatermain, in *Child of Storm*, admits of the Zulu girl, Mameena: 'This beautiful girl with the "fire in her head", this woman who was different from all other women I had ever known, seemed to have twisted her slender fingers into my heart strings and to be drawing me towards her.'

Haggard's African settings are of real places and real people. As Sandison says:

> What we are shown is not simply an imperial triumph
> against a bizarre native background but humanity absorbed
> with its squalid vices and petty absorptions in its
> honeycomb of racial and tribal compartments, struggling
> blindly with the incomprehensible and inexorable
> movement of which it is an unwilling part.[8]

The concern with the flux and change of human development and the search for purpose is common to all Haggard's fiction. It is therefore astonishing to find that Morton Cohen misses the pertinence of Haggard's allegorical tales to the modern human condition:

> Although Haggard was very much concerned with contemporary issues he was never really content with his own times. From a personal and spiritual standpoint he was not modern. He yearned for the past and spent much of his time investigating ancient cultures. He was an amateur antiquary. . . .[9]

Sandison has already rebutted this statement pointing out: 'One can hardly, after all, tax him (Haggard) with whimsical frivolity in his investigation of ancient cultures when his object was the profoundly sober one of a more honest understanding of his own nature and the nature of his time.'[10]

Haggard's concern with man's ambiguous status in the universe, a universe of chance and change, and his probing towards an elucidation of purpose and establishment of a 'great end', if indeed there was one to be found, is as old as mankind itself. That yearning to *know* will probably remain with us until, as the Zulus would say, the human race 'goes down into the blackness'. I believe, therefore, this is one of the subconscious keys to the immortality of Haggard's tales and a reason why the stories, in whatever historical setting he gave them, are timeless. And above all, overshadowing the pomp and circumstance of our unimportant egos, the rise of petty empires and civilizations, there emerges one factor in all Haggard's novels – the inevitability of death. This is seen, for example, in Ayesha's end; in the fate of the hero of *The Wanderer's Necklace*, blinded by the woman he loves and to whom he remains faithful to the last, and in *Nada the Lily, Allan Quatermain* and *Eric Brighteyes* where all the enterprises of great pitch and moment are finally made insignificant by death. Indeed, death seems the only certainty in life; it puts our paltry egotisms in a correct perspective.

In the last speech he was to make, in November 1924, Haggard tried to come to terms with his powerful imagination and his talent.

> Imagination is power which comes from we know not where. Perhaps it is existent but ungrasped truth, a gap in the curtain of the unseen which sometimes presses so nearly upon us. It means suffering, but it also means vision, and is not light better than darkness? Who knows its object? No man: but it may be that those who possess it are gates through which the forces of good and evil flow down in strength upon the world: instruments innocent of their destiny. For it seems to me as I grow old that the spirit of man is like those great icebergs which float in Arctic seas – towering masses of glittering blue-green ice, which yet hide four fifths of their bulk beneath the water. It is the hidden power of the spirit which connects the visible and the invisible: which hears the still small voice calling from the infinite. . . .[11]

Far from being a failure, Henry Rider Haggard has undoubtedly achieved a prominence given to few people. He was a successful farmer who was at one with nature and the land he loved; he was a profound agricultural reformer who pioneered afforestation work and the efforts to prevent coast erosion as well as propounding radical ideas on farming techniques which were in advance of their time; he expounded social reform which he thought would benefit the poor of the country and showed a special interest in child welfare; but above all, he was a successful novelist whose work stands out from his contemporaries not just as good escapist literature – mere romantic fantasy – but as serious exercises into man's nature and the evolution of the universe, that 'Eternal War between Flesh and Spirit', that search for some unity of process and purpose which forces the seeker into an 'Eternal Loneliness'. Haggard's voice from the infinite is still remarkably loud and clear.

CHAPTER 1

NORFOLK CHILDHOOD

The notice which appeared in the advertisement columns of the *Morning Post* on Tuesday, 26 June, 1856, was brief:

> Haggard – On the 22d inst., at Bradenham, Norfolk, the wife of W. Haggard Esq., of a son.

The son was Henry Rider Haggard who was the sixth son, and eighth child, of William and Ella Haggard of Bradenham Hall, near Thetford. He had been born at Wood Farm, a pleasant thatched house which stood to the north of Bradenham Wood on the Bradenham estate. It was to this farmhouse that Ella Haggard had decided to retire during her confinement. It was first suggested that the baby boy should be called Sylvanus but the idea was firmly rejected and the more conventional family names of Henry Rider were chosen. Mrs Haggard and her new son returned to Bradenham Hall early in August and within days the child developed internal troubles as a result of jaundice. A clergyman was hastily summoned and christened the boy in a big Lowestoft china bowl that happened to be handy. A proper christening ceremony was carried out on 22 September after the crisis had passed and Henry Rider had recovered.

The family into which Henry Rider had been born was a moderately wealthy, landowning family which claimed an ancient lineage. They claimed a descent from Sir Andrew Ogard, a Dane who settled in England during the reign of Henry VI. Sir Andrew's real name was Guildenstjerne but, on settling in England, he took as his surname the name of his place of birth, Aagaard in Jutland, which, through various phonetic renderings was finally settled as Haggard. He still bore, as his coat of arms, a golden star. The Haggards of

America also claim descent from Sir Andrew through one James Haggard who left England about 1698 and settled in Norfolk, Virginia. More directly, the American Haggards trace their descent from Nathaniel Haggard, born in Albemarle County, Virginia, in 1723. The family became prominent in the army, the Church and in politics, one of them becoming a state governor.[1]

The line of descent from Sir Andrew is extremely sketchy and the direct line of descent seems to start with David Haggard of Ware in Hertfordshire, whose will was proved in 1534. The Haggard family continued to be prominent in Ware and nearby Royston until William Henry Haggard (died 1813) moved to Norwich in 1760. It was his son William Henry Haggard Junior (1757–1837) who bought Bradenham Hall, Thetford. By a coincidence it seems that Bradenham Hall had once belonged to Sir Andrew Ogard through the ownership of his wife, but whether this was the reason why William bought the property cannot be proved.

It was William Henry who established the Haggards as 'squires of Bradenham'. He was an energetic barrister, a graduate of Emmanuel College, Cambridge, who married Frances Amyand whose father was the grandson of George II's surgeon and whose mother was the sole heiress of Thomas Rider of Twickenham. Thus the names Amyand and Rider became adopted as family names. William Henry's eldest son, William (1783–1843), became a justice of the peace and deputy-lieutenant of the county. He was apparently concerned in the banking business in Russia and in 1816 married Elizabeth, the eldest daughter of James Meybohm of St Petersburg (now Leningrad). A son, William Meybohm Haggard also trained as a barrister, became a justice of the peace, deputy-lieutenant of the county and chairman of the Norfolk Quarter Sessions. On 30 May 1844, he married Ella, the daughter of Bazett Doveton of the Bombay branch of the East India Civil Service. Ella had been born in Bombay on 16 June 1819 and spent her early years in India, the family not returning to England until 1840. William and Ella Haggard settled at Bradenham Hall, a red-brick Georgian mansion. It was a spacious house with ten bedrooms, three large reception rooms and bordered by an estate of 400 acres of well-timbered parkland through which ran the river Wizzey. It was not long before the children of William and Ella began to populate those ten bedrooms.

There were ten children in all; three girls and seven boys. The eldest was Ella Doveton, born on 10 March 1845; the eldest boy was William Henry Doveton, born on 25 June 1846; then came Bazett Michael, 29 September 1847; Alfred Hinuber, 17 April 1848; John George, 11 June 1850; Elizabeth Cecilia, 1 June 1852; Andrew Charles Parker, 7 February 1854; Henry Rider, 22 June 1856; Elenora Mary, 1 June 1858 and, lastly, Edward Arthur 5 November 1860. There is evidence that Ella also had a stillborn child which was buried in a corner of Bradenham churchyard. By Victorian standards the family was not unduly large.

William Meybohm Haggard, as head of the family, was a flamboyant squire of the old school, a kindly and paternal despot who, Rider wrote 'reigned at Bradenham like a king, blowing everybody up and making rows innumerable'. Squire Haggard, as he liked to be called, certainly indulged in his eccentricity. Even in the practice of law he obtained a certain notoriety through some amusing incidences, one of which Rider related. His father was prosecuting a man for stealing twelve hogs and in addressing the jury he did his best to impress upon them the enormity of the crime. 'Gentlemen of the jury,' he said, 'think what this man has done. He stole not one but twelve hogs, and not only twelve hogs but twelve fat hogs, exactly the same number, Gentlemen of the Jury, as I see in the box before me!' Rider added that tradition had it that the defendant was acquitted.

Squire Haggard treated his domestic servants abominably and the tenant farmers and workers on his estate little better. He would

> send back the soup with a request to the cook to drink it all herself, or some other infuriating message. He could pull at

the bells until the feet of connecting wire hung down the wall, and announce when whoever he wanted appeared that Thorpe Idiot Asylum was her proper home.

Rider continued:

It was the same with the outdoor men, especially with one Samuel Adcock, his factotum, a stout, humorous person, whose face was marked all over with smallpox pits. About once a week Samuel was had in to the vestibule and abused in a most straightforward fashion, but he never seemed to mind.

'I believe, Samuel,' roared my father at him in my hearing, 'donkey as you are, you think that no one can do anything except yourself.'

'Nor they can't, Squire,' replied Samuel calmly, which closed the conversation.

In spite of discourteous and abusive treatment of them, the servants attributed Squire Haggard's tempers as being 'only the squire's way'. They had, of course, little option in the semi-feudal society of Victorian Norfolk but to take such treatment with stoicism.

Squire Haggard and his family regularly attended at the parish church and his habit was to stand in the middle of the nave holding a very large old watch so that any latecomers were made aware of the enormity of their offence. The squire always read the lessons. He had a particular foible in that when he came to a piece containing biblical names he would read them through, pause and read them through again in order to try and render them in a better way. At the end of the service no worshipper would dare to stir until the squire and his family left the church. Then the squire would stand in the porch and watch the congregation emerge, counting them like sheep.

The squire was 'a Tory to the backbone' and he was once asked to contest the local parliamentary seat but, because of his business commitments, he declined. 'It is a pity,' wrote Rider, 'for I am sure that his strong personality, backed as it was by remarkable shrewdness, would have made him a great figure in the House of Commons and one who would have been long remembered.' Rider also acknowledged that: 'Notwithstanding his hot temper, foibles and tricks of manner, there was something about him that made him extraordinarily popular, not only as I have said in his household but in the outside world.'

Even so, life with Squire Haggard was difficult and the calming influence in the children's lives was their mother, Ella Haggard. In sharp contrast to her husband, Ella was a quietly spoken woman whom Rider described as 'an angel that had lost her way and found herself in pandemonium'. One of her daughters-in-law once asked her how she managed to make herself heard in the midst of the Haggard din. 'My dear,' she answered, 'I whisper! When I whisper they all stop talking because they wonder what is the matter. Then I get my chance.' Rider wrote not longer after her death:

> Of all women with whom it has been the writer's lot to be intimately associated, she was certainly the most charming as, taken altogether, she was the most brilliant. Beauty she did not possess to any remarkable degree, though the gentleness that characterised her face in youth grew with her years, and may be said to have reached its most complete development before her death.[2]

It was from his mother that Henry Rider undoubtedly drew his literary talents. She wrote poems and songs which were published in various journals and it was a year after Rider's birth that she published with Longman her first poem in book form entitled *Myra, or the Rose of the East: A Tale of the Afghan War*. The poem was in nine cantos and concerned the Kabul campaign of 1842. It also reflected on the 'mysterious law' or purpose of the universe which was one of the central themes that Rider was to develop in his fiction.

Time passes – silently but swift
And down its mighty current drift

The circling worlds on high;
We gaze upon them till some spark
Becoming till now, extinguished dark
   A blank leaves in the sky;
That which our hearts stand still with dread
We think, that orb's bright course is sped
   Our haven may be nigh;
And hush our souls in silent awe
And muse on thy mysterious law
Unknown Eternity.[3]

The year after her death Rider published with Longman a memorial volume *Life and its Author* which contained a memoir by him.

> *Life and its Author*, is undoubtedly the best that came from her pen; indeed, to the writer of this brief notice, it seems to have considerable merits; both in subject matter, conception and execution; the management of the heroic couplet being especially noteworthy. Therefore, among any who might wish to possess it, it is selected to stand as the literary memorial of a singularly pure and noble character – of one who was in truth, a good woman.[4]

The poem is a beautifully worded plea for humility during the period when science was becoming the new religion and the findings of Charles Darwin (1809–82) on the origin of the species and the law of natural selection were still being fiercely debated. Ella Haggard says that science can explain 'how' but not 'why'.

   Is Nature God? Are gases reigning laws?
   Atoms fortuitous – the Great First Cause?

She condemns the follies of the humanists who 'Adore their Dagon Lord Humanity'. However, Rider said, 'her earnest religion had no bitterness in it, it was all charity, as her life was all love and self sacrifice. . . .' It is interesting that, like his mother, Rider also became intrigued with the ideas raised by the evolutionary concept and it is indicative of his thinking that he chose to preface *Allan and the Ice Gods* (1927) with the verse by William Herbert Carruth:

> A fire mist and a planet,
> A crystal and a shell,
> A jelly fish and a Saurian
> And caves where the cave men dwell;
> Then a sense of law and beauty,
> And a face turned from the clod –
> Some call it Evolution,
> And others call it God.

Apart from these published memorials, there is evidence that Ella Haggard wrote a great deal more that is now lost. The Norfolk Record Office retains a 127-verse poem in the style of Longfellow's *Hiawatha* entitled *Bianca: a tale of Venice*. Rider, who was very close to his mother and admired her literary talents, wrote just after her death:

> Mrs Haggard, like many another woman, had her
> disappointments in life; it was, that owing to her endless
> cares and occupations, she was unable to devote herself to
> literature, a pursuit towards which she felt a strong natural
> inclination, whether this lack of opportunity was or was not
> a blessing in disguise cannot be now decided. Some who
> have experience of the rough path leading to any kind of
> literary success which can be called worth winning, may
> entertain their own opinions on the subject. That she
> possessed very considerable capacity for a literary career
> there can be no doubt. But circumstances were against her.
> During her early life and middle life the anxieties of a large
> family, with the home and local duties to which she
> earnestly devoted herself, and in her later years ever
> increasing in ill-health, effectually put a stop to such
> ambitions.[5]

Years later, in his autobiography, he wrote:

Her abilities were great; taking her all in all she was perhaps
the ablest woman whom I have known, though she had no
iron background to her character; for that she was too
gentle. Her bent no doubt was literary, and had
circumstances permitted I am sure she would have made a
name in that branch of art to which in the intervals of her
crowded life she gravitated by nature.

Rider and his brothers and sisters were an appreciative
audience for Ella Haggard's tales of life in India.

Many were the stories that our mother used to tell her
children of her girlish adventures in the East, of the long
journeys to and fro – then it took five months to reach it by
the Cape – and of the difficulties of the overland route that
she was one of the first to travel.

Summing up his mother's talents Rider recalled her greatest gift
as that of a conversationalist. 'She talked well, was a good
musician and an admirable correspondent. She sang sweetly and
drew with skill, and to the last was thoroughly acquainted with
the literary, religious, social and political questions of the day.'
Young Rider grew up with the tradition of the English
country squire firmly in him. His nephew Godfrey Haggard
wrote of him:

He had a deep sense as he walked over his land of the
generations that had worked it before him. He regarded
himself as one in an unbroken line of succession. He had a
genuine personal feeling of kinship, as he drained a plot of
marshy ground or wrestled with a piece of heavy soil,
towards his nameless predecessors who had coped, each in
their own way, with the same hard unyielding task.[6]

Like most country boys of his background, Rider learnt to ride at
an early age and would often trot round the Bradenham estate
with his father on his horse called Body-Snatcher. On such rides
Squire Haggard would teach him to know and love the land.
'When I am dead, boy,' the squire said during one of these
rides, 'you will remember these rides with me.' As well as

riding, young Rider was taught how to shoot, starting with a single barrel, muzzle-loading gun and progressing, as he grew older, to a breech-loading gun. 'Like the majority of country-bred boys I adored a gun,' he wrote. But that single barrel muzzle-loader nearly ended his life. He almost shot his brother Andrew with it while hunting for rabbits with Jack, his terrier. 'I did terrible deeds with that gun. Once even, unable to find any other game, I shot a missel-thrush on its nest, a crime that has haunted me ever since.' In addition he shot a farmer's best laying duck 'with results almost as painful to me as to the duck'. In middle age, Rider was to have an experience which made him give up shooting and vow never to kill a living animal again. But this was in the future and the young, carefree, Rider grew up learning the seasons – stalking through September fields looking for partridges and the occasional hares or, in October and November, standing in the pale sunlight while beaters, sticks tapping, moved forward to drive the pheasants to the guns. In Norfolk there were also the solitary watches in the marshes or through bog and morass in search of wild ducks and geese, or the brown woodcocks or grey snipe. Young Rider was also allowed to 'work' the dogs to retrieve game, crying out the strange, ages-old commands 'Go bet! Alorse! Hi-seek!'

Rider thought of himself at this age 'that on the whole I was rather a quiet youth, at any rate by comparison'. The comparison was with the other nine children especially the boys who were loud voiced and quick tempered like their father; it was a family in which rows seemed unending, but always without malice and quickly forgotten. Often a row would spring up when the family sat at some meal. Squire Haggard would rise majestically to his feet and say he would not be insulted in his own house. He would leave the room, banging the door loudly. He would then walk in a semi-circular direction through the rooms, each door banging behind him, until he entered the dining-room on the other side and resumed his seat, his temper being restored. As they grew older, the boys began to imitate this performance.

Rider recalled:

> I was very imaginative although I kept my thoughts to
> myself, which I dare say had a good deal to do with my
> reputation for stupidity. I believe I was considered the dull
> boy of the family. Without doubt I was slow at my lessons,
> chiefly because I was always thinking of something else.

His vivid imagination caused him many fears from which his
brothers and sisters were more or less free. For example, on 21
July 1869, his sister Ella married the Reverend Charles
Maddison Green and Rider was moved from his bedroom to a
little dressing-room wedged between the library and the east
bedroom and jocularly referred to as the sandwich room. It was
lined with books, had a solitary high and narrow window and
was stuffy and hot. Young Rider heard the sounds of the
wedding party die away, the guests depart and the family retire
for the night; heard a clock striking midnight and the creaks
and sighs of the now silent house. Suddenly he was aware of a
physical discomfiture, and once he thought he heard the swish
of a silk skirt. He recalled the tales of how Lady Hamilton, Lord
Nelson's mistress, used to sleep in the next room when she came
to stay with Nelson's sister, Mrs Bolton, at Bradenham, and how
Emma Hamilton used to love silk and stiff brocades.
Frightened, the boy pulled the bedclothes over his head and
after a while fell into an uneasy sleep in which he dreamt he was
a rat being chased by an enormous ferret with flaming eyes. He
sprang awake. The moon was shining brilliantly through the
window, lighting the room in its cold white light. He had raised
his hand when, looking at it in the moonlight, he was suddenly
overcome by the thought of death.

> Then it was suddenly that my young intelligence for the first
> time grasped the meaning of death. It came home to me
> that I too must die; that my body must be buried in the
> ground and my spirit be hurried off to a terrible, unfamiliar
> land which to most people was known as Hell. In those days
> it was common for clergymen to talk a great deal about

Hell, especially to the young. It was an awful hour. I
shivered, I prayed, I wept. I thought I saw Death waiting for
me by the library door. . . .[7]

While still a child, Rider suffered terrors from an old doll
with boot-button eyes, black wool hair and a sinister leer on its
painted face. An unkind nursemaid, playing on his fear of the
doll, used to frighten him into obedience by brandishing it.
This doll was known as She-Who-Must-Be-Obeyed, a name
which he later gave to his most famous creation, Ayesha, the
beautiful and terrifying *She*.

The family used to travel abroad quite often and one of the
first trips Rider made with them was to Dunkirk where Rider
and his brother Andrew engaged in fighting the local French
boys and the town resounded to such cries as '*Cochons
d'Anglais!*' and '*Yah! Froggie, allez à votre maman!*' until the
police were finally called in. Rider also recalled a trip on a river
boat on the Moselle and Rhône. Unmoved by the beauties of
the rivers, Rider retired to read a storybook but his father
dragged him out of his corner by the scruff of his neck
declaiming: 'I have paid five thalers for you to improve your
mind by absorbing the beauties of nature, and absorb them you
shall!' Implanted in him at an early age, Rider never lost the
urge to travel.

He began to take his first steps in formal education from the
governess employed to teach his sister Elenora Mary. He was slow
at learning but quite happy at his lessons. In May 1867 he
became, for two terms, the first pupil of the Reverend Henry
John Graham, curate of Hunstanton near Bradenham. But then
Squire Haggard moved his family to London, taking up
residence at 24 Leinster Square, W2, and Rider was sent to a day
school. The headmaster of this school was aided by a junior
master whom Rider grew to dislike intensely. He was a lanky,
red-haired, pale-faced man who was possessed of a violent
temper. On one occasion Rider amused his companions by
shaking his fist at the back of the master and the boys started to
giggle. The junior master wheeled round and demanded to

know the cause of the merriment. 'Some mean boy piped up', recalled Rider, 'please sir, because Haggard is shaking his fists at you.' The junior master gave Rider a beating which knocked him to the floor almost senseless. On returning home his condition was observed by his sister Ella who told Squire Haggard. The squire had an interview with the headmaster which resulted in the dismissal of the junior master. Rider met the master sometime afterwards in Hyde Park 'and so great was my fear of him that I never stopped running till I reached Marble Arch'.

Rider was sent to a second day school while Squire Haggard pondered over the boy's further education. The Reverend Charles Maddison Green, not yet married to Ella but accepted into the family circle, was asked to give Rider an examination to see what amount of knowledge the young boy had absorbed. The results were appalling. Rider had a painful interview with his father who told him that he was 'only fit to be a greengrocer'. When Rider told his brother Andrew, two years his senior, the only fraternal sympathy it aroused was 'I say, old fellow, when you become a greengrocer, I hope you'll let me have oranges cheap.'

Although mainly an outdoor boy, Rider began to read several popular romances of the day. He was not an avid or compulsive reader but he liked certain books.

I loved those books that other boys love, and I love them still. I well remember a little scene which took place when I was a child of eight or nine. *Robinson Crusoe* held me in his golden thrall, and I was expected to go to church. I hid beneath a bed with *Robinson Crusoe* and was in due course discovered by an elder sister and a governess, who, on my refusing to come out, resorted to force. Then followed a struggle that was quite Homeric. The two ladies tugged as best they might, but I clung to *Crusoe* and the legs of the bed, and kicked till, perfectly exhausted, they took their departure in no very Christian frame of mind, leaving me panting indeed, but triumphant.

Next to *Robinson Crusoe*, Rider liked the *Arabian Nights, The Three Musketeers* and the poems of Edgar Allan Poe and Macaulay. His two favourite novels were Charles Dickens' *Tale of Two Cities* and *The Coming Race,* a fantasy novel by Bulwer Lytton (the uncle of Sir Henry Bulwer, a Norfolk neighbour and friend of Squire Haggard who was to play a decisive part in Rider's life). Of *The Coming Race* Rider reflected: 'Only my delight in the last is always marred afresh by disgust at the behaviour of the hero, who, in order to return to this dull earth, puts away the queenly Zee's love.' Haggard's heroes would not bow down to Victorian scruples, if they loved a person from an alien culture they would not deny that love to meet the Victorian code of morality.

Haggard's boyhood was already paving the way for the future writer of romance. He encountered an old retired sea captain: 'I used to go and see him to listen to the long yarns which he was always ready to spin for me.' The sailor's supply of adventures was inexhaustible. On his finger the old man wore a strange gold ring from ancient Peru and he told Rider how he found it in a burial mound on the hand of a long-dead Inca. In the mound was a stone chamber where thirteen men sat around a stone table and even while the sea captain looked on, they turned to dust as the air disintegrated their centuries-old bones. Only the gold ring remained. Years later, Rider traced the ring, bought it and presented it to the British Museum: 'It was that ring and its story that made me a writer of romance', Rider told a friend.

When Rider was thirteen, Squire Haggard gave some serious thought to the boy's future. The squire's financial resources were strained through paying educational fees and allowances for his large family. William, the eldest boy, was at Oxford University, while Bazett was studying at Cambridge; Alfred was at Haileybury, Andrew was at Westminster and John George (Jack) was in the Royal Navy, and an officer's salary in those days had to be supplemented by a private income. Fees and allowances amounted to well over £1000 a year and the squire determined not to spend on Rider's education if the boy would not benefit from it. The squire had already come to this decision, influenced by the Reverend Green's examination, and it was felt that Rider completely lacked concentration and had failed to absorb enough general knowledge to meet even the modest requirements of the lesser public schools. It was remembered that Rider had made some progress when he had attended the Reverend Graham's school at Hunstanton but the Reverend Graham had left the village to become deputy rector of Garsington, a village several miles from Oxford. After some consultation with the Reverend Graham the squire decided that Rider would be sent to him as a boarder.

Rider was happy at Garsington and it made such a deep impression on him that he was to immortalize it as the village from which Allan Quatermain, his hunter-hero, came. Allan's father is described as rector of the village in the first chapter of *Allan's Wife* (1889). The rectory described in this book is the one in which Rider lived with the Reverend and Mrs Graham, while nearby stood the old house where 'Squire Carson' and his daughter 'Stella' lived.

> A little further down the road was a large house with big iron gates to it, and on the top of the gate pillars sat two stone lions which were so hideous that I was afraid of them. . . . One could see the house by peeping through the bars of the gates. It was a gloomy looking place, with a tall yew hedge round it; but in the summertime some flowers grew about the sun dial in the grass plot.[8]

Nearby lived a farmer and his wife who were kind to the young schoolboy. The farmer's name was William Quatermain. 'He was a fine handsome man of about fifty, with grey hair and aristocratic features, that came to him probably enough with his Norman blood, and he always wore a beautiful smock-frock.'[9] Such was the affection that Rider had for the farmer that he immortalized him as Allan Quatermain. For two years Rider stayed at Garsington and, it seems, his memories were entirely pleasant – bowling an iron hoop along leafy lanes, sitting in a hollow tree near the Norman church where 'this writer and a little fair-haired girl once taught each other the rudiments of flirtation'.[10] Mrs Graham later recalled Rider as 'the little, quiet, gentle boy'.[11]

Rider, aged fifteen years, was called back home and sent to a grammar school in Ipswich where he spent the next three years. He did not seem to enjoy the experience nor did he make friends there. He later wrote that Dr H. A. Holden, the school's headmaster, was 'the best thing about the school' and, in later life, Rider became very friendly with him when they became neighbours in Redcliffe Square, London. Certainly, Rider's first day did not augur well. It ended in a fight with a bigger boy named Phillips who was particularly insulting about Rider's hat. Although Rider came off worst he regained the respect of his fellow students by standing up for himself.

The only time Rider excelled at school work was when 'by some accident' he wrote a really fine set of Latin verses. The second master, a Mr Saunderson, knowing Haggard's reputation as a dunderhead, demanded to know from where Rider cribbed the verses. Rider denied 'cribbing' and was promptly accused of lying. Rider finally proved to Saunderson's satisfaction that he had, in fact, made up the verses himself and Saunderson summoned the whole school to apologize in public. Later Saunderson offered a special prize to the boy who could write the best descriptive essay on any subject. Rider chose to describe a medical operation, though never having witnessed one. Nevertheless, he won the prize.

Apart from becoming captain of the school's second football team, he did not recall much more about his school life except that the boys nicknamed him 'Nosey' in allusion to the prominence of his nose, a distinctive Haggard feature. He summed up his school life at Ipswich: 'I did not distinguish myself in any way at Ipswich – I imagine for the reason that I was generally engaged in thinking of other things than the lesson in hand.'

Just before his final term at Ipswich, during the summer holidays of 1872, Rider went to stay with a family in Switzerland to polish up his knowledge of French and 'with the able assistance of the young ladies of the house, I acquired a good colloquial knowledge of that language in quite a short time'. Towards the end of the summer he joined his parents at Fluellen on Lake Lucerne and then he and his brother Andrew walked to the top of the St Gotthard Pass to bid farewell to another brother, Alfred, who was about to start his career in the Indian Civil Service. Alfred was to marry in the following year, Alice Schalch, a daughter of a member of the council of the governor-general of India.

Back at Ipswich for his final term, Rider began to worry about a career. He took an examination for an army commission. Actually, he went with a friend who was taking the examination purely to keep him company and not because he wished to become a soldier. Rider blamed his lack of success in the examination on Euclid, or rather his lack of knowledge of the classical writer. 'Had I passed I might have gone on with the thing and by now been a retired colonel with nothing to do, like so many whom I know.'

Needless to say, Squire Haggard had very fixed ideas on what his son should do. He determined that Rider should enter the Foreign Office. But there was a difficulty. The entrance examination was a tough one and Rider would have to considerably improve his French before he could hope to pass. He was sent to a private tutor in London, a French professor who had married late in life to a school mistress. The professor was a liberal-minded man while his wife was a member of the Plymouth Brethren, a rigid religious sect which had originated at Plymouth in 1830 out of a reaction against the Anglican Church's principles. As a result, Rider was witness to many rows and squabbles so that he later wrote: 'the rows were awful. I never knew a more ill-assorted pair.' Realizing his son was learning little in these conditions, Squire Haggard sent Rider to Scoones, an institution in London which specialized in cramming people for examinations.

Rider was then eighteen, a young man in lodgings and alone in London. He took a room near Westbourne Grove which was run by a young widow and which 'did not turn out respectable' so he moved hastily into Davies Street. He commented: 'At this age I was thrown upon the world, as I remember when I was a little lad my elder brothers threw me into the Rhine to teach me to swim. After nearly drowning I learned to swim and in a sense the same may be said of my London life.'

One of the things Rider became interested in during his student days at Scoones was the spiritualist craze that was still at its height in London. Rider records that he became a 'frequent visitor at Lady Paulet's (*sic*) house at 20 Hanover Square'. This was Charlotte, Lady Poulett, wife of the fifth earl, who was a member of the Spiritual Athenaeum. Rider also mentions Maria, Lady Caithness, the second wife of the fourteenth earl who was one of the vice-presidents of the movement which centred around Daniel Douglas Home, a remarkable medium of the period whom Robert Browning immortalized as 'Mr Sludge, the Medium'.

Rider witnessed some spectacular events at some of the séances that he attended. Forty years later he was to write:

> To this day I wonder whether the whole thing was illusion,
> or, if not, what it can have been. Of one thing I am
> certain – that spirits, as we understand the term, had
> nothing to do with the matter. On the other hand I do not
> believe that it was a case of trickery; rather am I inclined to
> think that certain forces with which we are at present
> unacquainted were set loose that produced phenomena
> which, perhaps, had their real origin in our own minds, but
> nevertheless were true phenomena.

After witnessing some inexplicable physical phenomena, Rider gave up spiritualism, 'bearing in mind its effect upon my own nerves, never would I allow any young person over whom I had control to attend a séance.' He decided that

> in short, spiritualism should be left to the expert and
> earnest investigator, or become the secret comfort of such
> few hearts as can rise now and again beyond the world,
> making as it were their trial flights towards that place where,

as we hope, their rest remaineth. To most people that door should remain sealed, for beyond it they will find only what is harmful and unwholesome.

It was also during this period, in the spring of 1875, that Rider was taken to a ball in Richmond. 'There I saw a very beautiful young lady a few years older than myself to whom I was instantly and overwhelmingly attracted.' Rider fell violently in love as only a teenage boy can. He went to considerable lengths to find out who this girl was and where she lived; he managed to get her address from a butcher's shop as 'it occurred to me that even a goddess must eat'. For awhile all seemed well with the world and Rider and the girl, Lilith, were constant companions. Then Squire Haggard, with his usual characteristic abruptness, decided to change the course of his son's life again.

During the summer of 1875 the Haggard family went to Tours for a holiday and Rider joined them, travelling via Paris. The last time he had visited the French capital it had been lying in ruins after the terrible destruction of the Paris Commune in 1870. Rider remembered:

> A young Frenchman, whom I knew, taking me to a spot backed by a high wall where shortly before he had seen, I think he said, 300 Communists executed at once. He told me that the soldiers fired into the moving heap until at length it grew still. On the wall were the marks made by their bullets.

At Tours Rider was immediately despatched to stay with an old French professor named Demeste to continue to improve his knowledge of the language. Then came Squire Haggard's impetuous decision. The squire had learnt that his Norfolk neighbour and friend, Sir Henry Bulwer, had been appointed Lieutenant-Governor of Natal in South Africa. He immediately wrote to Sir Henry asking whether he would find a job on his staff for Rider; after all, the squire had reflected, it was by no means certain that Rider would pass the examinations for the Foreign Office and this might be a heaven-sent opportunity. Sir

Henry, surprisingly, agreed to accept Rider sight unseen providing he immediately report to him in London and sail, almost at once, for Africa.

Rider found himself bidding farewell to his parents and returning to London where he also bade farewell to Lilith, 'the girl with the golden hair and violets in her hand'.

A letter, dated 16 July followed him from his parents offering the young man advice.

> Be careful always to get a very clear understanding of Sir
> Henry's directions so as to make no mistake which might
> reflect on you. Make him repeat anything you are in doubt
> about – if you can. This I give you as a general hint only,
> which may be useful, and do not forget what I said about
> order and punctuality

wrote his mother. His sisters, Elizabeth Cecilia (Cissie) and Elenora Mary, added their signatures to the letter and there were messages from his father and brother Jack wishing him well.

He was nineteen years and two months old when, early in August 1875, he set sail for Africa. His mother had composed a poem on his leaving which ended:

> So, go thy way, my child! I love thee well;
> How well, no heart but mother's hearts may know –
> Yet One loves better, – more than words can tell –
> Then trust Him, now and ever more; – and go![12]

CHAPTER 2

AFRICA

Rider arrived at Cape Town in mid-August 1875. He was a tall youth, six feet high with a slight frame, blue eyes, brown hair and a fresh complexion. The Zulus were to name him Lundanda u Ndandokalweni which meant 'the tall one who travels in the heights' and which was shortened to Indanda. His sister Ella thought him 'conceited' at the time. A local Cape Town newspaper reported the arrival of a 'Mr Waggart'.

Sir Henry Bulwer and his staff went to Government House, Cape Town, on the morning of 17 August expecting to meet Major-General Sir Garnet Wolseley GCMG, KCB, who had been acting-Governor of Natal. Wolseley was still 'up country' in Natal and, for a while, Bulwer stayed at the Cape. The following day, 18 August, Rider seized the opportunity to write to his parents. He was still uncertain what his duties were to be on Bulwer's staff.

> I am getting on all right, though my position is not an easy one. I find myself responsible for everything, and everybody comes and bothers me. However, it all comes in the day's work. I don't know yet if I am private secretary, but I suppose I am as nobody else has appeared. I make a good many blunders, but still I think I get on very well on the whole. I expect I shall have a tremendous lot of work at Natal as the Chief told me that he was going to entertain a good deal, and all that will fall on my shoulders in addition to business. We are very good friends and shall, I think, continue to be so, as he is not a captious or changeable man. . . .

As a postscript Rider added: 'My mother will pity me when I tell her that I've got to get servants. Where on earth am I to find servants, and who am I to ask about them?'

The party set off for Natal, the journey from the Cape taking four or five days steaming by boat along the green and beautiful coastline of south-east Africa to Port Natal. There was some difficulty landing as Durban harbour at this time was not sufficiently dredged to admit sea-going vessels. A reception committee welcomed the new Lieutenant-governor and Rider had to scribble Bulwer's official reply to their speech of welcome as the ship lay rolling at anchor off the harbour mouth.

After a short stay in Durban, Bulwer and his party made their way to Pietermaritzberg, the administrative capital of Natal. They left at 10 a.m. on the morning of 1 September 'and came up the fifty-four miles over most tremendous hills in five and a half hours, going at full gallop all the way in a four horse wagonette', wrote Rider to his mother on 15 September. The party comprised Sir Henry Bulwer, Mr Theophilus Shepstone, who was the Secretary for Native Affairs in the colony, Mr Napier Broome, the colony's administrative secretary (called the colonial secretary), and a man called Beaumont who had been private secretary to Sir Benjamin Pine whose retirement as governor had led the way to Bulwer's appointment. Between Pine's retirement and Bulwer's arrival, the affairs of Natal had been governed by Wolseley. With this party came the wide-eyed 19 year-old Norfolkman.

Of the men in that four-horse wagonette, it was Theophilus Shepstone who was to be influential in Rider's subsequent career. Born in 1817, Shepstone had been brought up in South Africa from the age of three. He spoke Xhosa and Zulu with great fluency, was violently anti-Boer and dedicated to the idea of British Empire and the belief of a 'civilizing' mission. He had been made Secretary for Native Affairs in 1856 and was still influential in colonial policy towards the Africans. A few years before Bulwer's arrival he had been the chief architect in suppressing an uprising by the Zulu chieftain Langalibalele. Of Shepstone, Rider wrote 'personally he was known and almost

worshipped by every Kaffir* in the land'. This was hardly true.
The Zulu had given Shepstone the name Sompseu which Rider
had translated as 'mighty hunter'. It was, however, the name of
a legendary Xhosa hunter (so although not a literal translation,
the spirit of the translation was there) but in Zulu eyes the name
meant something entirely different. It was well known that
Shepstone was mortally afraid of elephants and could not even
face one behind the bars of a zoo. The Zulu name which so
impressed the young Englishman (and which he immortalized
in his books) was therefore a derisory one – a piece of sarcastic
humour on the part of the Zulu. They had little cause to like
Shepstone, let alone worship him.

On the journey to Pietermaritzberg Rider did not have much
chance to view the beautiful scenery of Natal. 'Some of the
scenery was very fine,' he told his mother, 'but we were so
choked by the dust, which was so thick that you could not see
the road beneath you, that we did not much enjoy it.' Later,
Rider was enormously impressed by the countryside of Natal
and neighbouring Zululand.

> Indeed on the whole I think it the most beautiful of any
> that I have seen in the world, parts of Mexico alone
> excepted. The great plains rising by steps to the
> Quathlamba or Drakensberg Mountains, the sparkling
> torrential rivers, the sweeping thunderstorms, the grass fires
> creeping over the veld at night like snakes of living flame,
> the glorious aspect of the heavens, now of a spotless blue,
> now charged with the splendid and many coloured lights of
> sunset, and now sparkling with a myriad stars; the wine like
> taste of the air upon the plains, the beautiful flowers in the
> bush clad kloofs or on the black veld in spring – all these
> things impressed me, so much that were I to live a thousand
> years I never should forget them.

* Kaffir is a derogatory Boer term for southern Africans (including the Zulu)
originating from the Arabic word *kafir*, or unbeliever. It was widely used by
new colonists in the mistaken belief that it was correct terminology for the
native Africans.

Nor did he forget, for in many of his novels, such as *Jess, Nada the Lily, Marie, Child of Storm* and *Finished*, he painted the South African landscape in vivid colours.

The party arrived at Pietermaritzberg to find the citizens of the town gathered to welcome them. At Government House a regiment of soldiers were drawn up on the lawn and struck up 'God Save the Queen' as soon as the carriage stopped. A salute was fired from the nearby fort and the prominent citizens came forward to officially welcome the governor 'and, at last, we were left alone to clean ourselves as best we could'. In a letter to his mother, 15 September 1875, Rider observed:

> Government House is a very pretty building, not nearly so large as the Cape Government House, but far from small. I, who have to look after it, find it too large. I have a large bedroom upstairs and my office in the Executive Council Chamber. The day after we arrived, the swearing in ceremony was held in a room where the Legislative Council sit in the Public Offices building. It was a very swell ceremony indeed, and I had to go through an extraordinary amount of scraping, bowing, presenting and pocketing, or trying to pocket, enormous addresses, commissions etc., etc. After it followed a levée, which tried my patience considerably, for these people came so thick and fast that I had no time to decipher their, for the most part, infamously written cards, so I had to shout out their names at haphazard. However, that came to an end too at last, and we drove off amidst loud hurrahs.

By now Rider had learnt his exact duties. Bulwer did not appoint him, as Rider expected, as his private secretary for, although he had a good opinion of Rider, he wanted an older man to help him; someone who could talk to people as a man of their own standing and who was experienced in the work. 'I am not in the least disappointed', wrote Rider. 'Indeed, now that I see something of the place, and of the turbulent character of its inhabitants, I should have much wondered if he had made a fellow young as I am private secretary.' This meant that Rider was still, to a great extent, dependent on Squire Haggard for an allowance. 'I am sorry, very sorry, still to be dependent on my father, but you may be sure, my dear mother, that I will be as moderate as I can. At any rate I shall cost less than if I had been at home.' Rider became Bulwer's general factotum.

> Of work I have plenty here, but my chief trouble is my housekeeping. I have all this large house entirely under me, and being new to it find it difficult work. I have often seen with amusement the look of anxiety on a hostess' face at a dinner party, but, by Jove, I find it far from amusing now. Dinner days are black Mondays to me. Imagine my dismay the other day when the fish did not appear and when, on whispering a furious inquiry, I was told the cook had forgotten it! Servants are very difficult to get here, and one has to pay £5 a month at the lowest.

Having settled into the routine of Government House, Rider diligently applied himself to learning about the peoples of South Africa and began to keep notebooks in which he soon displayed a growing literary talent. Even his letters home hint of the profession in which he was to excel, such as the account of a buck (springbok) hunt given in a letter home dated 14 February 1876.

> I got out for a day's buck-hunting the other day to a place about twelve miles off, a farm of fertile plain (about 12,000 acres). The owner of it, a very good fellow, is one of the few people who preserve their buck.
>
> The way you shoot is this: three or four guns on good horses ride over the plain about fifty yards apart. If an oribé gets up, you have to pull up and shoot off your horse's back, which is not very easy till you get used to it. Sometimes you run them as I did, but it wants a very swift horse. I had dropped a little behind the others, when in galloping up to join them my horse put its foot into a hole and came to the ground, sending me and my loaded gun to my head some five or six yards further on. I had hardly come to my senses

and caught my horse when I saw an oribé pass like a flash of light, taking great bounds. I turned and went away after him, and I must say I never had a more exciting ride in my life. Away we went like the wind, over hill and down dale, and very dangerous work it was, for being all through long grass the holes were hidden. Every now and then I felt my horse give a violent shy or bound, and then I knew we had nearly gone into some bottomless pit; if we had, going at that rate the horse would most likely have broke his legs or I my neck. And so on for about two miles, I gaining very slowly, but still gaining on the buck, when suddenly down he popped into a bush. It is curious how rarely one does the right thing at the right time. If I had done the right thing I should have got my buck – but I didn't. Instead of getting off and walking him up, I sent one barrel into the bush after him and gave him the other as he rose. By this means I hit him very hard but did not kill him. However, I made sure of him and struck the spurs into my horse to catch him. To my surprise he only gave a jump, and I found myself embedded in a bog whilst my wounded buck slowly vanished over a rise. I went back in a sweet temper, as you may imagine.

At Government House Rider met many men who, within the next few turbulent years, were to carve their names in South Africa's bloody history. Men such as General Sir George Pomeroy Colley (then a mere untitled colonel) who, arrogantly underestimating the Boers, was to meet his death at the famous battle of Majuba Hill. There was Ederic, Lord Gifford, who, as a colonel, fought with distinction in the Zulu Wars. But perhaps the most interesting personality was a 62-year-old Cornishman, John William Colenso, Bishop of Natal. Colenso compiled the first Zulu–English dictionary, a Zulu grammar, a manual and bilingual reading texts and went on to translate the New Testament into Zulu, portions of the Old Testament and the Anglican *Book of Common Prayer*. The Zulus affectionately called him Sobantu – Father of the People. 'He is a very strange man', observed Rider, 'but one you cannot but admire, with his intellect written on his face. I dare say that my father has met him in Norfolk where he was a rector; he recognised my name the first time I saw him.'

Among Rider's friends was a man named H. Bernard Fynney, who was the chief interpreter for the colony and utilized his fluent Zulu to write ethnographical pieces on the nation: 'From him I gathered much information as to Zulu customs and history which in subsequent days I made use of in *Nada the Lily* and other books.' Rider was to acquire a passable knowledge of the Zulu language, and his notebooks began to fill.

During May 1876, he accompanied Sir Henry Bulwer on a trip to a Zulu chieftain named Pagete who gave a ceremonial dance in the governor's honour. Pagete was a fairly powerful chieftain whose kraal was the centre of a population of 15,000 Zulu. Rider wrote a letter from Pagete's kraal dated 13 May describing the dance.

> It was a splendidly barbaric sight. The singing was the finest part of it. The last royal salute was also imposing; it is made by striking the assegais on the shield. It commences with a low murmur like that of the sea, growing louder and louder, till it sounds like far-off thunder, and ending with a quick sharp rattle. . . .

Rider was to use the notes he made to describe the dance in vivid detail in what he records as the first article he ever wrote for publication. The article was to appear as 'A Zulu War Dance' in the July 1877 issue of *Gentleman's Magazine*, but this was not the first of Rider's articles to be published. His first article was to be about Britain's annexation of the Transvaal Republic entitled 'The Transvaal' which appeared in the May 1877 issue of *Macmillan's Magazine*.

Ever since the Dutch settlers at Cape Town had surrendered to Britain in 1806, South Africa had become a maelstrom in which Britons, Boers (the word means 'farmers' and was applied by the British to the Dutch settlers who colonized South Africa from the mid seventeenth century) and native Africans clashed and fought with each other with monotonous regularity. The

British take-over of the strategic Cape Colony was followed by a suppression of the more democratic form of Dutch government and an attempt to extirpate the Dutch language in favour of English. In 1820 came the introduction of thousands of British colonists in an effort to 'swamp' the Dutch. The British colonial authorities were particularly high-handed in their treatment of the Boers, even to the extent of dictating what ploughs the Dutch should use in farming. Finally, in 1836, over 12,000 Boers left their homes and began to push into the interior of South Africa. Their leader, Andries Pretorius, stated: 'We would rather live for ever in a wilderness than under the Union Jack.'[1]

The story of the Great Trek was later to inspire Rider in writing *Marie* (1912). Some of the Boers crossed the Orange River and founded the Orange Free State as an independent republic. Others pressed into Natal, the special preserve of the great Zulu empire. The Boers clashed with the Zulus until, finally, at Blood River in 1838, in a ferocious battle they slaughtered 3000 Zulus with a loss of only six men due to the fact that they were armed with guns and the Zulus with assegais. This established a Boer community in Natal centred on Pietermaritzberg as capital of The Free Province of New Holland in South East Africa. They named the town in memory of Piet Retief and Gerrit Maritz who had been killed by the Zulus. Almost at once, in 1843, the British annexed The Free Province of New Holland. At first the Boers tried to fight for their new land but they were overcome by the superiority of new British settlers flooding into the community. Once more the Boers left their homes and began to trek further into the interior of the country.

They crossed the Vaal River and established a new Boer republic which they named the Transvaal. At first, Sir Harry Smith, the Governor of Natal, tried to quash Boer independence having already forced the Orange Free State to accept British 'protection'. But in 1852, at the Sands River Convention, Britain recognized the independence of the Transvaal. It was a republic of independent farmers with its economy based purely on agriculture. Its capital was Pretoria, named after Andries Pretorius, and its parliament was the Volksraad. The Transvaal retained full independence while the Orange Free State continued to be an autonomous state within the British Empire.

In 1872 Thomas Francois Burgers was elected President of the Transvaal. He was a former minister of the Dutch Reform Church who had been educated in Europe. He tried to liberalize the strict Calvinist attitude of the Boer religion which created friction among the more conservative adherents.

Britain had not accepted Boer independence with good grace and still retained territorial ambitions. The imperial dream was to seize control of the majority of territory on the African continent and unite it as the sub-continent of India had been seized and united. Therefore, a reasonable excuse was needed to annex the Boer republic. The discovery of diamonds and gold was to give an added incentive and spell the final destruction of the independence of the Transvaal. At first the Transvaalers tried to keep the discovery a secret but Burgers began to allow miners to move into the country and exploit its mineral wealth. Many Boers, disliking his liberal policies and foreseeing British intervention in the discovery of gold ('This gold will cause our country to be soaked in blood', warned Piet Jouberts), refused to pay tax. In February 1875, Burgers was forced to go to Europe (where he married a Scots woman in London) to seek money in order to build a railway to the coast on which the gold could be shipped.

Disraeli and the Conservatives had been returned to the British parliament in 1874 as staunch supporters of the imperial concept. Lord Carnarvon had been placed as head of the Colonial Office and was concerned with the 'Balkanization' of southern Africa. He felt there were too many colonies and semi-independent locations as well as the Transvaal and Orange Free State. The answer, Carnarvon felt, was in federation under the British Crown. He was no stranger to the federation policy for he had played a leading role in the federation of Canada in 1867. But when the idea of federation was put to the British territories of southern Africa, they rejected it. George Colley was despatched on a diplomatic mission to the Transvaal to test Boer reaction to the idea of federating with British territories. Burgers and his government treated Colley carefully, for they knew that Britain would not hesitate to annex the Transvaal by force. For some years up to 1876 the Boers made diplomatic noises.

Finally, in August 1876, a South African Conference was assembled in London and, although the Transvaal was not represented, President Johannes Brand of the Orange Free State threatened to withdraw if Britain started to talk about federating the Boer territories. The conference was also attended by Theophilus Shepstone and during its sitting Lord Carnarvon informed him that Britain's plan was to use the excuse of a growing Zulu threat of invasion against the Transvaal to annex it. Shepstone was to be in command.

The Zulu threat had developed in June 1876 and in a letter dated 6 July Rider mentions that trouble was brewing between the Zulus and the Transvaalers. Burgers had been increasingly harassed by Zulu cattle raids along his borders and had organized an army to fight a Basuto chieftain named Secocoeni (Sekukuni) of the powerful baPedi clan, a vassel chieftain of Cetywayo, the Zulu King. Secocoeni had led much of the skirmishing. The campaign against the Basuto was a fiasco, the Boers, brave fighters in defence of their own farms, saw no reason to fight in a state war and Secocoeni easily beat the troops sent against him. The Boer campaign was marred by a number of atrocities committed by some mercenaries commanded by a Prussian Captain von Schlickmann which caused an outcry to be made against the Transvaal. Rider wrote:

> Secocoeni is a tributary of, and allied to, Cetewayo the Zulu
> king, who has of late been on the worst of terms with the
> Boers, so that it is more than probable that he and his thirty
> thousand armed men supposed to be hovering like a
> thunder-cloud on the borders of Natal, will take an
> opportunity to have a shot at them too: if he doesn't he is a

greater fool than 'Cetywayo the Silent' is generally
supposed to be.

He also pointed out that the Swazi, counted on by the Boers
as allies against the Zulu, did not appear to be friendly with the
Boers any more. The reason for this was that the Boer
commandos had been carrying off Swazi cattle having been
unable to steal cattle from Zululand. Rider added 'if they patch
up their differences with the Zulus and a united attack is made
by this threefold power, Lord help the Dutch. War here
between white and black is a terrible thing. No quarter is given
and none is asked.'

For Carnarvon and the Colonial Office, this was the excuse to
annex the fabulously wealthy territory of the Transvaal; it would
seem as if the British were stepping in to save the Boers from
being annihilated by the Zulu armies. On 23 September 1876,
Shepstone set sail for Cape Town with a Royal Commission in
his pocket and secret instructions from Carnarvon. He was Sir
Theophilus Shepstone now, having received a knighthood in
August, perhaps in anticipation of the event. But when
Shepstone finally reached Natal, he found that the Zulus had
not followed up their advantage of the defeat of the Boer
commandos by Secocoeni's Basuto, and there was a comparative
peace between the Transvaal and Zululand.

In a letter home on 6 October Rider told his parents of his
pleasure at hearing that Shepstone had been knighted and
confessed that he was writing some articles. 'Don't say anything
to anybody about my having written things in magazines', he
implored. In a subsequent letter, on 2 December Rider had
exciting news for his parents. Sir Theophilus Shepstone had
asked him whether he wanted to join his mission to the
Transvaal. Shepstone had asked Sir Henry Bulwer who,
although not entirely happy about it, had decided to let Rider
go if he so wished.

He (Shepstone) wants me to come with him for two reasons.
First, we are very good friends and he was kind enough to
say he wished to have me as a companion. Second, I

41

imagine there will be a good deal of what is called the champagne and sherry policy up at Pretoria and he wants somebody to look after the entertaining. It will be a most interesting business. . . .

CHAPTER 3

THE ANNEXATION

Shepstone's special commission to the Transvaal set off in mid-December 1876. Rider left Pietermaritzberg on the afternoon of 15 December with three other members of the party. Two of them travelled on horseback and two on an ox-wagon. It was raining heavily. The next morning they had caught up with the main party consisting of eight wagons, each with a span of sixteen oxen. In this historic group was, of course, Shepstone, with Colonel T. E. Brooke RE acting as his chief-of-staff. There was Melmoth Osborn (1833–99) who was soon to be knighted and made British Resident in Zululand. Osborn knew a great deal about the Zulus and had been an eye-witness to the battle of Tugela River when the forces of Cetywayo encountered those of his adversary and brother Umbelazi in 1856. Osborn had hidden on a kopje (a low hill) in the middle of the battlefield. Rider eagerly noted down the stories that Osborn told him of the affair and recreated the battle in *Child of Storm* (1913). Also among the commissioners was Major Marshal Clarke (1841–1909), also to be knighted later, who was to distingish himself during the First Boer War and continue in the diplomatic service ending as Resident Commissioner of Southern Rhodesia from 1898 to 1905. The rest of the party, apart from Rider, consisted of Morcom, afterwards Attorney-General of Natal, Rider's Zulu-speaking friend, H. B. Fynney, Captain James Henderson, a Dr Lyle, who was medical officer to the commission, and a Lieutenant Phillips who commanded an escort of twenty-five Natal Mounted Police, a force which in later years he rose to command.

Perhaps the most interesting member of the expedition was a

Swazi warrior named M'hlopekazi who was called Umslopogaas. The *Natal Witness* of 26 October 1897, said that he was the son of Mswazi, king of Swaziland, who in his youth had belonged to the Nyati Regiment, the crack corps of the country. He had come to the British in Natal as an ambassador from his father's court about 1850 and had stayed there, becoming a special aide to Shepstone. Umslopogaas always carried a battle-axe with him which he called Inkosi-kass, the chieftainess, and sometimes he would refer to it as 'Groanmaker'. Rider observed:

> He was a tall, thin, fierce-faced fellow with a great hole above his left temple over which the skin pulsated, that he had come by in some battle. He said that he had killed ten men in single combat, of whom the first was a chief called Shive, always making use of a battle-axe. However this may be, he was an interesting old fellow from whom I heard many stories that Fynney used to interpret.

They were interesting enough for Rider to copy down and recreate Umslopogaas as a Zulu warrior who featured in many of his African tales commencing with *Allan Quatermain* (1887). In later years, when Rider and his books were famous, Lady Hely-Hutchinson, wife of the governor of Natal, asked Umslopogaas whether he was proud that his name should appear in books which were read all over the world. The warrior replied with dignity: 'Inkosi-kass, to me it is nothing. Yet I am glad that Indanda [Rider] has set my name in writings that will not be forgotten, so that when my people are no more a people, one of them at least may be remembered.'[1] Umslopogaas died in 1897 in the manner of a warrior, getting the women of his family to take him from his bed and lay him on the floor of his hut to die lying on his mother earth in the custom of his people.

It took Shepstone's party thirty-five days to trek over the 400 miles to Pretoria. It was Rider's first introduction to long-distance African travel and he greatly enjoyed it, although it was a trip full of hardship. On the very first day out two of the oxen had to be slaughtered because they were found to have the red-water disease. Then the following day they could only travel two and a half miles before a thunderstorm struck them and they had to outspan until it passed. Their camp became drenched. The next night they camped at the foot of the Karkloof heights which Rider felt was surely one of the coldest spots in the world. Another day's trekking brought them to the Mooi River, then on to Escourt, to Colenso and northward.

On 20 December Shepstone had sent a message on ahead to President Burgers informing him of the coming of his commission to the Transvaal. He told Burgers that the purpose of his visit was to discuss the threat to the Transvaal made by the Zulu and other African nations and devise ways and means of preventing a war breaking out. He did not mention that the Royal Commission in his pocket gave him powers to annex the Transvaal Republic 'in order to secure the peace and safety of Our said colonies and of Our subjects elsewhere'. Burgers was naïvely enthusiastic and told Shepstone 'we shall agree with anything you may do in conjunction with our Government for the progress of our State, the strengthening against our native enemies and for the general welfare of all the inhabitants of the whole of South Africa'.[2]

Christmas Day 1876 was a particularly hot one. Rider wrote:

> It seemed queer, riding along in the heat over those desolate
> African plains, gun in hand, to think of the people at
> home, and the holly decked rooms, the warm fires and
> church bells. We never realised what it means until we
> become wanderers on the face of the earth – the old home,
> the old faces and the Christmas Days of our childhood.[3]

The party finally trekked into Newcastle where Rider bought a pony for £8. On the afternoon of 2 January 1877 the party recommenced their journey towards the Transvaal border. The first people they encountered as they crossed into the republic was a Boer family and some sixty other people who said they were refugees from Wakkerstrom. They had just been raided by Zulus who had killed fifty African deserters from the Zulu armies.

Rider recorded in his diary:

It is very difficult to convey an impression of the monotony of journeying over the great Transvaal wastes. Day after day we passed over vast spaces, stretching away north, south, east and west, without a tree, a house or any signs of men, save here and there a half beaten wagon track. And yet those wastes, now desolate, are at no distant date destined to support and enrich a large population, for underneath their surface lie minerals in abundance, and when the coal of all Europe is exhausted there is sufficient stored up here to stock the world. Also, save in some places where water is scarce, the virgin soil is rich beyond comparison.

Next day we saw about a thousand head of springbok, bounding along with a succession of springs of about eight feet into the air, coming down as lightly as cotton wool. We chased this troop and fired at them but they would not let us get within six hundred yards.[4]

A deputation of Boers met the commission at the Vaal River and, as a mark of respect to a representative of a foreign government, they fired a salute. There is an oft repeated story that the Zulu king, Cetywayo, hearing of this sent a message to Shepstone asking if it was true that the Boers had fired *at* his wagon. Cetywayo is claimed to have said: 'Had one shot been fired I should have said – what more do I wait for – they have touched my father [Shepstone]. I should have poured my *impis* over the land and the land would have burned with fire.' Although a highly improbable story, it certainly strengthened Shepstone's diplomacy in playing up the fear of a Zulu attack.

The Boers were generous with their hospitality as the party journeyed towards Pretoria. During one halt at a Boer farm, the farmer invited Rider to *opsit* with his daughter, a *mooi mesje* (a pretty girl). Rider promised he would until Osborn explained to him that to *opsit* was a Boer custom which was tantamount to an engagement ceremony. A Boer boy and girl would sit opposite each other with a burning candle in between them starting in the late evening. If the Boer girl burnt a long candle which lasted until dawn, the wedding was on. If she burnt a short candle, the boy would have to leave when the candle burnt out, and there was no wedding.

The party arrived at Pretoria, the capital, on 22 January. The British settlers and miners gave Shepstone a rousing welcome. A camp was pitched in Market Square. President Burgers and the Transvaal Government gave a formal address of welcome to which Shepstone replied, seemingly hinting at what was to come:

> Recent events in this country have shown to all thinking men the absolute necessity for close union and more oneness of purpose among the Christian Governments of the southern portion of this continent; the best interests of the native races, no less than the peace and prosperity of the white, imperatively demand it, and I rely on you and upon your Government to cooperate with me in endeavouring to achieve the great and glorious end of inscribing on a general South African banner the appropriate motto *'Eendragt maakt magt'* (Unity makes Strength).[5]

A few days later a committee was formed to discuss the relationship of the Transvaal with the African nations. Osborn and Henderson represented the British while Vice-President Paul Kruger and Attorney-General Edward Jorrissen represented the Transvaalers. This was merely a piece of by-play while Shepstone began to sound out Burgers about annexation. There was no doubt that the republic was being grossly mismanaged. The national debt was £215,000 and the well-intentioned but incompetent Burgers had recently incurred a £90,000 debt to build his cherished railway to Lourenço Marques. Balanced against this was the projected wealth of the Transvaal (it was estimated that £200,000 *millions* of gold alone could be mined over the next fifty years) which was only beginning to be exploited. The gross mismanagement was a matter of domestic policy which Vice-President Kruger had promised to correct. He was forthright in his blame of Burgers for the chaos.

Shepstone's lever was not the chaotic state of the Transvaal

Government but the threat of a Zulu invasion. It was true that along the borders of the Transvaal the Basuto, Swazi, Bechuanas and the Zulu were making war-like noises. Cetywayo had mobilized 40,000 warriors, many of whom were celibates yearning to take a wife, a course of action denied to the individual warrior until he had 'washed' his assegai in blood. Shepstone's suggestion was that the Zulus would never dare attack the British and that if Britain annexed the Transvaal it would prevent the annihilation of the Boers by the Zulu. To the European nations, however, Britain would present their annexation of the republic as, in the words of Wolseley, being 'evidently intended to defend the native (African) against European (Boer) aggressors'. The Boers would be shown to the European nations, to quote Queen Victoria, as 'a horrid people, cruel and over bearing'.[6] Burgers was weak and vacillating and, according to Rider:

> The better educated Boers also were for the most part satisfied that there was no hope for the country unless England helped it in some way, though they did not like having to accept help. But the more bigoted and narrow-minded among them were undoubtedly opposed to English interference, and under their leader, Paul Kruger, who was at the time running for the President's chair, did their best to be rid of it.

The Volksraad were divided. Rider wrote:

> Members of the Volksraad and other prominent individuals in the country who had during the day been denouncing the Commissioner in no measured terms, and even proposing that he and his staff should be shot as a warning to the English Government, might be seen arriving at his house under cover of the shades of evening, to have a little talk with him, and express the earnest hope that it was his intention to annex the country as soon as possible.[7]

The Boers were not the only people to practise deception. While in public Shepstone was saying that the British would respect the treaty guaranteeing the Transvaal its independence, he wrote to Burgers on 9 April: 'If I could think of any plan by which the independence of the State could be maintained by its own internal resources, I would most certainly not conceal that plan from you.'[8]

Rider was able to report that, superficially, 'life at Pretoria was very gay during this annexation period'. There were fifty-nine social functions given for the British commission; dances, dinners and cocktail parties and all held within two months. It was 'champagne and sherry' politics with a vengeance. Underneath, of course, was a growing tension as the politicians sought to manipulate for the various ends. Rider was witness to the general antagonism towards the British. He saw a Boer watch the British hoist the Union Jack at their camp in Market Street. The man suddenly ran forward shouting: 'O father, O grandfather, O great grandfather, rise from the dead and drive away these red handed wretches who have come to take our land from us, the land which we took from the *swartzels* (black men).' The Boer attempted to drag down the flag but some of his compatriots restrained him. Rider admitted 'there was much to justify this attitude of the Boer', but, being a young man and not educated in politics, he persuaded himself that 'our intervention was necessary' to prevent southern African being plunged into war. That the great mineral wealth of the Transvaal had something to do with British colonial attitudes did not occur to him and a few years later, when he came to write his account of the annexation (*Cetywayo and His White Neighbours*) Rider continued to ascribe altruistic motives to British territorial ambition rather than a desire for material gain.

The intense dislike felt by the Boers towards the British, which in the light of Boer history is surely understandable, was emphasized one night when Rider and Morcom were writing despatches in a room of the building which was to become Government House. The room had large windows opening on to a verandah and the two young men had not drawn the curtains but were working in the lamplight. Shepstone came in and admonished them 'saying we ought to remember that we made a very easy target against that lighted background'.

In a letter to his father, dated 15 March, Rider wrote:

> matters have been rapidly advancing and drawing to a close. The (Volks) Raad, after making a last move at once futile and foolish, has prorogued itself and left matters to take their course. Things are also looking much more peaceable, and I do not think that there will be any armed resistance. At one time an outbreak seemed imminent, in which case we should have run a very fair chance of being potted on our own stoep. . . .

In the same letter Rider assured his parents that troops and guns (field artillery) were on the way to the Transvaal and he had asked Shepstone whether he could take the next batch of despatches home. Although Rider made no mention of the fact in his letter, he was anxious to return to England 'to bring a certain love affair to a head by a formal engagement, which there was no doubt I could have done at that time'. The girl he wanted to marry was, of course, Lilith with whom he had corresponded since going to Africa. He told Shepstone the reason behind his request to go home and Shepstone, understandingly, agreed. But it seems that Squire Haggard, as perverse and domineering as ever, learnt about his son's proposed engagement and sent Rider 'a most painful letter'. Rider was to write later:

> The words I have forgotten, for I destroyed the letter many years ago immediately upon its receipt, I think, but the sting of them after so long an absence I remember well enough, though some four and thirty years have passed since they were written, a generation ago.
> They hurt me so much that immediately after reading them I withdrew my formal resignation and cancelled the passage I had taken in the post cart to Kimberley en route for the Cape and England. As a result the course of two lives

were changed. The lady married someone else, with results that were far from good.

Haggard replied to his father's letter on 1 June: 'I do not think it will be of any good to dwell any more on what is to me, in some ways, at least, a rather painful subject' and thereon the matter was closed. However, the paths of Lilith and Rider were to cross again, and cross in tragic circumstances.

The last move of the Volksraad, which Rider mentioned as 'futile and foolish', appears to be the announcement that the Transvaal had made a peace treaty with the chieftain Secocoeni (Sekukuni) which would then render British 'protection' unnecessary. Even Rider recorded: 'The news, of course, was very important, since, if the Transvaal Government had really induced Secocoeni to become its subject, one of the causes of the proposed British intervention ceased to exist.' In answer to this claim Shepstone immediately produced a letter dated 16 February which he said came from Secocoeni.

> For Myn Heer Shepstone – I beg you, Chief, come help me, the Boers are killing me, and I don't know the reason why they should be angry with me; Chief, I beg you come with Myn Heer Merensky. I am Secocoeni.

The Reverend A. Merensky was a well-known German missionary at Botsabelo who added a letter stating that Secocoeni had refused to sign any peace treaty with the Volksraad.

In response to Shepstone's cynicism about the treaty, Burgers appointed a commission to investigate it. This consisted of Holtshausen, a member of the executive of the Transvaal Government, van Gorkom, who had been born in Holland but settled in the Transvaal, and Osborn and Clarke, representing British interests. Rider was seconded to the commission to act as its secretary. They were to go to Secocoeni's kraal and discover whether the chieftain had, in fact, signed the treaty. They set out on 27 March, going first to Fort Webber to see Commandant Joachim Ferreira who had negotiated the treaty.

They closely questioned Ferreira's interpreters and found that the treaty had been about the boundary line of Secocoeni's country, the number of cattle he possessed and other trifling matters. Secocoeni, said the interpreters, had positively refused to place himself under the jurisdiction of the Transvaal Government. The commission then set out for the chieftain's kraal.

> All that day we rode through wild and most beautiful country, now across valleys and now over mountains. Indeed I never saw any more lovely in its own savage way, backed as it was by the splendid Bluebird range rising like a titanic wall, its jagged pinnacles aglow with the fires of the setting sun. At length, scrambling down the path, in which one of our horses was seized with the dreaded sickness and left to die, we entered the fever-trap known as Secocoeni's Town and rode on past the celebrated fortified kopje to the beautiful hut that had been prepared for us.

They were received by Swasi, Secocoeni's uncle and guest-master who led them, amidst the curious eyes of the Africans, to a reed-hedged courtyard in which stood a splendid hut, floored in limestone concrete with a verandah round it. The interior walls were painted in red ochre with various designs. It reminded Rider of Greek art. 'Indeed, these Basutos gave me the idea that they were sprung from some race with a considerable knowledge of civilisation and its arts.' Very few white men had come to Secocoeni's kraal and Rider was very interested in the African customs and habits. But he admitted that the kraal was 'an uncanny kind of place. If you got up at night, if you moved anywhere, you became aware that dozens or hundreds of eyes were watching you. Privacy was impossible.'

> On the morning following our arrival, after a night so hot that sleep was almost impossible – for at that season, the place, surrounded as it was by hills, was like a stewpan – we rose and, quite unwashed, since water was unobtainable, ate more chunks of half-cooked sheep, which we flavoured

with quinine. Then after combating demands for brandy, whereof the fame had spread even to this remote place, we surrendered ourselves into the charge of the astute-faced Makurupiji, the fat Swasi, and of the general of the forces, an obese person called Galock, with a countenance resembling that of a pig. These eminent officers conducted us for nearly a mile, through a heat so burning that we grew quite exhausted, to the place of the *indaba* or talk.

Secocoeni turned out to be a middle-aged man with twinkling black eyes. He was seated on the hide of a bull under a shady tree, clothed in a tiger-skin kaross and a cotton blanket, and wearing on his head an old felt hat. He shook hands with the delegation and then sat on his bull hide and took no further part in the proceedings. All the questioning was done, in African fashion, through his 'tongue' – the chieftain Makurupiji. The *indaba* took place before a hundred petty chieftains and took four hours. It was very tiring for Rider, sitting in the blaze of the sun, trying to take down what was said as it was rendered from Sesutu into English and English into Sesutu.

The result of the four hours of talking was that the treaty between Secocoeni and the Volksraad was proved to be a fraud. When this had been demonstrated beyond possible denial Commandant Ferreira, who was supposed to have negotiated the treaty, rose in a rage and took Holtshausen and van Gorkom with him back to the kraal. After that the British were allowed a 'private' interview with Secocoeni, the petty chiefs withdrawing, but Makurupiji still continued as his chief's 'tongue'.

When the three Britons returned to the kraal they found that the Boers had already departed for Pretoria and had left no guide. Rider says 'then began a series of mysterious delays'. When they asked the Africans to supply guides they were given several feeble excuses. Osborn then took a tough line with Swasi who produced two young warriors called Sekouili and Nojoiani who were immediately renamed 'Scowl' and 'No-joke'.

The party moved off that evening, coming to the crest of the first mountain ridge soon after the moon had risen. The trail forked here, one division running over the mountains and the other following the line of a deep valley. The party stopped to discuss which route to take. Sekouili and Nojoiani favoured the mountain path as did Osborn and Clarke. Rider wanted to go along the valley; he argued it would be more scenic. Osborn said with a laugh: 'Oh! let the young donkey have his way.' The young donkey saved their lives for Sekouili and Nojoiani had been ordered by their chief to lead the white man along the mountain path where a group of Basuto warriors were waiting to ambush them. They subsequently pleaded with the white men to retain their services because they could not return to Secocoeni for fear of their lives.

As the party went down the valley they saw a Basuto warrior watching them and later heard war horns being blown. But the rest of the journey continued without incident. Rider wrote the next day:

> It was sombre, weird, grand. Every valley became a
> mysterious deep, and every hill and stone and tree shone
> with that cold, pale lustre that the moon alone can throw.
> Silence reigned, the silence of the dead.

The story of the attempted ambush was later told to Rider by a friendly Boer named Deventer (De Winter) and the implications were much wider.

> He said that it was the accident of our choosing the lower
> path that in fact saved our lives, as on the upper one the
> murderers were waiting. When we emerged from it the Boer
> Commission and Mr A. (Ferreira) had, he added, crossed
> the great valley and reached the further range of hills, where
> they were met by some troopers from the fort. Here, by the
> blowing of the horns that we had heard, or otherwise, – for
> these natives have very strange and effective means of
> communication – knowledge came to Mr A. that in some
> unexpected fashion we had escaped the ambush and were
> riding towards him across the valley. Thereon, said
> Deventer, he lost all control of himself and called for

volunteers to shoot us down in the second nek. Then, according to him, Holtshausen – who, by the way, was one of the best fellows I ever knew, a very honest and straightforward man, and who, like Mr Van Gorkom, had no suspicion of any of these things – intervened with great effect, shouting out that if this wicked deed were done he 'would publish it in every Court of Europe.'

The Boer, Deventer, at the time asked that the information should not be made public because he was in the service of the Transvaal Government and the information was certainly prejudicial to his government.

The party reached Fort Webber and Osborn and Rider journeyed towards Pretoria on their own, Clarke having other business to attend to. The two men trekked to Middleburg on what Rider described as 'a fearful and sleepless journey'. The oxen fell down in the yokes and, after a while, they found they had no provisions left, only a single pot of jam. They opened and ate this.

> While we were thus engaged an eagle sailed over us with a koran or small bustard in its claws. I shouted and it dropped the koran, which, thinking that it would serve for supper, I secured and tied to my saddle, unfortunately by its head, not by its feet. We rode on and I noticed that the eagle and its mate followed us. In the end the jerking of the horse separated the koran's head from its body, so that the bird fell to the ground. In a moment the eagle had it again and sailed away in triumph.

The two exhausted men finally made it to their camp in Pretoria. Rider had obtained the services of a personal servant, a Zulu named Masooku, who rushed out of Rider's tent crying in Zulu: 'He has come back! By Chaka's head I swear it! It is his voice – his own voice that calls me – my father's – my chief's!'

They arrived back on about 9 April and reported to Shepstone that the treaty had been a bluff by the Volksraad. It now seemed to Shepstone that there was no need to delay any longer with the annexation. On that day, 9 April, he informed the Transvaal Government of the action he planned. On 11 April he sent a message to the Zulu king, Cetywayo, that he had heard rumours that the Zulus intended to invade the Transvaal but the Transvaal had now become a British possession and to attack it would mean attacking the British. Cetywayo obligingly replied: 'I thank my father Sompseu for his message. I am glad that he has sent it because the Dutch have tired me out and I intended to fight them once and once only and to drive them over the Vaal.'

On 12 April 1877, the members of Shepstone's commission to the Transvaal marched to Market Square and stood on the steps of the Volksraad building. Osborn stepped forward and began to read the official proclamation of annexation in a voice that trembled and Rider had to step forward and help him with his papers. In describing the scene in *Finished* (1917) Rider said that Osborn broke down and he completed the reading which was received by the cheers of the crowd 'that, of course was largely composed of English folk or of those who were not unsympathetic'.

After the reading Rider was told to take copies of the proclamation to various offices in the city and in front of one of them a group of disgruntled Boers barred his way and showed no signs of allowing him to pass. 'Mynheeren,' said Rider politely, 'I pray you let me pass on the Queen's business!' The Boers laughed and contined to bar his way. After repeating his request, Rider raised his foot and stamped it deliberately on the foot of one of the Boers, who drew back with an exclamation and then let the young Englishman by. Rider half expected to be shot as he passed them.

The immediate reaction of the Boer population in the Transvaal was a shocked bewilderment. When Major Clarke went to Leydenburg, on the same day, to take official command of the Transvaal Volunteers, who constituted the Boer army and whose headquarters was there, he found the Boer troops passive. He ordered the Republican flag to be lowered and the British flag to be hoisted in its place. To his surprise his orders were carried out but the Boers repented their inaction soon afterwards and made an attempt on Clarke's life. It was three weeks later that the 1st Battalion of the 13th Regiment of Foot (later the Somerset Regiment) marched into Pretoria.

On 24 May, Queen Victoria's birthday, the British flag was hoisted over Pretoria for the first formal occasion. The flag was hoisted by Rider with the aid of Colonel Brooke who lifted it from the ground and broke it. On 17 June Rider wrote to his father:

> It will be some years before people at home realise how great an act it has been, an act without parallel. I am very proud of having been connected with it. Twenty years hence it will be a great thing to have hoisted the Union Jack over the Transvaal for the first time.

Whether his son had done 'a great thing' or not, Squire Haggard was more concerned that Rider had become £25 overdrawn. Rider had to write and apologize on 1 June for a miscalculation but added 'horses, arms and servants cannot be had for nothing, and I had to provide myself with all. If I get any pay for this business that will at all enable me to do so, I hope that you will allow me to remit the £25.' He was able to report that he now had an official job. Osborn had been appointed Colonial Secretary for the Transvaal and Rider was to be his English clerk with a salary of £250. He also expected to be appointed clerk to the governor's executive council 'which will be worth nominally £100 per annum but in reality only £50'. Rider's financial troubles were more settled as he had also been informed that a godparent had left him a legacy of £500. He was able to write to his father, 'I have now got my foot on the first rung of the ladder and D.V. [*Deo volente*] I intend to climb it.'

Shepstone was now the idol of the empire while Burgers, the impractical president, delivered a formal protest against the annexation and retired under protest to Cape Town to live with his wife and four children, on a British pension, and to write his memoirs. He died on 9 December 1881. The British public were now extremely interested in the Transvaal, their newest colony, and Rider's first article 'The Transvaal' was published in the May 1877 issue of *Macmillan's Magazine*. In this article, the young Rider expressed the belief that 'it is our mission to conquer and hold in subjection, not from thirst of conquest but for the sake of law, justice, and order'. He believed, with the ardour of youthful inexperience, that England had a 'high mission of truth and civilisation'. Rider also displayed a strong anti-Boer prejudice, a prejudice which took him some years to grow out of, and which was probably a reflection of Shepstone's own narrow prejudices, for Shepstone greatly influenced his young protégé. Justice John G. Kotzé was clearly puzzled by this prejudice which was out of keeping with Rider's character. He wrote: 'Haggard could not, however, be persuaded into visiting the homes of the Boers. He was strongly prejudiced against them, although they never offended him in any way.' He added: 'This was a pity for Haggard's own sake, for, had he understood the Boers, he would have written of them with better knowledge and spirit.'⁹ Rider's article later annoyed Sir Bartle Frere, newly appointed as Governor-General of South Africa, who was afraid it would affect his subsequent 'pacification' of the Boers.

On 22 May Shepstone had established a High Court of Justice in the Transvaal under Mr Justice John G. Kotzé, a respected jurist in the British service in South Africa. In August the Master and Registrar of the High Court died and Shepstone decided to appoint Rider, then barely twenty-one years of age, with no legal training at all, to the post. In spite of the lack of experience and the fact that he, with Kotzé, were the legal custodians of a bitter and resentful population of Boers, Rider threw himself into the job with enthusiasm. The work steeled him; not only were his duties concerned with sorting out legal problems to present to the court and administrating the court but he had to supervise the implementation of its decisions. In a letter to his mother dated 4 March 1878, he added a postscript: 'I have a pleasing duty to perform early tomorrow – go and see a man executed.' The man was a Swazi chieftain who was responsible for killing a Mr Bell. The Swazi was 'a most dignified and gentlemanlike person'. Rider claimed that the High Sheriff was sick and retired and the executioner was drunk and that he (Rider) had to force the drunken man to perform the execution. Justice Kotzé's version considerably differs.

> Haggard came into my chambers, which were next to his own room, on the previous day, and told me he wished to be present at the execution early on the following morning . . . I intimated to him that . . . there appeared to be no objection to his presence. . . . Everything was in readiness, and when the condemned man was brought from the cell and mounted the platform Sir Rider, before the final drop, was overcome and moved away towards the corner of the yard. The Sheriff . . . an old sailor . . . was not the kind of man to be overcome in the discharge of his duty. . . . The sentence was carried out by the executioner without any hitch. Later that same morning Sir Rider himself mentioned to me that he felt queer and upset and could not look to see the end. Mr Juta, the Sheriff, also told me that Haggard's nerves had failed him.[10]

Since there was only one judge Kotzé and Rider were forced to set out on a circuit of the Transvaal towns and settlements to perform their duties. Kotzé was to write: 'To my pleasant surprise, I may say astonishment and admiration, this genial, high spirited and romantic young man . . . proved himself to be an excellent cook. He prepared our evening meal, dishes which would have done credit to a first class chef.'[11] On the first circuit young Rider distinguished himself by rescuing Kotzé from a quicksand; later on the trip a thick mist forced the men to sit in their wagon until it cleared, whiling away the time by reading a play or two of Shakespeare, each taking it in turn to read an act.

By the end of October, Kotzé and Rider had completed their first circuit and were back in Pretoria having sworn in civil authorities, heard innumerable cases and prepared for the court's civil terms which began in November. Rider wrote to his parents shortly afterwards: 'Do you know one quite gets to like this sort of life. It is a savage kind of existence but it certainly has attractions, shooting your own dinner, cooking it – I can hardly sleep in a house now, it seems to stifle one.'

There was still a considerable amount of unrest: the Boers were determined to drive out the *rooineks* (rednecks) as they called the British. Also, the Africans were once more massing their armies and Rider told his parents that 'the Zulus are panting for war' and quite accurately forecast that 'we are on the eve of a vast native war . . . if it should happen the results would be terrible beyond words'. He hoped that any war with the Zulu would be staved off until April 1878, 'because the horse sickness would render all cavalry useless at this time of year.' In a letter to his mother on 10 December, Rider says he is sure that war will come.

> That it will be a terrible fight there is no doubt; the Zulus
> are brave men, as reckless about death as any Turk. They are
> panting for war, they have not 'washed their spears' since
> the battle of Tugela in 1856 when the two brothers fought
> for the throne, and when the killed on one side alone
> amounted to 9,000 men. They will come now to drive the
> white men back into the 'Black Water' or to break their
> power and die in the attempt.

By the time he penned this letter he had already 'taken the shilling' as a cavalry volunteer and received a commission as a lieutenant in the Pretoria Horse. Of the Boers he wrote in a letter dated 11 February to his mother: 'We are rather in a state of excitement (as usual) as the Boers are making some manifestations against us, and even talking about summoning the Volksraad.'

Vice-President Paul Kruger had returned to the Transvaal after a futile trip to London in May 1877, to demand the repeal of the annexation. Following the months of British rule, the Boers realized that Shepstone's promises that the annexation did not mean a loss of self-government nor the ability of the Boers to make their own laws, were false. Shepstone had imposed an autocratic administration and now the Boers were determined not to relinquish their freedom without a fight.

On 4 March 1878 Rider wrote home that 'our most pressing danger now is the Boers. They really seem to mean business this time.' During 1877 Rider published another article in the September issue of the *Gentleman's Magazine* entitled 'A Visit to Chief Secocoeni'. Of the storm which greeted this publication, Rider wrote:

> I am one of the marked men who are to be instantly hung on account of that Secocoeni article I wrote. Some spiteful brute translated it into Dutch with comments and published it in the local papers. The Boers are furious; there are two things they cannot bear – the truth and ridicule. . . . You would not know me again if you could see me as I appear in the *Volksteem* leaders. However, it amuses them and does not hurt us. I only hope that when the chief comes back (we expect him next Monday) he will take strong measures. He has been too lenient and consequently they have blackguarded him up hill and down dale.

In the midst of this rising storm the Colonial Office confirmed Rider's appointment as Master and Registrar of the High Court of the Transvaal at £400 per annum. He wrote on 7 April with some satisfaction to his father: 'I believe I am by far the youngest head of department in South Africa. I have also the satisfaction of knowing that my promotion has not been due to favouritism.'

By June Rider had made a staunch friend of a young man of his own age, Arthur D. Cochrane, who had been sent to the Transvaal as a crown agent to investigate the finances of the colony for the British Government. Cochrane became known to the Zulus as Macumahzahn (Watcher by Night) and this name Rider borrowed as the Zulu name of his hero Allan Quatermain. The two became lifelong friends and built a three-roomed bungalow together in Pretoria which they named The Palatial. It was to become more famous as Jess's Cottage in his novel *Jess*

(1887). On 2 June Rider wrote to his father asking if he could
have the £500 left by his godparent which his father was holding
in trust for him, and guaranteeing a 6 per cent return on it. He
had decided to settle in Pretoria, he told him.

It was during this period that he received a letter from Lilith.
She could no longer wait for him to return from Africa. She had
met someone else and was going to marry him.

> It was a crushing blow, so crushing that at the time I should
> not have been sorry if I could have departed from the world.
> Its effects upon me also were very bad indeed, for it left me
> utterly reckless and unsettled. I cared not what I did or what
> became of me.

The Africans had now started openly skirmishing with British
troops but these were small tribal affairs which were easily
contained and gave the British military commanders a false
sense of security. On 2 June Rider told his father:

> there is, however, a still blacker cloud over us now. Sir
> Garnet's (Wolseley) famous thunder cloud of thirty
> thousand armed Zulus is, I think, really going to burst at
> last. It must come some time, so I think it may as well come
> now. We shall have to fight like rats in a corner, but we shall
> lick them and there will be an end of it. I do not think a
> Zulu war will be a long one; they will not hide in kloofs and
> mountains, but come into the open and fight it out.

The Zulu War did come, precipitated by a British ultimatum
to Cetywayo. In the autumn, Sir Henry Bartle Edward Frere,
Governor-General and High Commissioner of Native Affairs in
South Africa, arrived in Natal to assess the situation. Frere had a
reputation as a colonial administrator and adventurer who had a
powerful sense of the 'civilizing responsibility' of the British
Empire. He was a linguist and an able soldier who had
distinguished himself in the Indian Sepoy Rebellion of 1857.
On 16 November Frere issued an ultimatum to the Zulu king
telling him to disband his armies. He went further, striking at
the very roots of Zulu sacred tradition. He demanded that the

Zulu military system be abandoned, that Zululand should be opened up to white missionaries and that a British Resident be established to advise Cetywayo. There was only one way which Cetywayo could interpret the ultimatum – it was the death knell for Zulu independence. He refused to answer it.

On 11 January 1879 Frere gave authority to his military commander (Lieutenant-General Frederic Augustus Thesiger, 2nd Baron Chelmsford) to move British troops into Zululand. The war was inevitable. Even Rider afterwards admitted 'this ultimatum was a mistake'.

Lord Chelmsford assured Frere that the conquest of Zululand would be quick and easy. It took eight months of bitter fighting. Chelmsford took 5000 British troops, 1200 cavalry recruited from the colonists, and a large body of native levies. They entered Zululand in three columns. On the morning of 22 January the Zulu army attacked the British camp at Isandhlwana – knobkerries and assegais against British regiments armed with modern weapons. There were 1800 men in the camp. By late afternoon only fifty-five of the Europeans were left alive. It was a defeat that British arms had never suffered before. Rider, who knew Captain Edward Essex, one of the survivors of the battle, used the story in *The Witch's Head, Finished* and *Black Heart and White Heart*. Of the versions he used, the one published in 1893, *The True Story Book*, was the most accurate and the proofs were personally checked by Essex who was then a colonel.

On the morning of 24 January Rider was in his garden in Pretoria when he heard the shrill excited voice of an old Hottentot washerwoman talking to a Basuto cook. Curious, Rider asked her what the news was. 'Ah! Baas, bad news, very bad. Cetywayo the king has attacked the *rooibatjes* (redcoats) down in Zululand and killed them by the hundreds. Yes, yes – they lie like leaves upon the plain – red winter leaves – steeped in blood.' Rider was startled and asked when this had happened. The woman told him that the battle had taken place two days before. Rider was immediately cynical. 'Where is the man who can run, or the horse that can gallop over two hundred miles of veld in thirty hours – even to bring bad news?' Uneasy, however, Rider went to Government House and saw Osborn who had not heard any news. But Osborn didn't dismiss the story out of hand and told Rider that Africans had ways of sending messages over long distances of which the white men knew nothing.

Twenty hours later an exhausted horse and rider galloped into Pretoria with the news of the British defeat.

CHAPTER 4

AFRICA AT WAR

The shock of the British defeat by the Zulu army at Isandhlwana completely stunned the British residents in Pretoria. On 26 January a few hours after he had heard the news, Rider sat down and scribbled a letter to his father.

> I write one line in great haste to tell you of the terrible disaster that has befallen our troops in Zululand. One of the camps – Rorke's Drift, has been eaten up by the Zulus, about four hundred and fifty white men killed, regulars, and both Colonel Durnford and all the officers under him killed, except Gardner. Newcastle Rifles cut down with the exception of three. Osborn's son-in-law dead, and his family wandering in the veldt. We are sending to their assistance. I have just now sent all the money I have in gold to help the people. Cochrane is in laager at Utrecht. Sir Theophilus Shepstone has lost probably three, certainly one son. I suppose that all the natives will rise. There is a rumour we have gained a victory since, but unconfirmed. I suppose that most white men will have to turn out, especially if the Boers joined the Kaffirs. Don't be alarmed, however, and *don't* publish this.[1]

Written as the initial news reached him, Rider was then unaware that twice as many British soldiers had been killed as he had thought and that the 'victory' which was rumoured was a battle at Rorke's Drift, a mission station nearby Isandhlwana, where he had mistakenly thought the major engagement had taken place. Rorke's Drift, a station run by Otto Witt, was serving as a hospital and there were thirty-six patients there in the charge of Surgeon Major Reynolds. Also stationed there were eighty-six men of 'B' Company, 2nd Battalion of the 24th Foot (afterwards the South Wales Borderers) commanded by Lieutenant Gonville Bromhead. As news of Isandhlwana reached the outpost, followed by the news that three regiments of Zulus under Dabulmanzi, one of Cetywayo's best generals, and consisting of 4000 warriors were descending on the station, Lieutenant John Chard of the Royal Engineers took command as senior officer. There were several desertions from the post but with little more than 100 effective men, Chard held the Zulu *impis* at bay for over twenty-four hours, expending 20,000 rounds of ammunition. After this time the Zulus, who had not eaten or slept for several days, pulled out of the fight and, keaving nearly 500 dead behind, continued on their way. Chard lost fifteen men and two more were to die within a few days. It was a stalemate rather than a victory. For the defence of the mission station an unprecedented eleven Victoria Crosses were awarded to the survivors.

Two days after the initial news, and after he had a chance to talk with survivors, Rider wrote a longer letter to his father about the defeat and summed up 'it was the old story of under estimating your enemy'.[2] Rider's account is substantially accurate although certain details are inaccurate such as his nomination of Bromhead as commanding Rorke's Drift and designating him as 'captain'. Rider, who was then the adjutant of the Pretoria Horse Volunteers, added:

> You and my mother must not be alarmed, my dear father, when I tell you that I shall very likely go down to the border with a volunteer troop shortly. The emergency is too great, and mounted men are too urgently needed for us to hang back now, especially when one's example may bring others. If I should, and if anything should happen to me, it must be and I am sure will be your consolation that it will be in doing my duty.

Rider did not go to the border to join Colonel Frederick Weatherley's troops. The Pretoria Horse were ordered to stay in Pretoria to safeguard the town. It was fortunate for Rider, for

Colonel Weatherley's command was annihilated by the Zulus at Hlobane.

The reason for the order for the Pretoria Horse to stay in the town was the growing threat from the Boers. The defeat of the British by the Zulus had boosted their morale and many of the Boer leaders were calling for action to throw the British out of the Transvaal while their army was embroiled in the Zulu campaign. A large Boer encampment, overlooking Pretoria, was established to intimidate the town on 17 March. Some 4000 Boers assembled at Kleinfontein.

The Pretoria Horse made an attempt at a military display by placing a cannon in Church Square. Some Boers, with a sense of humour, removed the cannon during the night and in the morning it was found trained on Colonel Owen Lanyon's home with a pumpkin in its muzzle.

Sir Theophilus Shepstone had left for England at the end of January to discuss the deterioration of the situation and Owen Lanyon had succeeded him. With the worsening situation with the Boers, Sir Bartle Frere, the High Commissioner, was asked to come to Pretoria and, until his arrival on 12 April, Layton tried to fend off the Boers with talk of incorporating the Vierkleur with the Union Jack and other sops towards the Boers' demand for independence.

In the meantime Lieutenant H. Rider Haggard of the Pretoria Horse was ordered to take a detachment and watch the Boer encampment at Kleinfontein. Rider organized spies within the Boer camp itself and each night these men would sneak out and report to him. The Boers discovered the presence of the British and one day a commando of thirty to fifty men surrounded Rider's force of six or eight. His men were billeted in a nearby inn at this time. The Boers entered and took up positions round the inn. Rider and his men, acting on strict instructions not to be drawn into a quarrel or do anything unless attacked first, tried to sit it out looking unconcerned.

> I began to wonder whether we had another five minutes to live. It was then that the ready resource of one of my

sergeants, a fine young fellow called Glyn, saved the situation. One of the Boers paused in a furious harangue to light his pipe, and having done so threw the lighted match on the floor. Glynn, who was standing amongst them, stepped forward, picked up the match, blew it out, and exclaimed in tones of heartfelt gratitude and relief, '*Dank Gott!*' [Thank God].

The Boers stared at him, then asked, 'For what do you thank God, Englishman?'

'I thank God,' answered Glyn, who could talk Dutch perfectly, 'Because we are not now all in small pieces. Do you not know, Heeren, that the British Government has stored two tons of dynamite under that floor? Is this a place to smoke pipes and throw down matches? Do you desire that all your wives should become widows, as would have happed if the fire from that match had fallen through the boards on to the dynamite underneath? Oh! thank the Lord God. Thank the Lord God!'

Now the Boers of that day had a great terror of dynamite, of the properties of which they were quite ignorant.

'Allemagte!' said one of them. 'Allemagte!' echoed the others.

Then they rose in a body, fearing lest we had some devilish scheme to blow them up. In a few minutes not one of them was to be seen.

Rider and his men returned to Pretoria. The situation did not improve and a few days later there came reports that the Boers were planning an attack on the town. Captain E. Jackson, Rider's commanding officer, and the only other senior officer of the Pretoria Horse, had been sent on some mission and Rider found himself in charge of the defences. He posted his men and waited until dawn brought the news that the Boers had drawn off.

When Sir Bartle Frere arrived on 12 April to talk with the Boer leaders, Paul Kruger and Piet Joubert, Rider was given command of the guard of honour which met him and escorted him into Pretoria. Rider ordered his troop to 'present arms' and then found, to his embarrassment, he did not know how to rescind the order. He shouted in stentorian tones 'Put 'em back again!' With broad grins, his soldiers obeyed.

Frere managed to get on well with Paul Kruger but made it clear that the annexation of the Transvaal could not be revoked. Nevertheless, he promised to forward a Boer petition to London. In the meantime, Frere instructed Lanyon to prepare to give the Boers greater self-government and to make the Dutch language 'official' and allow the Boers to conduct their affairs in it. These concessions made the liberal leaders of the Boers decide to 'wait and see' the future policy of Britain towards them. Also, heavy British reinforcements were pouring into South Africa *en route* for Zululand. It was, therefore, not a good time to attack the British.

Rider was not happy with the developing situation in the Transvaal and the departure of Shepstone. Colonel William Owen Lanyon was perhaps the worst possible choice to govern the new territory. The Boers called him Lang Jan (Long John) and he had the appearance and manner of an arrogant blimpish martinet. Goggle-eyed with a monocle, a drooping moustache, and hair plastered on his domed head. . .![3] He preferred to rule by the sword and was no diplomat. Lanyone despised the Boers as a 'semi-civilised people who think of leniency and forebearance as a sign of weakness and fear'.[4] As for the High Commissioner, Sir Bartle Frere, Rider's opinion of him was 'a great administrator and *almost* a great man'. Frere, who had been friends with Rider's mother when they were young together in India, criticized Shepstone for his anti-Boer attitude. Rider, under Shepstone's influence, resented this.

Perhaps it was this unhappiness with his new masters that made Rider give up his job at the height of the alarms. He decided to join his friend, Arthur Cochrane, in buying 3000 acres of land near Newcastle, in Natal, some 200 miles from Pretoria. With the land, which was purchased from Melmoth Osborn, came a house named Hilldrop. The two young men decided to go into ostrich farming. Cochrane immediately went down to Newcastle and began to put the farm to rights and start buying the ostriches. Rider had to put in his resignation to the government in May and serve out his notice. His immediate superior, Justice J. G. Kotzé wrote to him on 24 May: 'The Civil Service in the Transvaal offers no inducement for young men of ambition or ability, and hence farming if properly conducted affords a far better prospect to those willing and able to work.' By August 1879 Rider was free and took his things down to Newcastle. He then boarded a ship for England, to return for a visit after an absence of four years. He also wanted to conclude some business on behalf of Cochrane and himself.

On the way home Rider visited his brother John George (Jack) who was stationed at Ascension Island as the First Lieutenant on HMS Flora. Jack had bought a large turtle as a present for Squire Haggard and he asked Rider to take the animal back to Bradenham. Rider did so, but the turtle managed to escape in the London docks and was never heard of again. Rider also had another duty to perform. He had been appointed the guardian of young John Osborn, the 16-year-old son of Sir Melmoth who was to be Resident British Commissioner in Zululand following the final defeat of the Zulu armies and the imprisonment of Cetywayo. Osborn replaced the first British Resident, a man named Wheelright, in March 1880. Rider had been asked to place young Osborn in whatever school he might think fit. John Osborn was to complete his education, go back to Zululand in a government post and die, tragically, a few years later.

It was early August when Rider arrived in England and it is significant that he did not go immediately to Bradenham to see his mother and father. The problem was Squire Haggard. Rider felt that someone should prepare the way for his coming, especially for his leaving the government service and indulging in a business speculation. He went down to Devonport to see his brother Andrew, whose regiment was stationed there. On 11 August Andrew wrote to his father:

> Rider has been stopping with me two or three days. He
> expects to be able to get home to Bradenham at the end of

the week. I have talked over his plans with him carefully and
am of the opinion his step has been a very wise one. As far as
I can judge his speculation is a thoroughly sound one and I
fancy when you have seen him, and heard what he has to
say, that you will agree that he has done well and not
thrown up the service from mere caprice. I do not think he
will ever return to Pretoria in an official capacity, and I
think it will make his stay at home a much pleasanter one to
him and you all if he is not pressed to do so. He is looking
very well and hearty and it strikes me his years of foreign
service have developed his ideas so as to make him a sharp
fellow, who is by no means likely to take an important step
like this without good, weighty reasons. He would 'entre
nous' like me to join him in his enterprise. If I could get the
cash together, about a thousand, I should not be at all
averse to doing so.[5]

The way having thus been prepared, Rider set off home. The
letter had had no effect on the dictatorial squire. Rider wrote
later:

My father did not welcome my reappearance with whole
hearted enthusiasm. He remarked with great candour that I
should probably become 'a waif and a stray' or
possibly – my taste for writing being already known – 'a
miserable penny-a-liner'. I am sure I do not wonder at his
irritation, which, were I in his place today, I should certainly
share. He saw that I had thrown up my billet and he had no
faith in the possibilities of African farming.

The rooms of Bradenham resounded with the squire's bellows
of outrage. In the meantime, since Rider had gone home,
Andrew had received no reply to his letter. He wrote to his
father again:

As I have not heard anything from home since Rider went
there, I write to ask what you think of him and his plans. I
hope you will agree with me that he is not such a fool as we
thought him – I think more highly of his investment the

more I think of it! The mill I think is an excellent idea, and I should like very much to put five or six hundred pounds into it. I am living now in a state of genteel
poverty – devilishly but deucedly poor; why should not I have a little enterprise? You talked about a year ago with me about putting my money into land in
England – yielding what? Three or four per cent. Well, I do not see in the least why Rider's concern (if he sticks to ostriches and the mill) should not yield forty or fifty per cent. Suppose I put six hundred into the concern.[6]

Squire Haggard's reply was brief and to the point. Any attempt by Andrew to give up his army career and go into any hair-brain scheme with Rider would have no parental sanction at all. The row about Rider's future was continuing when Rider's sister Elenora Mary brought a girlfriend to stay at Bradenham for the week.

The girl was a former schoolfellow of Mary's named Marianna Louisa Margitson. She was young, a few weeks from her twentieth birthday which she was due to celebrate on 6 October, and she was pretty. Louie, as she was called, was an orphan. Her father had been Major John Margitson of the 19th Regiment, a prominent landowner in south Norfolk, at an estate called Ditchingham, near Bungay on the Suffolk border. Margitson had died in Switzerland in 1868 and, with her mother already dead, Louie had been brought up by William Hartcup of Upland Hall, Bungay, and his wife Jane, who was Louie's aunt. Squire Haggard was to have his next shock – for before the week was out Rider and Louie announced they wanted to get married. In fact, so hurried was their plan that when Louie wrote to her guardian she spelt his name *Ryder*.

On 21 December Rider wrote to his brother William, who was then attached to the British embassy in Teheran.

Next, my dear Will – *je vais me marier* – to such a brick of a girl, Louie Margitson. They are certain to have told you all about her in their letters from home, so I will only say that I love her sincerely, as I think she does me, and that, unless something untoward occurs to dash the cup from my lips, I think we have as good a prospect of happiness as most people. She is good and sensible and true hearted, and every day I see her, I love and respect her more. She is a woman who can be a man's friend as well as his lover, and whom I would trust as I would very few. She is willing to come to Africa, so we propose returning there shortly, i.e. as soon as we can get satisfactorily married.[7]

Louie won old Squire Haggard's heart and he gave his blessing. The next step was difficult. At first Louie's guardian, Hartcup, gave his consent and then, as he found out what prospects Rider had, he withdrew it. He began to place difficulties in the way and Rider wrote to Louie in the first week of December:

I tell you fairly I don't like the present state of affairs a bit more than you do. I think that my supposition that your uncle is doing it to give you another chance is probably correct. Do you wish to avail yourself of it, my sweet?

Louie told her guardian and aunt quite clearly that she loved Rider and intended to marry him, moreover, she would accompany him to Africa. Hartcup's reply was to make Louie a ward in chancery. Rider wrote to her:

There are evidently rocks ahead of us, it is the dickens and all when one has to deal with lawyers in these matters. I am so very glad to see, love, that you are prepared to take a line of your own, and to back me up if it should come to any difference of opinion. Two things are very clear. 1. That I do not see my way clear to stopping in England until next October. [When Louie would come of age on her twenty-first birthday] 2. That I will not leave England without you. So the sooner that your respected uncle makes up his mind to treat the matter on that basis the more comfortably we shall get on together. If it comes to the worst, we must go to Court, that is all, though I should be sorry if we are driven to it. We are not children to be played with, as the Kaffirs say. . . .

But Rider and Louie were forced to court and it was not until February 1880 that the case came before V. C. Mallins who ruled in favour of the marriage. Hartcup had tried to make out that Rider was an impecunious young man with no prospects who was 'latching' on to Louie who would soon be inheriting Ditchingham and its estate. Mallins, while ruling that the marriage could take place, stipulated, however, that Hartcup was still to continue as guardian but, as a counterbalance, also appointed Louie's more sympathetic maternal aunt, Mrs Hildyard as co-guardian. Hartcup continued to make things difficult for the couple, getting the marriage postponed from May until August. He fought each item of expenditure, even the £115 for Louie's wedding dress. Finally, on 11 August, Louie and Rider were married in the church at Ditchingham by the rector, the Reverend William Edward Scudmore. The Hartcups were not present.

During this period Squire Haggard had met all the expenses for his penniless son, arranging insurance, writing to friends for loans and meeting the initial expenses of married life for the couple. Rider's concern about money, and the fact that he had been in England longer than he anticipated, made him have second thoughts about his future. He wrote to Sir Garnet Wolseley who had now taken over from Lanyon in the Transvaal, and asked for his old job back. Wolseley replied: 'that arrangements are in contemplation which prevents your reinstatement in the office of Master of the High Court of the Transvaal'. His old boss, Justice Kotzé, wrote on 27 June:

> . . . you speak of seeking employment in the Civil Service
> out here. Abandon the idea and take the following
> suggestion into careful consideration. Why not read for the
> Bar? You have a splendid opening in the Cape Colony or at
> the Diamond Fields. It will not take you more than three
> years. . . .

Napier Broome also advised Rider against returning to South Africa to take up ostrich farming. 'No gentleman ever did any good in Natal', he wrote. 'You may take this as you like now, but if you lay it by and read it ten years hence, or at any rate remember it, you will find I am right.'

There was also a letter of advice from another colleague, Colonel Brooke.

> You say nothing of when the marriage is to take place but I do trust it will induce you to give up going back to South Africa for farming purposes. For you to take up such a calling is to my mind simply wicked. You are capable, and you know it, of making a name for yourself either at the Bar or in official life. Go to South Africa if you like – but go in some position in which you will be able to stamp the name of Rider Haggard on the history of future generations. This you only require the will to do.

Rider not only required the will but someone who would offer him such a post. Unfortunately, there was no one.

During this tempestuous period, beset by the responsibilities of marriage and his future financial security, Rider heard that a great friend of his, a fellow student from Scoones named Justin Sheil, was going to become a Trappist monk of the Cistercian Order. Rider, as a young man, was greatly prejudiced against Catholicism and, in particular, the idea of people being shut up in monasteries or convents seemed to horrify him. He wrote to Sheil, who was then in Mount St Bernard's Abbey, Leicester, and tried to dissuade him from 'wasting his life in a monastery'. Sheil wrote a sharp letter back.

> You have used hard words and you will let me add that I think it unworthy of a man of your mental ability to live year after year confronted by the Catholic Church (*pulchritudo tam antiqua et tam nova*) and be content to derive all your knowledge of it from some vulgar Protestant pamphlet, and all your ideas of its institutions and ways from what I suppose you were told in the nursery.

A week before Rider was married, on 3 August, Sheil wrote to congratulate him on the forthcoming ceremony. By this time Sheil had taken his vows as Brother Basil. He added: 'I should like to have been at your wedding and seen your bride.' After Rider and Louie returned from their honeymoon in the Lake District, they went to the monastery and saw Brother Basil. Even then Rider tried to get him to give up monastic life. 'Many have scolded me and lectured me', replied his friend; 'you are the first who ever came here to try to snatch me from what you believe to be an intolerable fate.' Rider's friendship with Brother Basil continued until 1893 and Rider used to send him copies of his books. Brother Basil became Procurator General of his Order. He developed a tendency to consumption and died on 11 May 1893, in Rome where he had gone for his health. Many years later Rider, in his autobiography, showed that Brother Basil had left a profound mark on his thinking. Perhaps it was the start of Rider's serious thinking about the course and purpose of the universe. Brother Basil, he observed, had lived a hard life seeking the truth through his religion, but so had the holy men of Egypt and the Tibetan monks. 'That which was, still is and shall be while the world endures; *not in one religion but in many.*'

The time was coming when Rider could not delay the return to Africa any longer. The news from Cochrane was not good. The ostriches he had bought were dying, the fodder crops had failed and the oxen were going down with lung sickness and red-water fever. On top of that, labour was short and there were various other complications; one he did not enumerate was a tempestuous love affair he was having at the time. In November 1880, the newlyweds sailed for South Africa.

They arrived at Cape Town in December after an arduous voyage in which they encountered a gale not far from the Cape. Mr and Mrs Haggard brought a strange entourage with them: there was Louie's elderly maid, Lucy Gibbs, Stephen Lanham, a young groom from Bradenham who was immortalized as Job in *She*; three dogs, two parrots and a Norwich-built coach. From Cape Town they journeyed to Durban and from Durban they went inland to Pietermaritzberg where they stayed for some weeks with Sir Theophilus and Lady Shepstone.

The news that greeted them was grim. A few days before their arrival the Transvaal Boers had declared open insurrection. The Volksraad was summoned and a triumvirate executive was elected consisting of Paul Kruger as Vice-President (no president was elected); Petrus Jacobus Joubert as Commandant-General of the Boer forces; and Marthinus Wessel Pretorius, because of his name, as a figurehead. A Boer army had been organized consisting of 'commandos'; one 'commando' was sent 'to lie close to Pretoria', a second 'commando' was sent to a strategic point between Pretoria and the Natal border, along a roadway by which any big reinforcement of British troops from Natal would have to travel, and, lastly, a third 'commando' was sent to Heidelberg, to declare it the new capital of the Transvaal Republic and run up the *Vierkleur*, the republican flag, once more. A declaration was then sent to the British administration stating that although the Boers did not wish to spill blood, they were prepared to fight to restore their domestic freedom. They were, in fact, prepared to accept some sort of federal union with the rest of South Africa with the British in control of all external affairs affecting the country as a whole. The declaration was given to Sir William Owen Lanyon, who was in Pretoria. He was told that he had forty-eight hours to reply. Lanyon's reaction to the Boers, whom he called 'those inflated toads' was 'they are incapable of united action, and they are mortal cowards, so anything they do will be but a spark in the pan'.[8] He was soon to regret those words.

British complacency turned to annoyance when, on 20 December, a commando of 200 Boers under Commandant Frans Joubert, straddling the Pretoria to Natal road, stopped a column of 240 men of the 94th Regiment *en route* to reinforce Pretoria. Under a white flag, a Boer officer told the colonel in command that the Transvaal was a republic again and the movement of foreign troops beyond this point, known as Bronkhorst Spruit, would be prejudicial to its interests. If the British advanced it would be considered an act of war. The colonel replied by signalling his men to form a skirmishing line. The Boers opened fire. Some fifty-seven soldiers died and over a hundred were wounded, of which twenty more died within a few days. The others were taken prisoner. Afterwards British pride found the statistics hard to swallow and it was given out that the Boer commando had numbered over 1500 men. It was the first time that the Boers displayed their almost uncanny marksmanship and proved their fighting capabilities.

With the outbreak of the Boer War, Rider was dubious about proceeding to Hilldrop which was on the Transvaal border. It was Louie who insisted they should go. On 2 January she wrote to her London solicitor: 'We've got this far OK, but we're detained by the Boer outbreak which began as we were about to start up country. We hope it will be safe to venture forth this week.' There was another worry for Rider – Louie had announced she was three months pregnant.

On the evening of 9 January, Rider and Louie had dinner with Sir George and Lady Colley at Government House in Pietermaritzberg. George Pomeroy Colley was not only Governor of Natal but Commander-in-Chief of the British forces there and he was to command the army which was about to move against the Boers. At the dinner was another lady, and the other guests were officers and members of Colley's staff. Within six weeks, as Rider recalled, only Lady Colley, Louie and himself were to be alive of that band who sat down to dinner that evening. The unkown lady died soon after but all the men, with one exception, were to be killed at the great defeat at Majuba Hill. The exception was Colley's young adjutant, with whom Rider conversed that evening. This young man was to fall at the battle of Laing's Nek shouting to another Eton boy: 'Come along, Monck, *Floreat Etona!* We must be in the front rank!'[9]

The next day 10 January, after paying £135 to get their furniture to Hilldrop due to the inflationary war prices, Rider and Louie set off for Newcastle, accompanied by coach, dogs, parrots and servants. The same day Colley set off to take up his command.

On 19 January from Escourt Louie wrote to her father-in-law:

The roads are in a positively fearful state. I walked a good

78

part of the way, in fact we all did, as it was quite as hard work hanging on driving as walking. Yesterday we came here, not half such a tiring day, as the roads were comparatively very good – if we are not detained by rain we expect to get to Newcastle next Saturday. At almost every stage we meet fugitives from the Transvaal, but they all seem to consider Newcastle as safe.

They eventually reached Hilldrop where Cochrane gave them an enthusiastic welcome. Rider was reunited with his Zulu servant, Mazooku. Everyone was given a Zulu name by the Zulu workers on the farm and Rider recalled that his wife was named as 'a pretty white bead with a pink eye' while her servant Lucy Gibbs became 'a worn out old cow who would have no more calves'. Rider could not recollect whether anyone dared to translate the name from Zulu into English for her.

The Hilldrop estate, Rooipoint, covered 3000 acres lying between the suburbs of Newcastle and the Ingagaan River. In the centre of the estate rose a flat-topped hill from which the estate took its name – Rooipoint or Red Point. Rider soon installed a steam-driven grinding mill, which he had shipped out from England, and Cochrane and he decided to make their own bricks: 'Our energy, I remember, astonished the neighbourhood so much that Natal Boers used to ride from quite a distance to see two white farmers actually working with their own hands.'

The main business was the ostriches which were ill-tempered creatures and quite likely to attack people. Cochrane was injured and a native barely escaped with his life. There were many problems to ostrich farming and Rider recalled one experience whereby an ostrich swallowed a bone which stuck in its gullet. He and Cocrane had to operate on the unfortunate bird without an anaesthetic.

I only hope that such another job may never fall to my lot, for that ostrich was uncommonly strong and resented our surgical aid. However, we got the bone out and the creature recovered. Imagine our horror when, a few weeks later, it appeared with another bone immovably planted in exactly the same place!

There were also oxen and wagons on the farm which Rider and Cochrane hired out to raise extra money. Some hundreds of pounds were invested in oxen. After one trip the man who had hired their oxen came back without them and said that they had all died in the bush after eating a poisonous herb called 'tulip'. Rider reflected: 'We often wondered if *tulip* really accounted for their disappearance from our ken.' During the spring of that year, Cochrane and Rider made hay which was, with the continuing war a profitable business: 'I remember selling the result of about a month of my own work for £250, and never in all my life have I been prouder of anything than I was of earning that money, literally by the sweat of my brow.'

The prospects for the farm had definitely taken an upward swing but the happy life on the farm was marred with the warfare taking place a few miles away. On 30 January Rider wrote home: 'We have chosen a bad time to come to Natal. Louie is wonderfully plucky about the whole thing, but it is very anxious work for me.'

Sir George Colley's troops had begun their advance into the Transvaal from Newcastle on 24 January, the day after sending an ultimatum to Joubert to disband the Boer army. Twelve miles from Newcastle, at Mount Prospect, a camp was established. The Boers were reported to be a short distance away at a place called Laing's Nek. On 28 January Colley decided to attack.

The first news of the disaster reached Rider on the afternoon of 28 January. It came in a letter from the Resident Magistrate of Newcastle, W. H. Beaumont.

> I am sorry to say the troops failed this morning in their attack on the Nek and had to retire to their wagon laager after heavy loss. We have no further particulars. I do not think that Newcastle is in any danger. The signal for alarm in town is a bell; but should I think there is any occasion for it I will send out a runner to warn you.

It was the second British disaster of the war. Seven officers and 70 non-commissioned officers and men were killed while 111 men were wounded. Two British soldiers were taken prisoner. On the Boer side only 14 were killed and 27 wounded.

However, even after Bronkhorst Spruit and Laing's Nek the British continued to underestimate the Boer army and belittle them. What could these semi-civilized, illiterate farmers teach British soldiers about war? *The Times* pompously reported the defeat at Laing's Nek: 'The engagement was not a defeat. We simply failed to take the position.'[10]

Colley retired into his camp but two days later Rider wrote 'there will be a fearful engagement'. He added: 'We have got all our things safely and made the place quite pretty, but, somehow, one can take no pleasure in anything with blood being shed like water all around.'

In early afternoon of 8 February the residents of Hilldrop farm could hear gunfire coming from a hill about ten miles distant. It was a hill known as Schuins Hooghte, straddling the Newcastle to Standerton road near the Ingogo River. A native boy arrived to tell Rider that the English had been hemmed in here and 'before night came they would all be dead'. Colley, in fact, had put his men into a bad position whereby they were surrounded by a commando led by Nicholas Smit. The firing lasted until 9 p.m. when the British troops withdrew under cover of darkness leaving arms, ammunition and supplies for the victorious Boers. The British counted seventy men dead, sixty-five wounded and one taken prisoner compared to the Boers' loss of eight dead and ten wounded, of whom two were to die later.

Criticism of Colley's generalship in the face of three defeats was now being voiced. Sitting at Hilldrop that day, listening to the rattle of the guns, Rider wrote to his mother thanking her for a letter which

has come at a most anxious time, I may say, awful time. While I read it the air was alive with the roar of cannon and the crash of Gatlings. The Boers have attacked our camp up

on the mountain, with what result we are entirely ignorant,
but the fighting lasted more than two hours, and was
evidently most severe and many a man has lost his life. Sir
George Colley's advance has indeed been a fatal one. The
best we can hope for is that the camp has been able to hold
its own; the worst that it has been taken, in which case Natal
is at the mercy of the Boers, and God help us all. Last night
we slept in our clothes ready to make a bolt for it, as there
was a report the Boers were coming in to Newcastle.
Meanwhile reinforcements are straggling along the roads
and goodness knows if they will get here before being cut up
piecemeal.[11]

After this defeat at the Ingogo River, Rider and Cochrane
posted native scouts around their farm and took to sleeping with
loaded revolvers and rifles and with six horses always saddled.
One night they heard the thunder of horses' hooves but they
passed by in the distance. They later learnt it was a Boer
commando raiding nearby farms for provisions. Fortunately for
Rider, the commando missed Hilldrop. One can imagine the
propaganda value of the Boers capturing Haggard, the man who
had actually hoisted the Union Jack over the capital of Pretoria
when the British annexed the Transvaal. The thought must have
occurred to Rider for he decided that the situation was
dangerous, with the Boers making raids into Natal, and that
they should move, temporarily, into the greater protection of
Newcastle. At one stage he discussed with Cochrane the idea of
forming a volunteer company and Louie told him: 'Do what
you think is your duty – I'll take my chance.' Rider later wrote:

> Never did I admire any woman more than I did her upon
> that occasion. In all circumstances, which included in her
> case the imminent birth of a child, I thought, and think,
> her conduct in this matter, and indeed, through all these
> troubles, little less than heroic.

By mid-February Rider, Louie and Cochrane were able to
return to Hilldrop when British reinforcements marched into

Newcastle and the threat of a Boer invasion of Natal (a threat which never occurred to the Boers) receeded. The disembarking of Brigadier General Sir Evelyn Wood and thousands of fresh troops gave the imperial cause a fresh boost. Throughout this time the Boer army had laid siege to isolated British garrisons within the Transvaal at Pretoria, Potchefstroom, Standerton, Lydenburg, Rustenburg and Wakkerstrom. Now there seemed a hope of relieving these garrisons and asserting British military authority over the Boers. In the meantime, secret negotiations were going on in which Kruger had more than once expressed his willingness for a settlement whereby the Transvaal would resort to its position as a republic under the suzerainty of the British Crown.

On Sunday 27 February Louie was sitting on the verandah at Hilldrop when she suddenly heard the boom of guns coming from a hill called Spitz Kop by the Boers but which was more generally known under its Zulu name Amajuba – the hill of the doves. Majuba Hill overlooked a Boer encampment and Colley, determined to win one engagement against the enemy, had led a force of twenty-two officers and 627 men to occupy it and, from its strategic point, to fire down on the Boers. The Boers were commanded by Petrus (Piet) Joubert himself who replied to this attack by advancing up the hill against Colley's defensive positions. It was to be the last disaster for the British army in the war and although the losses were less, the significance of the battle was greater than the disaster at Ishandhlwana. The Boers lost only one man dead and six wounded. The British losses were six officers and ninety men killed, seven officers and 125 wounded and seven officers and forty-nine men captured. Among the dead was General George Pomeroy Colley.

Rider and Cochrane rode to Newcastle later that Sunday to try to get news of what the gunfire meant. The news was a great shock. It was the most shattering defeat that the British soldiers had suffered, underlined by their superior attitude to the Boer. 'The state of affairs out here is really becoming serious', wrote Louie to Rider's mother on 7 March. 'We are told that the troops now in camp at the "Nek" are perfectly panic-stricken

by the continual defeats they have sustained and that in the last
engagement, when poor Sir George Colley lost his life, the
officers had the greatest difficulty getting their men to stand.'

Such rumours of cowardice on the part of the ordinary soldier
were the only reasons that British colonials could put forward for
the defeats. But Louie, showing a surprising lack of prejudice,
added:

> In spite of the Boers being rebels one cannot help admiring
> the way in which they are conducting this affair. Their
> coolness and pluck are wonderful, and they have not made
> one false move yet. Add to this the fact that they are all
> splendid shots and you will agree that it is no mean foe with
> whom we have to deal, though this is what our officers and
> men would not at first believe.[12]

Louie was remarkably astute in noting: 'Poor Sir George Colley
had paid dearly for his rashness, but, humanely speaking, it was
far better for him to die as he did fighting bravely at the head of
his men than to live with a lost reputation.'

In spite of the worsening situation, Rider and Cochrane were
still trying to improve the farm and Rider was rising at 6 a.m.
each morning to go out and take part in the haymaking. The
ostriches were doing well, although they occasionally lost a bird
for one reason or another.

On 21 March news reached them that an armistice with the
Boers had been negotiated and signed at O'Neill's Farm near
Laing's Nek. A royal commission was to be set up under the new
South African High Commissioner, Sir Hercules Robinson,
which would discuss the terms of the peace. Robinson asked
Rider and Cochrane whether the royal commission could rent
Hilldrop for £50 a week and use it as a base for their sittings
because the farm, on the Transvaal border, was an ideal
geographical location. Rider and Cochrane agreed, Rider
stipulating that Louie must be allowed to retain the use of one
bedroom because her baby was expected in June, although he
expected the commission to be gone by that date.

It was ironic. Rider was the man who had hauled the British

flag over Pretoria to symbolize the British annexation of the country. Now his farm was to be used in which to discuss the British withdrawal from it.

April and May were busy months at Hilldrop. There was the arrival of the commission but, in addition, Rider's brother John George (Jack) arrived for a visit and soon after came George Bromefield, a ward of Squire Haggard, who had arrived to become a partner in the farm. In the midst of all this hustle, on 23 May, Louie gave birth to a son – Arthur John Rider – who was to become known as Jock. Rider was awakened by Louie towards 5 a.m. and, once convinced the baby was to arrive earlier than expected, promptly set off for the doctor. But the doctor had gone away on holiday. At 5.45 a.m. Rider's first child was delivered by a native woman with Louie's maid, Lucy Gibbs, having hysterics in a corner of the room. Joyfully, Rider wrote to his father on the following day: 'The child is a very perfect and fine boy, he weighed nine pounds just after birth, and is a very well-nourished child. He has dark blue eyes and is a fair child with a good forehead.' He added: 'The Royal Commission are still in the house . . . we don't know what is going to happen here. If it is war, I only hope it will not be until Louie is well enough to travel down country.'

Among the letters of congratulations which arrived was one from Sir Theophilus Shepstone from Pietermaritzberg on 16 June. As the man who engineered the annexation of the Transvaal, there was a bitterness in his humour.

> Fortunately everything that is born in a stable is not a horse, or your boy would be either a Boer or a Royal Commissioner; the latter he may become, but the former never. I suppose you will call him Joubert or Jorissen but Bok would make a shorter signature; for shortness I think I should prefer Juhan and for respectability Cetywayo.

Juhan was a great Zulu chieftain and warrior. Shepstone goes on to say:

> There is nothing to be said about the Transvaal that would

have the slightest effect just now; the humiliation is determined upon and must be endured; natural causes and natural proceeses are all that can now be looked for to bring about amelioration. The next thing to look forward to is the effect that this humiliation to the British flag will produce at the Cape. The Transvaal rebellion was not a Transvaal question; at the next general election in the Cape Colony the Dutch element will predominate in their Parliament, they will adopt Dutch as the official language, and they will ask England to withdraw, and threaten vaguely if she does not. I can see no escape from the logic of facts which she has created; she must withdraw and if from the Cape why not from Ireland or Canada or anywhere else?

By 3 August, the royal commission had agreed on thirty-two articles of a peace treaty between Britain and the Transvaal which agreed to recognize the Transvaalers 'complete self-government, subject to the suzerainty of Her Majesty'.[13] The Vierkleur flag of the Boer republic was ceremonially raised by Joubert in Pretoria, at the site where Haggard had raised the British flag, on 8 August. But the signing of the peace treaty had not taken place at Hilldrop. The draft had been made and the commissioners had left the farm on 3 June to conduct the rest of their negotiations in the Transvaal.

Like the majority of British colonists, Rider was unhappy at what he considered a 'sell-out' by Prime Minister Gladstone to the Boers. As early as 3 May he had written to his mother 'that we are seriously debating clearing out of this part of the world. I am sorry to say that every day that has elapsed since I wrote has only strengthened my conviction that henceforth we can look for no peace or security in South Africa.' By 30 July Rider had reached a decision and wrote to his father: 'I must now tell you that after thoroughly thinking the matter over I have made up my mind to return to England next month . . . what brings me back in such a hurry, however, is the state of the country.' Rider had also written to Sir Bartle Frere on 6 June in which he deplored the attitude of the British Government in leading all these hundreds of thousands of men and women to believe that they were for once and for ever the subjects of Her Majesty, safe from all violence, cruelty and oppression, we have handed them over without a word of warning to the tender mercies of one, where natives are concerned, of the cruellest white races in the world. . . .

He went further:

Lastly there are unfortunate English inhabitants, three thousand of whom were gathered during the siege in Pretoria alone, losing their lives in a forsaken cause. I can assure you, sir, that you must see these people to learn how completely is their ruin. They have been pouring through here, many of those who were well to do a few months since, hardly knowing how to find food for their families.

Frere wrote on 20 July thanking Rider for 'one of the best accounts I have read of the present miserable state of affairs in the Transvaal'. The 'sell-out' seemed to reinforce Rider's anti-Boer prejudice. As Rider grew older, and his philosophy of life and people matured, he deeply regretted that prejudice: 'I now know that there is much to admire in the Boer character, also that among them were many men of real worth.'

The Haggards began to pack their belongings. Cochrane, who was suffering from a prolonged attack of dysentery, decided to accompany them back to England. It was decided to leave the farm in the charge of George Bromefield who would run it with the aid of a Mr North, an engineer, who was 'a very respectable man who has the advantage of experience of the country'. Rider derived a small income from the farm for a few years because it was not until 29 April 1883, that the partnership between Rider, Cochrane and Bromefield was legally dissolved.

Again came the subject of Rider's future. At first he and Cochrane made plans to go to Vancouver Island, Canada. He wrote to his mother:

I dare say you will wonder at this, but there are several

reasons, first we both like Colonial life, next it is a satisfaction to earn one's own living, thirdly, and chiefly, I am very anxious to form connections with some country in which it is possible for a man of moderate means to start his children in some respectable career in which they can earn their own livelihood, and have a fair chance of getting on in the world. This I had hoped to do in Natal – but events have been against us.

The idea was apparently dropped after Rider's brother, John George (Jack) talked the two young men out of it.

Before they left Hilldrop they had a sale of the furniture they had imported from England and because many items were rare in Natal they managed to fetch good prices. A second-hand grand piano, bought for £40, was sold for £200 and other items went at proportionally good prices.

The leave-taking was sad, especially when Rider said good-bye to his Zulu servant Mazooku, whom he eventually immortalized under his own name in *The Witch's Head* (1885). Mazooku solemnly gave Rider his redwood knobkerrie which is still retained by Haggard's heirs today.

So at last we bade farewell to Hilldrop. . . . I remember feeling quite sad as we drove down the dusty track to Newcastle, and the familiar house, surrounded by its orange trees, grew dim and vanished from our sight.

There my son had been born; there I had undergone many emotions of a kind that help to make a man; there I had suffered the highest sort of shame, shame for my country; there, as I felt, one chapter in my eventful life had opened and closed.

On Wednesday 31 August Rider, Louie and Cochrane watched the shores of Natal recede from the decks of the SS *Dunkeld*.

CHAPTER 5

LAW AND
LITERATURE

On the journey back to England, Rider, Louie and baby Jock spent two weeks in Madeira. They then returned to Bradenham where Squire Haggard had a few words to say about the accuracy of his prophecies on the subject of his son's future. Why had he left the safety of the Colonial Office to undertake such a hair-brained scheme as ostrich farming? Rider and Louie managed to overcome the squire's irate temper. But there was still a problem . . . what was Rider to do? His old chief Kotzé had written the year before 'why not read for the Bar?' But that meant that Rider would have to live off the finances provided by Louie's estate at Ditchingham for three years. It galled Rider but there was no other prospect. The Bar it would be. Squire Haggard approved. At last his son was beginning to show some sense.

One Sunday, during the autumn of 1881, while Louie was wheeling Jock in the garden of Bradenham, Rider went into the library where his brother Andrew, home on leave from his regiment, was reading the manuscript of a novel he had been writing. His mother and a friend named Bessie Ravenshaw were providing his audience. The novel was entitled *Ada Triscott* which was eventually to be published by Hurst & Blackett in 1890. Andrew, in fact, was to publish several volumes of French history, some novels and poems. Rider had no great opinion of *Ada Triscott* but did not inform Andrew of the fact. Andrew, like most of the Haggards, disliked criticism.[1] After a while, the audience drifted away leaving Andrew alone with Rider. Andrew asked his younger brother what he was going to do. Rider told him. He had decided to qualify at the Bar and then go to Africa again. 'I should read for the Bar and fill up your time writing', advised Andrew. He then launched forth on his own literary exploits.

By December of that year, Rider, Louie and Jock had moved into a furnished house in Norwood, South London, so that Rider could attend a crammer course for the entrance examinations to Lincoln's Inn. At the same time he realized that South Africa, due to the recent war, was a subject of heated discussion. At one stage he wrote an indignant letter to *The Times* expressing his views but it failed to appear. He decided that people did not know the real facts of the situation and embarked on the writing of a book which would tell them what really happened. He surrounded himself with Blue Books, governmental reports, and other reference works and eventually produced a work of fact which was interspersed with much opinion. He entitled it *Cetywayo and his White Neighbours, or Remarks on Recent Events in Zululand, Natal and Transvaal*. He bought a copy of *Athenaeum* magazine and made a list of publishers from its advertising columns. He wrote a covering letter and sent the manuscript to publishers pointing out that as the Zulu king, Cetywayo, was also visiting London shortly, there would be 'a ready sale' for 'an opportunely published work'. He added: 'The book is written in as interesting a style as I can command and would be published under my own name.'

Rejection followed rejection until, on 18 May, 1882, there came a letter from Trübner who informed him that 'if you will send us a cheque for the sum of £50 sterling we will undertake to produce an edition of seven hundred and fifty copies'. Although he could ill afford it, Rider sent off his cheque and on 22 June 1882, the book was published. It had a mixed reception from the critics.

The *British Quarterly Review, Vanity Fair*, the *Spectator* and *Saturday Review*, were generous in their praise of it. But the *Daily News* seized on Rider's ill-disguised anti-Boer prejudice and noted that Rider 'is shocked at the *retrocession of the Transvaal* and thinks we have not yet seen the end of the troubles in store for us, owing to our neglect to persevere in the work of exterminating the Boers'.[2] Rider, however, received personal letters of congratulation from Lord Randolph Churchill, Lord Lytton and Lord Carnarvon. Carnarvon, the Colonial Secretary at the time of the annexation, thought 'The English public was so deceived by misrepresentations of the annexation of the Transvaal that the real history was never understood; and the humiliating surrender of it was accepted in partial ignorance at least of the facts.'

By mid-April, 1884, *Cetywayo* had sold only 154 copies and Trübner's wrote to Rider on the 17th of the month:

> You will no doubt consider the account a most
> unsatisfactory one, as we do, seeing that we are out of
> pocket to the extent of £82 15s 5d. Against this, of course,
> we hold the £50 advanced by you, but we fear that we are
> never likely to recover the balance of £32 15s 5d.

In fact, Messrs Trübner did recover the money and more besides for when Rider became famous the remainder of the edition sold out rapidly. A second edition with new material was published in 1888 and on 20 October 1899, the section on 'The Transvaal' was published in a paperback format as *The Last Boer War* and sold over 30,000 copies. At the same time an American edition appeared as *A History of the Transvaal*. The second edition of *Cetywayo* received some good notices and the *Saturday Review* said:

> the Introduction is very well worth reading by anyone
> whether he knows the book or not, and the book by anyone
> who wishes to be acquainted with one of the most ghastly
> stories of injustice and imbecility combined that recent
> times have seen.[3]

Rider was to see one of his prophecies come true. He had written in the 1882 edition 'it is now quite within the bounds of possibility that they (rulers of the British Empire) may one day have to face a fresh Transvaal rebellion, only on a ten times larger scale'. The Second Boer War was to erupt in 1899, the Boers being provoked by the aggressive attitudes of the British colonists in the rest of southern Africa, and among the British soldiers killed was Rider's own nephew. But the Second Boer War could not have been averted by Britain militarily conquering the Transvaalers in 1881. The causes of the Second Boer War were the fruits of the very policy of imperial acquisition which Rider so ardently advocated.

With the publication of *Cetywayo*, Rider was considered something of an expert on South Africa and he contributed a series of six articles to the *South African* ranging from the history of the Transvaal, the advisability of the restoration of Cetywayo, to the prospects of confederation.[4]

> Whilst at Norwood a little incident occured which resulted in my becoming a writer of fiction. At the church which my wife and I attended we saw sitting near to us one Sunday a singularly beautiful and pure faced lady. Afterwards we agreed that this semi-divine creature – on whom to the best of my knowledge I have never set eyes again from that day to this – ought to become the heroine of a novel. So then and there we took paper, and each of us began to write the said novel. I think that after she had completed two or three folio sheets my wife ceased from her fictional labours. But, growing interested, I continued mine, which resulted in the story *Dawn*.

Rider originally entitled his novel *Angela,* after its heroine, and while he was working on it the couple decided to move to Louie's estate at Ditchingham. Louie was pregnant again and so, in December 1882, they moved to Ditchingham House which, it was felt, would be an ideal place for her confinement and for Rider to continue his law studies and writing activities. Moreover, they could live cheaply at Ditchingham because they would have no rent to pay. The second child, a girl, was born on 6 January 1883, and she was named Agnes Angela Rider, the Angela was after Rider's fictional heroine.

Rider worked hard on the novel.

> How to compose a novel I knew not, so I wrote straight on, trusting to the light of nature to guide me. My main object

was to produce the picture of a woman perfect in mind and body, and to show her character ripening and growing spiritual, under the pressure of various afflictions. Of course, there is a vast gulf between the novice's aspiration and his attainment, and I do not contend that Angela as she appears in *Dawn* fulfils this idea; also, such a person in real life might, and probably would, be a bore. . . .[5]

Rider admitted that 'before I had done with her, I became so deeply attached to my heroine that, in a literary sense, I have never quite got over it'.

Rider wrote a second draft of the novel, 554 pages of closely written foolscap, and he retitled it *There Remaineth a Rest*. He showed it to Mr Trübner, his one contact with the publishing world, who replied: 'You can write – it is certain you can write. Yes . . . I will get the book published for you.'[6] But Mr Trübner did not feel he could publish the book himself. Rider sent it to several publishers who were not interested. Eventally James Payne of Smith & Elder decided to send the manuscript to the novelist and biographer John Cordy Jeaffreson who wrote to Rider on 27 April 1883, making a detailed criticism of the novel and encouraging him to rewrite it. He told Rider 'I have read your story deliberately and read it with considerable interest, which would of course have been greater had I read it in type'.

Your opening chapters have a superabundance of action, and several highly dramatic positions, but they lack dramatic interest, i.e. the interest that comes from an exhibition of the influence of character upon character. Novels being what they are just now, it is small praise to say that Angela's love-story is better than two-thirds of the stories that are published. I could say much more in its favour. Still I urge you not to publish it in its present rude form. Indeed, the story has caused me to take so much interest in its writer that I could almost *entreat* you not to publish it.

I take it you are a young man. You are certainly a novice in literature; and like most beginners in the really difficult

art of novel-writing you have plied your pen under the
notion that novels are dashed off. Inferior novels are so
written, but you have the making of a good novelist in you,
if you are seriously bent on being one. It would therefore be
ill for you in several ways to make your debut with a tale
that would do you injustice. I don't counsel you to try again
with new materials. I advise you to make your present essay,
what it might be made, a work of art and a really good
performance.

You have written it with your *left hand* without strenuous
pains; you must write it with your *right hand*, throwing all
your force into it. If you produce it in its present crude state
you will do so only to regret in a few weeks you did not burn
it. If you rewrite it slowly with your right hand –
suppressing much, expanding much, making every
chapter a picture by itself, and polishing up every sentence
so that each page bears testimony to the power of its
producer – the story will be the beginning of such a literary
career as I conceive you to be desirous of running. Get the
better of the common notion that novels may be dashed
off – by remembering how often Lord Lytton rewrote
'Pelham', thinking over every part of it, now compressing
and now expanding the narrative, before he ventured to give
it to the world. Go to Charles Dickens rooms in the S.
Kensington Museum and observe the erasures, the
insertions, the amendments of every paragraph of his
writings.

Rider sat down on 15 May 1883 and began to rewrite the
manuscript. By 5 September the same year he had finished the
493 foolscap sheets. 'I toiled at that book morning, noon and
night with the result that at length my eyesight gave out, and I
was obliged to finish the writing of it in a darkened room.'[7] He
wrote off to Jeaffreson and asked him to recommend a
publisher. Jeaffreson, without seeing the rewritten manuscript,
wrote to Arthur Blackett of Messrs Hurst & Blackett, stating that
he had read the first draft and had advised Rider to rewrite it

so that every chapter should be in harmony with its best and strongest parts. He has acted on my advice, and if the result of his renewed labour answers my anticipation, he has produced a work that will make your reader rub his hands and say 'This will do'.

Arthur Blackett soon wrote to Rider.

We shall be very happy to undertake the publication of your novel on the following terms. To produce the work at our own expense and risk. To pay you the sum of £40 on the sale of four hundred copies and £30 on the sale of every hundred copies after. The title *Angela* has been used before. . . .

The novel was finally named *Dawn* and it appeared in an edition of 500 copies on 21 February 1884. It was produced in three volumes. Rider noted:

In most quarters it met with the usual reception of a first novel by an unknown man. Some reviewers sneered at it, and some 'slated' it, and made merry over the misprints – a cheap form of wit that saves those who practise it the trouble of going into the merits of the book. Two very good notices fell to its lot, however, in *The Times* and in the *Morning Post*, the first of these speaking about the novel in terms of which any amateur writer might feel proud though, unfortunately, it appeared too late to be of much service.[8]

The Times had enthused:

Dawn is a novel of merit far above the average. From the first page the story arrests the mind and arouses the expectation. . . . This is, we repeat, a striking and original novel breathing an elevated if somewhat exaggerated tone.[9]

The *Athenaeum* said 'He lacks neither imagination nor courage, and his achievement is such as need not call a blush to the cheek of the most melodramatic story writer.'[10] *Pall Mall Budget* felt the book 'somewhat undisciplined' although it was 'above the average of first books'.[11] *Academy*, while feeling the book was 'too long' said 'it is well written, it has considerable interest of plot, and the characters are not borrowed'.[12]

Jeaffreson wrote in May, having read *Dawn* in its published version, to invite Rider to dinner.

> We could talk all round the literary question over a cigar in my study after dinner. Could you succeed in literature? Certainly, up to a certain point: unquestionably up to the point you indicate, though you might never earn as much money as the two novelists you mention; for in that respect they have been singularly fortunate. But you may not hope to succeed in a day. You might become famous in a morning; but you may not entertain the hope of doing so. You must only hope to succeed by degrees – by steady work, slow advances, and after several disappointments.

Rider was now totally bitten by the literary bug. Although he still worked hard at law, and found it a very lonely period in his life ('since my friends were African, and Africa was far away'), he commenced work on his second novel. He called it *Eva, or a Tale of Love and War* and it consisted of 377 foolscap pages. After trying to get magazines interested in publishing it as a serial, for there was money to be made in serialization, he sent it to Hurst & Blackett and they agreed to publish it on the same basis as they had *Dawn*, in three volumes with the same remuneration. It was published on 18 December 1884 under the title *The Witch's Head*. Rider said that after it had been published 'the editor of a leading monthly told me that he would have been delighted to run the book (serially) had it fallen into the hands of his firm'.[13]

Generally, the reviewers were enthusiastic:

> Its reception astonished me, for I did not think so well of the book as I had done its predecessor. In that view, by the way, the public has borne out my judgement, for to this day three copies of *Dawn* are absorbed for every two of *The Witch's Head*, a proportion that has never varied since the two works appeared in one-volume form.[14]

George Saintbury, writing in *Academy*, said: 'That Mr Rider Haggard has very considerable powers as a novelist was evident from his rather extravagant book *Dawn*, and it is still more evident from *The Witch's Head*'.[15] *Literary World* admitted, somewhat begrudgingly that 'some parts of the novel are really good'.[16] The *Boston Literary World* described it as an 'extraordinary novel'.[17] A pirated American edition of the book came out early in 1885 from which Rider received no royalties at all.

While Rider had been working on the book Louie had given birth to her third child, another daughter, named Sybil Dorothy Rider, the name Dorothy being taken from the heroine in *The Witch's Head*. Dorothy, as she was always called, was born on 25 March 1884 at Ditchingham. It was time, Rider felt, to take stock of his literary career. He found that, so far, *Dawn* and *The Witch's Head* had made him the sum of £50 whereas *Cetywayo* had cost him £50. The profit, therefore, was nil. It was no way for a 28-year-old married man with three children to provide security for his family. Rider and his family were still existing on the income from his wife's estate, a depressing fact which was heightened by the realization that even this income was insecure. The estate was suffering from the general agricultural recession and times were extremely difficult. He dismally contemplated his future as he strode around the estate with his bull-dog Caesar, carrying a twisted walking stick of umzimbet wood which reminded him of Africa.

> I came to the conclusion that I would abandon the making of books. The work was very hard, and when put to the test of experience the glamour that surrounds this occupation vanished. I did not care much for the publicity it involved, and, like most young authors, I failed to appreciate being sneered at by anonymous critics who happened not to admire what I wrote, and whom I had no opportunity of answering. It is true that then, as now, I liked the work for its own sake.[18]

He finished his law studies, passed his exams and was

awarded his certificate on 3 October 1884 by Spencer H. Walpole at Lincoln's Inn. He was then called to the Bar on 26 January 1885. 'I determined to abandon the writing of fiction and devote myself entirely to my profession', he wrote. He, with his family, moved back to London, to a small house in Gunterstone Road in West Kensington, and with them went Agnes Barber, a school friend of Louie's who volunteered to help with the children. They managed to let Ditchingham House and Rider secured a job in the office of a distant relation, Sir Henry Bargrave Deane, who afterwards became a judge of the Probate and Divorce Division. Rider had decided to specialize in Probate and Divorce Law and he was all set to throw himself into his career.

But, travelling to London with one of his brothers, a conversation occurred which was to lead to the foundation of Rider's literary career, a career which he had announced he had given up. The brothers were discussing *Treasure Island*, by Robert Louis Stevenson, which had just been published and was a resounding success. Rider did not think the book was so remarkable. His brother, indignantly, bet him a shilling that Rider could not write 'anything half as good'.[19] Writing on a pedestal desk brought from Ditchingham House, Rider occupied the evenings and weekends of six weeks writing an adventure story which he entitled *King Solomon's Mines*.

After he had finished Rider took the story round to several publishers, including Hurst & Blackett, but no one was interested in the tale. One publisher, rather unkindly, forwarded his reader's report to Rider.

> We approached this book with feelings of curiosity – we left it with those of loathing and disgust. Never has it been our fate to wade through such a farrago of obscene witlessness . . . in conclusion we must enter our protest against the multiplication of books like *King Solomon's Mines*. Nothing which has ever appeared in the *Pall Mall Gazette* or *Town Talk* is likely in the hands of the young, to do so much injury as this recklessly immoral book.[20]

Rider finally sent the manuscript to Cassell who sent it to the poet and critic W. E. Henley, who was editor of their *Magazine of Art*. Henley was enthusiastic about the story and showed it to a friend of his, the 42-year-old Scottish writer, historian, mythographer, poet and journalist, Andrew Lang. Lang was London editor of *Harper's Magazine* and, by coincidence, Rider had already been in touch with him having submitted a short story entitled 'Bottles' to the magazine. Lang had replied on 28 March 1885:

> Your paper 'Bottles' has reached me as London editior of *Harper's*. I am much pleased by it, but I am unable to accept anything except by permission of the American editor. . . . I am glad to take this opportunity of thanking you for the great pleasure *The Witches' Head* has given me. I have not read anything so good for a long while.

'Bottles', recalled Rider, was eventually retitled 'The Blue Curtains' and appeared in the *Cornhill Magazine* before it was collected in volume in *Smith and the Pharaohs* (1921).[21]

Rider was not long delayed before he heard from Lang about his adventure story.

> I have got as far as Sir Henry's duel with the king. Seldom have I read a book with so much pleasure: I think it perfectly delightful. The question is, what is the best, whereby I mean the coiniest way to publish it? As soon as possible I will find out what *Harper's Boys Magazine* is able to do. I believe that all boys' magazines pay hopelessly badly. There is so much invention and imaginative power and knowledge of African character in your book that I almost prefer it to *Treasure Island*.[22]

With the recommendation of both Henley and Lang, John Williams, the editor of Cassells Company wrote accepting it for publication. In an interview in his office Williams offered Rider a choice of £100 for the entire copyright or a 10 per cent royalty agreement. This was to be a £50 advance on account of royalties to be calculated 'at the rate of ten per cent on the published price of the book on all copies sold by them during the continuance of the copyright, reckoning thirteen copies as to the twelve.'[23]

Rider admitted:

> After my previous experiences as an author, £100 on the nail had great attractions. I had no particular belief in the story which I had thrown off in my leisure hours as a mere *jeu d'esprit*, especially after its rejection in other quarters. Even Mr Lang's kind expression of opinion carried no conviction to my mind, for I did not understand all that it meant coming from such a source.[24]

Rider told Williams he would settle for £100 in outright payment and Williams left the office to get the appropriate contract.

> As it chanced, however, there sat in the corner of the room a quiet clerk, whom I had never even noticed. When the editor had departed this unobtrusive gentleman addressed me.
>
> 'Mr Haggard,' he said in a warning voice, 'if I were you I would take the other agreement.'
>
> Then hearing some noise, once more he became absorbed in his work and I understood that the conversation was not to be continued.

Rider realized that the clerk must have first-hand knowledge of Cassell's estimation of the worth of the book and when Williams returned Rider told him he had changed his mind and would accept the royalty agreement. It was the wisest move of his life.

The book was published on 30 September 1885. Max Pemberton recalled a certain publisher sitting next to him at a dinner party that day who turned to him and said: 'There's a silly story of a diamond mine published today . . . by a man named Rider Haggard. They offered me this book six months ago and I declined it. Some fool has bought it as you will see – and I'm sorry for him.'[25] By December, Cassell's had had to reprint *King Solomon's Mines* four times. It sold 12,000 copies in the first twelve months alone and has never been out of print since it first appeared.

The reviewers were full of praise. The *Athenaeum* said it was 'one of the earliest books of the season, and we shall be surprised if it does not also prove to be the best'.[26] *Academy* said it was 'a boys' book of the first class, which holds the attention from the first page to the last'.[27] *Vanity Fair* felt it was not just a boys' adventure and recommended 'this clever and highly exciting story' to all its readers.[28] The *Spectator* judged it superior to works by Jules Verne and Herman Melville and said the author was 'a story teller of no common power'.[29] *Public Opinon* felt 'it stands as a work of art'.[30] In an unsigned piece in the *Saturday Review*, Lang said 'to tell the truth we would give many novels, say eight hundred (that is about the yearly harvest), for such a book as *King Solomon's Mines*'.[31] In America, where a limited edition of 500 copies was issued by Cassell, the *Book Buyer* said 'we cannot recall a bit of modern fiction to equal it'.[32]

Rider bathed in praise from the literary establishment of the day. From Skerryvore, Bournemouth, Robert Louis Stevenson wrote to Rider that he had received a copy. 'I know not who did this good thing to me; and so I send my gratitude to headquarters and the fountainhead.' Stevenson said that in the book he found flashes of a fine, weird imagination and a fine poetic use and command of the savage way of talking: Subsequently Stevenson wrote to give Rider some advice.

> You rise in the course of your book to pages of eloquence and poetry; and it is quite true that you must rise from something lower; and that the beginning must infallibly (?) be pitched low and kept quiet. But you begin (pardon me the word) slipshod. If you are to rise, you must prepare the mind in the quiet parts, with at least an accomplished neatness. To this you could easily attain. In other words, what you have still to learn is to take the trouble with those parts which do not excite you.

In another letter Stevenson added:

> Further reflection on *King Solomon's Mines* makes me think
> you are one who gets up steam slowly. In that case, when
> you have your book finished go back and rewrite the
> beginning up to the mark. My case is the reverse: I always
> begin well, and often finish languidly or hurriedly.
>
> PPS – How about a deed of partnership?

But Rider never met Stevenson although they corresponded
infrequently over the years.

Among his distinguished fans was the man he felt had
'sold-out' British interests in the Transvaal, the former prime
minister, Gladstone, and a young boy who was to become a
famous prime minister of the future – Winston S. Churchill.
The young Winston wrote to Rider on 11 February 1888 to
thank him for sending him *Allan Quatermain*, the sequel to
King Solomon's Mines. 'I like *Allan Quatermain* better than
King Solomon's Mines; it is more amusing. I hope you will
write a great many more books.' At the same time, Winston's
aunt, Lady Constance Leslie wrote to Rider asking whether she
could bring the boy to meet him.

> I don't wish to bore so busy a man as yourself, but will you,
> when you have the time, please tell me, shall I bring him on
> Wednesday next when Mrs Haggard said she would be at
> home. . . . He really is a very interesting being, though
> temporarily uppish from the restraining parental hand
> being in Russia.

While waiting for *King Solomon's Mines* to be published,
Rider spent the summer vacation at Ditchingham, although not
at Ditchingham House which had been let, but at Dewton, a
farm on the estate where he set to work and wrote a sequel to
the story entitled *Allan Quatermain*. He began the manuscript
on 17 July and finished the 256 foolscap pages on 28
September. His original title was *Zu-Vendis* which he then
altered to *The Frowning City* and finally to *Allan Quatermain*.

This sequel was bought by *Longman's Magazine* which ran it as a serial between January and August 1887, without illustrations.[33] The book was then published by Longmans Green in a 20,000 edition on 1 July 1887.

Rider returned to London in the autumn to continue his law practice, sharing chambers at No. 1 Elm Court with a Mr Kerr. For a while he reported Divorce and Probate cases for *The Times*, filling in for the regular reporter, an old barrister named Kelly, who was then on holiday. Cases were few and far between for a newly qualified lawyer and so Rider filled up his time by starting another book which he wrote 'upon an old teak table with a leather top'. Writing a book in such conditions was 'no easy task, since young barristers of my acquaintance, with time on their hands, would enter and scoff at my literary labours'.

The new book was set against the background of his life in Pretoria and he entitled it *Jess*. He started the first of the 254 pages of foolscap on 31 December 1885. The original draft of the latter part of chapter 26 was lost one evening when Rider was travelling home and although he advertised for it, the missing portion was never recovered and it had to be written from memory. Rider sold this as a serial to the *Cornhill Magazine* who published it between May 1886 and April 1887.[34] He then, recklessly, sold the copyright outright to Smith, Elder who published it in March 1887.

But before *Allan Quatermain* and *Jess* were published, Rider had written and published another romance which was to make the name of H. Rider Haggard known throughout the literary world and secure him his place in the history of English literature.

CHAPTER 6

'KING ROMANCE
HAS COME INDEED!'

Towards the end of March 1886 Rider arrived at the office of his newly appointed literary agent, Alexander Pollock Watt, in Paternoster Square, near London's St Paul's Cathedral. He carried a manuscript with him which he threw on the desk before Watt. 'There is what I shall be remembered by', he announced. The title of the tale was *She* and Rider was right. From the very first day of publication *She* was a bestseller, the subject of literary controversy and a book, which ninety years later, has hardly ever been out of print either in the UK or USA; a book that has been translated into over twenty languages, filmed nearly a dozen times, and made the subject of plays, an opera and a ballet.

Rider said he wrote the book in about six weeks. The manuscript bears the note 'Finish 18 March 1886' but where the notation of the commencement has been made a paper clip has torn away part of the day which reads 'Feb/86'. Even allowing that the book was started on 1 February Rider did indeed complete the remarkable book in six weeks. He says: 'Moreover it was never rewritten, and the manuscript carries but few corrections. . . . The fact is that it was written at white heat almost without rest, and that is the best way to compose.' It is also true, however, that Rider must have been constructing his tale for some time before he started the actual writing because he had been in correspondence with Andrew Lang, now a close friend and literary adviser, concerning certain details of the story, such as the Greek to be used and the ancestry of his hero, Leo Vincey. One of Lang's letters concerning the derivation of Vincey's name is dated 1 February 1886,[1] so Rider was not perhaps accurate when he recalled:

I remember that when I sat down to the task my ideas as to its development were of the vaguest. The only clear notion that I had in my head was that of an immortal woman inspired by an immortal love. All the rest shaped itself round this figure. And it came – it came faster than my poor aching hand could set it down.

But whether Rider worked out all or even some of the details of the story before he started to write it, he still had a career to follow while he was dashing down the tale. He recalls that he 'followed my profession, spending many hours of each day studying in chambers, or in Court where I had some devilling practice, carried on my usual correspondence and attended to the affairs of a man with a young family and a certain landed estate'. In spite of such pressures Rider had produced a book that took the literary world by storm.

She is a tale told by one Ludwig Horace Holly. The story starts when Holly, a student at Cambridge, is sitting in his room at midnight studying. A friend, Vincey, arrives with a strong-box and confides to the astonished Holly that he is dying and asks Holly to act as guardian to his son, Leo. After his death Holly is to take charge of the strong-box which he is to give to his son Leo on his twenty-fifth birthday. Vincey dies. Twenty-five years later the box is opened and in it is a broken potsherd inscribed with ancient writings. Leo Vincey learns that he is the sole descendant of an ancient family which traces its roots back to ancient Egypt and to Kallikrates, a priest of Isis who had deserted his temple and fled the country with Amenartes, daughter of Pharaoh. The two flee into the interior of Africa and encounter the immortal, beautiful white queen, revered as a goddess, and a strange pillar of fire. The goddess loves Kallikrates and promises to make him immortal if he stays with her. But he rejects her love for Amenartes and, in a fit of jealous rage, the goddess slays him. Amenartes escapes to bear Kallikrates' son, the ancestor of Leo Vincey, and enjoins him to 'seek out the woman and learn the secret of Life, and if thou mayest, find a way to slay her. . . .' If her son fails then she urges 'all of thy seed who come after thee' to avenge Kallikrates. There is a note by Leo's father to the effect that he has tried but failed.

So Leo, his guardian Holly and a manservant, Job, set out to Africa where, after sundry adventures, they are captured by natives – a tribe called the Amahagger. Billali, an old man from among the captors, reminds his comrades of the words of She-Who-Must-Be-Obeyed – that all white men captured in her country are to be brought to her. After another incident in which Leo is wounded trying to rescue his native guide, the party are taken across swamps and plains and led blindfolded through tunnels to the lost city of Kôr where She reigns. Holly alone is taken before She while Leo is taken to have his wound tended. The figure is veiled and commences to question Holly on the outside world. But her questions speak of the ancient Greeks and Egyptians as contemporaries. Holly is puzzled. Then the woman says she has lived in the lost city of Kôr for 2000 years, time is irrelevant, death cannot touch her. Her name is Ayesha and she has discovered the secret of immortality, contained in a Pillar of Fire in which she has bathed. Her only purpose in life is to await the return of the man she once loved, Kallikrates. She casts aside her veil and shows Holly her breath-taking beauty.

Holly is worried about Leo, who is now in danger of dying from fever. Ayesha promises to visit him. As she stands over the fever-racked body of Leo, she gasps. Leo has the features of the dead Kallikrates; he is the reincarnation of his ancestor, the priest,. the man for whom she has waited 2000 years. She restores Leo's health and then invites the Englishmen to a native ball which is illuminated by burning embalmed corpses. At this ball, Ustane, a native girl, whom it is hinted is a reincarnation of Amenartes, falls in love with Leo and is killed by Ayesha. Ayesha then takes Leo and Holly to her apartments and reveals the perfectly preserved body of Kallikrates – it is Leo, or rather an exact replica of him. Ayesha destroys the body with acid saying she need no longer guard her ancestor's remains now that her beloved has returned.

Leo is under her spell and Ayesha plans that he must become immortal by bathing in the Pillar of Fire. Ayesha, Leo, Holly and Job set off to cross a vast plain, scale a cliff and finally reach a cave in which the Pillar of Fire burns. Leo hesitates to enter and Ayesha, to encourage him, enters first. The flames shoot up around her . . . and as Leo, Holly and Job look on, she begins to age and shrivel. Has the flame's magic changed or can it be used only once in a lifetime? Ayesha's destruction is so horrific that Job dies of shock and Leo's hair turns white.

After helping Leo to return to England, Holly writes the tale ending:

> Here ends this history so far as it concerns science and the outside world. What its end will be as regards Leo and myself is more than I can guess. But we feel that it is not reached yet. A story that began more than two thousand years ago may stretch a long way into the dim and distant future.

Thus Rider prepares his readers for the three sequels that he was to write to this, his most enduring tale, although he delayed writing the first of those sequels for twenty years.[2]

Before actually beginning on his manuscript, Rider called upon Lang to help him with the Greek for the sherd of Amenartes. Lang replied 'My Greek prose has twenty years of rust on it but I'll get you a piece by an Ireland scholar.'[3] This was not apparently forthcoming because Rider turned to his old headmaster, Dr H. A. Holden, from Ipswich Grammer School, who happened to be one of the best Greek scholars of the day. Holden told Rider that to do the work justice he would like to be able to have six months of study before he ventured to write the particular Greek prose Rider required. Rider felt it was unnecessary for a man of Holden's learning. 'My dear boy,' replied his ex-headmaster, 'I have been soaking myself in the classics for over forty years, and I am just beginning to learn how little I know about them.' In March, however, Holden wrote to Rider:

Your task is not quite so big as one of the labours of
Hercules, but by no means easy without further data. Do
you want the Greek to be such as to deceive the learned
world into thinking that it is no forgery but a genuine bit of
antiquity? If so, the style will have to be taken into account:
it won't do to imitate Herodotus, though it is just
the bit suitable for his style, because of the date BC 200.

Finally, Rider managed to get the Greek translation which
was so excellent that, even today, it has impressed a Greek-born
scholar of ancient Greece with its accuracy of style and concept.[4]
Rider followed Lang's advice on the transition of Vincey's name
from Latin. Lang suggested 'Vindex, Vindici, Vincey would
knit'.[5] Rider was also meticulous on other background aspects
and for the Old English paragraphs he consulted 'my late friend
Dr Raven, who was a very great authority on monkish Latin and
medieval English'. Ironically, *The Times* reviewer decided to
attack the book by making a criticism of the Greek.

Rider's agent, Watt, was deeply impressed with the
manuscript and it was not long before he sold the serial rights of
She to the *Graphic* which ran the book from 2 October 1886 to 8
January 1887.[6] Longmans, Green would publish it in book form
at the end of the serialization. E. K. Johnson was commissioned
to prepare fourteen illustrations. In New York, *Harper's
Weekly* also agreed to serialize the story, commencing on 2
October, using several of Johnson's illustrations. They would
also publish the work in book form on 24 December 1886, in
their Franklin Square Library series. Because there was no
copyright enforcement with the USA, by the end of March
1887, I have discovered no less than thirteen different editions
of *She* in existence. Rider had the same problem with *King
Solomon's Mines* which, by 1890, had sold over 200,000 copies
in various American editions and on which Rider only received
£13 in royalties. According to a 1904 edition of *She* produced by
George Munro of New York, Munro claims to have published
an edition in May 1886. It would have been impossible to have
pirated *She* at this date and we can accurately assume that

Harper's Franklin Square Library edition was the first American appearance of the book.

When *She* was in proof form for serial publication, Rider showed it to Andrew Lang. On 12 July Lang wrote to Rider:

> I have pretty nearly finished *She*. I really must congratulate you; I think it is one of the most astonishing romances I have ever read. The more impossible it is, the better you do it, till it seems like a story from the literature of another planet. I can't give a better account of the extraordinary impression it makes upon me; as to the Public I never can speak.

However, Lang has his reservations and criticisms.

> You really must look after the style, more when it comes out as a book. I would also, if it is not impertinent, reduce the comic element a good deal – it is sometimes so sudden a drop as to be quite painful. For my own part (and I am pretty sure many readers will agree) there is too much raw heart . . . and other tortures. I'm saying pretty much what I would say in a review, only beforehand. I'd like to see it polished up a bit and made more worthy of the imagination in it.

Two days later Lang wrote again to tell Rider to guard from facetiousness.

> I'm sure the note about a monograph on Ayesha's Greek pronunciation for the use of public schools, will show the Public you are laughing – a thing I never can help doing, and the B[ritish] P[ublic] hate it.

Lang was not keen on the scene in which Holly, Leo and Job are captured by the Amahagger and introduced to some gruesome cannibalistic rituals whereby the trio's native guide is about to be killed by placing a ceremonial red-hot cooking pot on his head: 'I've never heard of it, historically, and even now I'm not sure whether it is one of the cannibal myths.' He thinks the episode should be modified 'in the selling interest of the book'.

Rider took Lang's advice in this matter and when the book form came out it differed considerably from the serial form. The comparative passage reads thus:

The *Graphic*	First book edition
. . . they had reached the spot where Mahomed was struggling and then – even now I can scarcely bear to write it – there was one awful heartrending shriek, ending and smothered in a hissing sound, and the next thing I saw was the poor wretch, broken loose from his captors, in the despairing effort of a hideous death, and rushing and rolling in the darkness beyond the lamps, the red hot pot jammed upon his head, completely covering it from view.	. . . they had reached the spot where Mahomed was struggling. He fought like a fiend, shrieking in the abandonment of his despair, and notwithstanding the noose around him, and the efforts of the men who held his legs, the advancing wretches were for the moment unable to accomplish their purpose, which, horrible and incredible as it seems, was to put the red hot pot upon his head.

Lang also urged Rider to look after the style of the book. 'When I say style, I mean that it is risky to bring in colloquialisms with abruptness, after flights into the ideal.' The day after this letter Lang completed his painstaking reading of the proofs and wrote again.

> I have just finished *She,* previously I skipped a bit to get to the end. I certainly still think it the most extraordinary romance I ever read, and that's why I want you to be very careful with the proofs before it goes out in a volume. I will read them over again and annotate. I'm perfectly certain most of the chaff about Gladstone must go, it entirely disturbs the mood of the reader – any reader can be a judge

of that much. I nearly cried over Ayesha's end. But how did she come to Kôr? There is a difficulty about Leo. He is not made a very interesting person. Probably he was only a fine animal. Anyhow that can't be helped now and never could perhaps. I dare say Kallikrates was no better. But some of the chaff in awful situations lets one down too suddenly. I'd take other fellow's advice about it, in some of the marked places. I hope they find *She* in Thibet and all die together. By George, I'd have gone into the fire and chucked *She* in too, perhaps it would have picked her up again.

Rider took Lang's advice again and deleted the Gladstone reference and revised one or two minor points. It was not until twenty years later when he wrote *Ayesha: The Return of She* (1904) that he used Lang's idea of Leo and Holly finding She in Tibet where they were to die. Rider was so delighted with Lang's help and enthusiasm that he decided to dedicate the book to him. Lang wrote on 27 July:

It is awfully good of you to think of putting my name in *She* and I consider it a great distinction. The only thing is that, if you do, I shan't be able to review it, except with my name signed thereto and my honest confession. Probably I could do that in the *Academy*. It is rather curious (plagiarism on your side again) that I was going to ask you to let me dedicate my little volume of tales 'That Missionary' etc. to you.

The serialization of *She* in the *Graphic* attracted a great deal of attention but the avalanche of literary acclaim and criticism was reserved until the book was published on 1 January 1887. The first Longman's edition, priced at six shillings, did not carry any of E. K. Johnson's illustrations but it did carry an illustration (in two plates) of the sherd of Amenartes which Rider and Louie's friend, Agnes Barber had made. Agnes was now one of the family. She had come to live with Rider and Louie to help Louie with the children and then met Rider's brother John George (Jack). They were married on 28 January

111

1886. It was Agnes who had drawn the map for *King Solomon's Mines* and had enthusiastically helped Rider make up the sherd. It was shown to the antiquarian, Sir John Evans, who examined it through an eyeglass and finally remarked: 'All I can say is that it might possibly have been forged.' Rider eventually presented it to the Norwich Museum where it can still be seen.

With the appearance of the book came the reviews. Rider missed them because, by January 1887, he had decided to give up law and take a long holiday in Egypt. In the main, the reviewers were overwhelming in their praise of the book.

Lang, in fact, did review it in the *Academy* and told its readers that it was a rare experience for him and one which took him 'beyond the bounds of explored romanticism'. But he admitted 'it is hard to give any but a personal and subjective estimate'.[7] The *Athenaeum* described Rider as 'a story teller with a rare turn for romance'. The conception of *She* was 'original, weird, fantastic and certainly fascinating' but it complained that the treatment of the story was 'lamentably unequal' and that 'the language and dramatic force rarely rise to the level of a really great occasion'.[8] The *Saturday Review* thanked Rider 'heartily' for the production of *She* and told its readers that they would have 'no cause for complaint' if they read the romance.[9] The *Spectator* while admitting 'a dislike for Mr Rider Haggard's favourite literary method' conceded that *She* was 'very stirring and exciting' and showed 'remarkable imaginative powers'.[10] The *Pall Mall Budget* praised the 'energy and intensity of imagination' but deplored the 'bathos' and 'frequent torpors'. It likened Rider's conception to Dante and his writings to the *Daily Telegraph*.[11] *Public Opinion* said that 'Few books bolder in conception, more vigorous in treatment, or fresher in fancy, have appeared for a long time.'[12] *Murray's Magazine* called it 'a marvellously realistic tale of fantastic adventures'.[13] *Blackwood's Edinburgh Magazine* devoted three full pages to it.[14]

W. E. Henley, the man who had first 'spotted' *King Solomon's Mines* and shown the manuscript to Lang, informed the American readers of the *Critic* two months later that it is 'impossible in any house to attempt any conversation which is

not interrupted by the abominable introduction of *She* . . .
artist, author, pedant, politician, man of science, man of the
world, there is only one book that all of them just now are likely
to ask if you have read'. He added:

> Haggard has the gift of invention to such a point as to be
> practically a man of genius but he is not an artist. . . . I
> couldn't help regretting that Mr Rider Haggard is not Mr
> Stevenson and has not taken seriously to heart the
> difficulties of his profession.[15]

He admitted, however, that the book had to be read 'in a gasp'
and 'for my part I couldn't put it down until I had finished'.
   Queen praised the story's 'vividness and power'[16] while
Vanity Fair decided to produce a review in verse.

> This is the song of Ayesha.
> Weird, clever, exciting, full of strange
>   thoughts and true philosophy.
> Written by a dead Princess on a Cracked Pot.
> Price, six shillings for the lot.[17]

Wilkie Collins (author of *The Moonstone*, acclaimed the first
English detective thriller) praised it highly and Marie Corelli
wrote to Rider saying that she had been 'dazzled to my very
heart's core by the splendour of *She*'.[18]
   But there were critics who disliked the book. George Moore
thought *She* was 'paste' not 'crystal'[19] 'manufacture' not 'art',
while George Meredith said he could not even bear to read the
book (an excellent way to make a judgment!). Henry Sidgwick,
the philosopher, told Mary (Gladstone) Drew that he had read
it 'under protest and with firm resolve not to read any more
[novels which the public enthuse about]'.[20] But those who
disliked the tale were in a minority.
   Sir Walter Besant wrote to Rider the day after publication:

> While I am under the spell of Ayesha which I have only just
> finished, I must write to congratulate you upon a work
> which most certainly puts you at the head – a long way

ahead – of all contemporary imaginative writers. If fiction is best cultivated in the field of pure imagination then you are certainly the first of modern novelists. *Solomon's Mines* is left far behind. It is not only the central conception that is so splendid in its audacity, but it is your logical and pitiless working out of the whole thing in its inevitable details that strikes me with astonishment.

I do not know what the critics will say about it. Probably they will not read more than they can help and then will let you off with a few general expressions. If the critic is a woman she will put down this book with the remark that it is impossible – almost all women have this feeling towards the marvellous.

Whatever else you do, you will have *She* always behind you for the purposes of odious comparison. And whatever critics say the book is bound to be a magnificent success. Also it will produce a crop of imitators. And all the little conventional story tellers will be jogged out of their grooves – until they find new ones. . . .

Another letter came a few days later from Edmund Gosse, the author and literary critic.

I feel constrained to write again to you about *She* before the impression the book has made upon my mind in any degree wears off. In construction I think you have been successful to a very marvellous degree. The quality of the invention increases as you go on, and the latest chapters are the best. Indeed it does not appear to me that I have ever been thrilled and terrified by any literature as I have by pp. 271–306 of *She*. It is simply unsurpassable.

All through the book there are points which I have noted for the highest praise, the three white fingers on Ustane's hair, the dream about the skeletons, the meeting of the Living and the Dead, the Statue of Truth – these are only a few of the really marvellous things that the book contains. I was a great admirer and, as you know, a warm welcomer of *King Solomon's Mines* but I confess that exceedingly picturesque and ingenious book did not prepare me for *She*; and I do not know what to say, of hope or fear, about any future book of adventure of yours. I don't know what is to be imagined beyond the death of Ayesha.

Accept again my thanks for the gift of your book, which I put among my treasures, and now the expression of my sincere and cordial admiration.

PS May I say without impertinence, I think the style strikes me as a vast improvement upon that of KSM?

At a dinner of the Authors' Club, Gosse was later to say of *She*: 'I read [it] in a single night. It was impossible while the book was in my hand to take my eyes from a single page.[21]

Lang was so taken with *She* that he wrote a sonnet entitled 'She' and dedicated to H. Rider Haggard:

Not in the waste beyond the swamp and sand,
The fever-haunted forest and lagoon,
Mysterious Kôr, thy fanes forsaken stand,
With lonely towers beneath the lonely Moon!
Not there doth Ayesha linger, – rune by rune
Spelling the scriptures of a people banned, –
The world is disenchanted! oversoon
Shall Europe send her spies through all the land!

Nay, not in Kôr, but in whatever spot,
    In fields, or towns, or by the insatiate sea,
Hearts brood o'er buried Loves and unforgot,
    Or wreck themselves on some Divine decree,
Or would o'er leap the limits of our lot,
    There in the Tombs and deathless, dwelleth SHE![22]

Lang then parodied his sonnet with a work called 'Twosh' which he dedicated to 'Hyder Ragged'.[23] Lang then produced with W. H. Pollock a parody on the book, entitled *He: by the authors of 'It', 'King Solomon's Wives', 'Bess', 'Much Darker Days', 'Mr Morton's Subtler' and other romances*. The work was published anonymously by Longmans, Green on 23 February 1887. The dedication, in fact, is addressed from 'Kôr, January 30, 1887.' In front of the novelette, Lang's sonnet was published, which, since 1896 has appeared, unacknowledged, in subsequent editions of *She*. Amazingly a second edition of *He* was printed in March 1887.

Lang and Pollock's parody inspired many such works to be written. Most of them were confined to magazine pieces but several, like *He*, were of book length.[24] In April 1887, for example, Vizetelly published a book entitled *King Solomon's Wives*. The author was a young barrister, Sir Henry Charles Biron, who became a noted jurist, but this was not learnt until Ernest Vizetelly wrote a letter on the subject to the *Sketch* in 1921. New York publisher Norman L. Munro issued five parodies of Rider's work all within 1887. These were entitled *He, King Solomon's Wives, It, King Solomon's Treasures* and *Bess*. Munro ascribed their authorship to an American popular writer John de Morgan. It was not until 1891 that a copyright agreement with the USA protected writers from this sort of thing. The identical titles of the first two parodies to Lang and Pollock's *He* and Biron's *King Solomon's Wives* have caused several learned bibliographers to claim that Munro actually pirated these two works and that De Morgan wrote only the last three titles in the series. Some have even gone so far as to suggest that the British publishers pirated the titles and that De Morgan was the authentic author. However, this confusion has been due to the rarity of the titles so bibliographers have not been able to compare texts. The truth is that De Morgan's *He* is an entirely different, and full length novel, to Lang and Pollock's shorter parody. It may, therefore, be presumed that De Morgan's *King Solomon's Wives* is also a different book to Biron's parody.

An entire study might be made on the parodies of Rider's works for they continued with works such as George Forrest's 'The Deathless Queen'[25] and George R. Sims 'The Lost Author'[26] and many others. It is even known that James M. Barrie enjoyed *She* so thoroughly that he immediately wrote a skit on it.[27] And extensions of the *She* saga are still being made, the latest being *The Vengeance of She* by Peter Tremayne which has Ayesha returning to modern-day England in search of the reincarnation of Kallikrates.[28]

She not only inspired literary parodies but, starting with Lang's sonnet, caused several poetical works to be penned. The Comtesse de Bremont, for example, similarly wrote a sonnet 'She' which she dedicated to Sophie Eyre who played Ayesha in the original London stage production of the novel.[29] And yet another poem, 'To the Author of She', by Theophilus (Shepstone?) appeared in *Month*, September 1888.

A few short months after its publication, the book had become an institution. Stories about *She* abounded. The Reverend W. J. Loftie wrote to Rider.

> Are you acquainted with the story of the lady who wrote poetry? She had begun an epic –
> Man was made innocent and good, but he –
> when a visitor called. She left the paper on the table; the visitor came in, waited a little and departed. When she returned she found the couplet completed:
> Man was made innocent and good, but he –
> Would doubtless have continued so – but SHE.

By the time of Rider's death *She* had been adapted on the stage both in London and New York, was made into a ballet, and made into six different silent films.

Its success was such that, before and after Rider's death, many writers have tried to fathom deep meanings in the tale. One of the first to do so was an American named Leo Michael who wrote a study entitled *She, an allegory of the church*, which was published by Frank L. Lovell in 1889. He professed to see *She* as symbolic of the Christian world. Kôr was the modern world, Ayesha was the church, the sole guardian of truth and possessor of the secret of eternal life. Leo Vincey was its conscience and Holly was science. The origin of *She*, like the Church, is shrouded in the mysterious and Ayesha's passion for Vincey is symbolic of the weakness of the Church. In recent years Carl

Jung came to hold up *She* as a classic example of his concept of the feminine force in man, anima, the aggregation of all the feminine characteristics in him.[30] Nándor Fodor, the eminent Freudian, on the other hand, saw *She* as 'a beautiful allegory of the penalty attendant on our yearning to return to the womb'.[31] Morton Cohen also observes:

> *She* is undoubtedly a psychological allegory, and perhaps more so than most works of fiction because of the way Haggard let the tale write itself. Haggard, writing here before the birth of analytical psychology, innocently extends to the new scientists an invitation to his unconscious.[32]

He devotes several pages in his book to trying to track down the sources and influences in *She* which lead one into a morass of mythology, psychology and allegory; in trying to trace Ayesha as Asherab of the Old Testament to Queen Guinevere of Celtic legends. At the last moment Cohen tries to turn back from the confusion into which he has plunged with this passage: 'But the facts are that Haggard was neither writing a conscious parable nor preaching a moral sermon; as far as he was concerned, he was simply telling a tale.' Perhaps it is the *Athenaeum*, when reviewing the book, who gave the best advice: 'Whether he (Haggard) is a philosopher with a turn for allegory, the readers of *She* must decide for themselves.'[33]

While all the praise and acclaim were flattering to the ego, perhaps the best news for the practical and now professional author came in a letter from Charles Longman, his publisher, on 15 March 1887:

> I am glad to tell you that *She* keeps on selling capitally. We have printed 25,000 already and have ordered another 5,000 and I do not think we shall have many left when the printers deliver them . . . last week we sold over 1,000 copies!

She had placed the name of Henry Rider Haggard in the vanguard of resurgent romance writing. W. E. Henley commented:

Just as it was thoroughly accepted that there were no more stories to be told, that romance was utterly dried up, and that analysis of character . . . was the only thing in fiction attractive to the public, down there came upon us a whole horde of Zulu divinities and sempiternal queens of beauty in the Caves of Kôr.[34]

Andrew Lang put it more enthusiastically in a set of verses later that year which he dedicated to Rider and to Robert Louis Stevenson.

King Romance was wounded deep
   All his knights were dead and gone
All his court was fallen on sleep
   In the vale of Avalon!

Then you came from south and north
   From Tugela, from the Tweed;
Blazoned his achievements forth
   King Romance is come indeed![35]

CHAPTER 7

THE LURE OF EGYPT

By the end of 1886, with the still rising sales of *King Solomon's Mines* and the favourable prospects for his other novels, Rider had decided to give up law and launch himself into a full-time writing career. He also decided he wanted a holiday and it seemed an ideal time to visit Egypt, a country which had always held a great fascination for him. His brother, Andrew, was stationed there – a lieutenant-colonel commanding the Egyptian Battalion. There was also another incentive: Rider was already turning over in his mind the possibilities of writing a novel on Cleopatra. Louie was not keen on travelling, however, and decided that she should remain home with the children and so, for the first time in six years of marriage, Rider and Louie were parted.

Rider left England in January 1887, soon after the publication of *She* and went first to Paris where he visited the Louvre to examine the Egyptian exhibits. Then he took the train to Rome and on to Brindisi. It was a wearisome journey and he travelled in the company of Sir Victor Halston and his wife; they knew Rider's brothers William, Alfred and Arthur. The train to Brindisi broke down in the middle of the night and in the confusion Rider lost a portmanteau containing, among other things, his evening clothes. He felt quite ill by the time he arrived on the boat bound for Alexandria but was cheered to find on board the sister of Sir Henry Bulwer, with her sons, travelling to join her husband in Cyprus. There were also the Milners, a big game hunter named Jamieson who was going to Africa to join Stanley, and French the publisher. Rider was stimulated by the company and his ego was boosted when he found that most of them had read either *King Solomon's Mines* or *She*.

His brother Arthur met him when the boat docked and lost no time in introducing him to 'Cairo society'. Rider was soon bored by colonial society and wrote to Louie 'Notoriety has many drawbacks, I think, and as to literary matters, I am heartily sick of them.'[1] He toured the museum of Boulak where Brugsch Bey showed him the various treasures of ancient Egypt. More enthusiastic, he wrote to Louie 'It is impossible to begin to tell you the impression that all this has made upon me.'[2] He journeyed up the Nile to the ancient city of Luxor and then visited the tombs at Thebes.

In March Rider decided to return to Cyprus and visit Sir Henry Bulwer, who was High Commissioner for the island. From Government House in Nicosia he explored the island and was delighted with Famagusta 'that marvellous mediaeval walled town'. Rider wrote: 'Here in this beautiful island of Venus I trust, before turning to my tasks again, to have a little real holiday after a good many years of hard work.'

But Rider could not relax. To Louie he confided:

> I cannot tell you, dear old girl, how homesick I am – or how I want to see you and the kids again. I will never come on a trip of this kind again without you. I miss you very much and get quite lonely.

He was anxious to set to work on his projected novel *Cleopatra* and told Louie that he wanted to write it at Ditchingham and suggested they get rid of Mr Hampton, who was renting the house. 'I cannot tell you, my dear, what a pleasure it will be to me if I find myself in a position to give you back the home again which in a way you lost by marrying me.'[3]

By April Rider returned to England and to the biggest literary furore of the decade. The cause was basically Rider's attitude to his new profession. In the February issue of the *Contemporary Review* he had written an article entitled 'About Fiction'. It was reprinted in *Living Age*, the *Critic* and the *Ecletic Magazine*. Rider later admitted: 'It is almost needless for me to say that for a young writer who had suddenly come into some kind of fame to spring a dissertation of this kind upon the literary world over his own name was very little short of madness.'

It is a self-opinionated article, a pretentious, dogmatic attack on the literary world. Rider asserted, without diplomacy, that the world could do without three-quarters of the novels published. He attacked realism in novels and said that romance was the *ne plus ultra* of all art: 'really good romance writing is perhaps the most difficult art practised by the sons of man. It might even be maintained that none but a great man or woman can produce a really great work of fiction.'[4]

The literary world turned on Rider like a wolf pack. From March onwards came printed denunciations of his work and, more wounding, charges of cheap plagiarism. Rider had already been accused of plagiarism over *King Solomon's Mines* the year previously so the experience was not a new one.[5] What was new was the viciousness of the attack and the eminence of those who led it. It was W. T. Stead, the crusading editor of the *Pall Mall Gazette*, who was later to perish on the *Titanic*, who set things going with an article 'Who Is She and Where Did She Come From?'[6] He managed to sustain the attack in his journal for two months. Perhaps his anger at Rider was increased by the fact that he had appeared in Lang's parody *He* as 'old Pell Melli'. The *Literary World, Spectator, Whitehall Review, New York Post, Court and Society, London Journal* and even *The Times* were full of attacks on Rider's work. George Moore displayed great ingenuity by citing, as examples of Rider's plagiarism, passages from Bishop Hall's *Mundus Alter et Idem* to stories of Théophile Gautier. Amazingly enough, during all these attempts to attribute *She* and the creation of Ayesha to some other author, the critics managed to overlook a three-volume novel, published in London in 1834, entitled *Ayesha, the Maid of Kars*. The coincidence is too great to believe, and Rider, either consciously or subconsciously, derived Ayesha of Kôr from its title. But therein the similarity stops for *Ayesha, the Maid of Kars*, written by James Morier, bears no relation to

Rider's tale. The critics continued, however, to accuse Rider of 'lifting' works as diverse as Thomas More's *Epicurian* to the Japanese legend of *Urashima*. Most of the attacks were merely puerile such as 'The Culture of the Horrible: Mr Haggard's Stories'[7] and 'The Fall of Fiction'.[8]

The attacks had, of course, begun while Rider was in Egypt and his family and friends had come to his defence in his absence. Andrew Lang wrote a lengthy and lucid defence in an article on plagiarism for the *Contemporary Review* in June and Lord Curzon, who did not know Rider, also came to his defence. Rider sent off his own answer to the critics in a letter written from Cyprus before his return.[9]

His novel, *Jess*, which Smith, Elder published in March that year also came under attack and this time the critics delightfully found they had something to get their teeth into. Rider had enclosed some verses in the book which began 'If I should die tonight . . .' which were supposed to have been written by his heroine just before she died. Stead and the *Pall Mall Gazette* immediately took up these verses in an article 'The Song of Jess and Who Wrote It'[10] and it was shown that the verses had been published anonymously in the *Transatlantic* in March 1874, having in their turn been copied from the *Anglo-American Times* of 31 January 1874. The correspondence went from March into April with Louie, C. J. Longman, and James Stanley Little defending Rider[11] and Andrew Lang writing on 'The Ethics of Plagiarism'.[12] Rider's letter from Cyprus explained the verses. They had been sent to him while he was in South Africa by a 'lady friend', presumably Lilith. Rider had imagined them to be her own composition and had made use of them, as she implied he might do. Rider's mistake was that in using them he gave no indication that they were not his own composition.

Rider's main guilt lay in one thing: his intemperate attack on the literary establishment. In later years he was to write:

There are two bits of advice which I will offer to the youthful author of the future. Never preach about your trade and, above all, never criticise other practitioners of that trade, however profoundly you may disagree with them. Heaven knows there are critics enough without your taking a hand in the business. Do your work as well as you can and leave other people to do theirs, and the public to judge between them. Secondly, unless you are absolutely driven to it, as of course may happen sometimes, never enter into a controversy with a newspaper.

At the time Rider did not take these attacks lightly: 'About this time I must have become rather sickened of the novel writing trade and despondent as regards my own powers'. In fact he wrote off an application to rejoin the Colonial Service in some capacity but was refused. Lang admonished him for the idea and wrote to him 'If you jack up Literature, I shall jack up Reading!'[13] Lang also hit back at Rider's critics in a piece of doggerel:

> The Critics, hating men who're Dabs
>   At drawing in the dibs
> Declare that Haggard cribs his crabs,
>   And so they crab his cribs.[14]

During this period Rider and Louie had been living in a larger house which they had rented at 24 Redcliffe Square, near Earls Court. In spite of literary establishment hostility he was elected to the Savile Club, a gathering place for prominent literary men of the day, in which he was to meet some who were to be his lifelong friends, including Rudyard Kipling. On Saturdays he would join a select group of friends for luncheon, including Lang, Edmund Gosse, Eustace Balfour, William Loftie, and R. M. Stevenson, a cousin of Robert Louis Stevenson.

By early May 1887, Rider had managed to come to an amicable agreement with the lessee of Ditchingham House: Mr Hampton moved out and the Haggard family returned. 'I remember,' recalled Rider, 'my disgust when on arrival there an invitation to be present in Westminster Abbey on the occasion of the Jubilee of Queen Victoria was forwarded too late for me to be able to avail myself of it. Although I do not greatly care for

such pomp and circumstance, that was a ceremony which I
should have liked to see.'

On 27 May Rider sat down in his study in Ditchingham
House and began *Cleopatra*. He finished it on 27 August. The
publisher, Charles Longman, now a firm friend, thought very
highly of the book and paid a large sum for the outright
copyright. During this period Rider made several financial
miscalculations against the advice of his agent, A. P. Watt. He
also sold *Jess* and *Colonel Quaritch VC* for outright sums and
Watt eventually stepped in to sort out matters, getting the
publishers to abrogate their agreement on condition Rider
write two other stories for them. These were to be *Mr Meeson's
Will* (1888) and *Allan's Wife* (1889). While Longman liked
Cleopatra, Lang was not so keen. 'You will loathe me for the
advice,' he wrote, 'but if I were you I'd put *Cleopatra* away for
as long as possible, and then read it as a member of the
public. . . .' Lang, as usual, was profuse in his advice and
detailed what should be done to give the book greater impact.
Rider did not recall taking Lang's advice and the story appeared
serially in the *Illustrated London News* from 5 January to 29
June 1889, before Longman published an edition of 25,000
copies on 24 June 1889.

Rider dedicated this volume to his mother 'because I thought
it was the best book I had written or was likely to write'. He
wrote the dedication on 21 January 1889 and sent it to his
mother for her approval. His mother, now aged seventy years,
was growing increasingly frail and her eyesight was failing.
Nevertheless, she replied:

> Dearest Rider, I cannot object to your appreciatory
> dedication if you really think you inherit your literary tastes
> from me. Perhaps you do, from me and mine, for there was
> much intellectual power on my side of the family, but your
> inventive imagination has brought our obscure and
> unknown attempts to the surface. Circumstances, in my
> case, have always been steadfastly against me, a little
> disappointing I must confess, now in the evening of my life,

when the shadows are closing and blotting out the bright
but perhaps foolish gleams which brighten my youth.
Thanks, dear boy, for the pleasure you have given me. I fear
I cannot manage to visit to you – I am very helpless you
know. . . .[15]

On 24 June, when *Cleopatra* was published, Rider sent her a
copy but she could hardly see to open it. Squire Haggard wrote
to him:

This morning came a beautiful copy of *Cleopatra*, which
your mother, with my assistance opened herself and herself
(for though it strained her eyes for the moment a bit, I
would not help her in it, for I knew you and she would like
her to do it best herself) read the dedication which gratified
much her maternal heart – even unto tears.

On 29 June Ella Haggard wrote to her son Rider:

My dearest Rider, I have only a few minutes to write and
thank you for your charming gift, but I must not let the
week pass over without my doing so. I think it is got up as
well as possible, and the Dedication is most successfully
accomplished, which must be as gratifying to you as to me. I
have not thoroughly looked at the illustrations, but see that
they are very much more to be liked than those of the
Illustrated News. Thank you greatly for your excellent work,
my dear son. It certainly redounds greatly to you, dearest
Rider, whatever the critics may say, and I have no doubt
they will do their worst. But I think posterity will do justice
to your production. I will write no more as I cannot easily
add to this.

Ever your most affectionate Mother,
Ella Haggard[16]

It was the last letter that Rider received from his mother. She
died on 9 December 1889. Her death affected Rider deeply and
years later he felt unable to talk about it to his daughter Lilias.[17]
As a memorial, he wrote a moving tribute to her in a memoir

which introduced one of her poems published by Charles Longman in 1890.[18]

From 29 July to 26 December 1886, Rider was writing a 'contemporary novel' entitled *Colonel Quaritch VC* the background of which paralleled Rider's own background very closely. He sold serial rights to Messrs Tillotson of Bolton who released it for serialization in June of 1887 in the *Newcastle Chronicle, Yorkshire Post, Liverpool Daily Post* and a journal called *England*. It was published in book form by Longman on 3 December 1888. Certainly his depression about writing as a career did not stop his prodigious output. Having produced *Cleopatra* and *Colonel Quaritch VC*, he wrote *Mr Meeson's Will* which the critics promptly accused him of plagiarizing from *Les Nouvelles Amoureuses* by Charles Aubert. Ignoring them as the best policy, he produced another Allan Quatermain adventure entitled *Maiwa's Revenge* which he finished on 10 November 1887, and which was published by Longman on 3 August 1888. Giving himself only two weeks rest, he then plunged into another novel, *Beatrice*, commencing it on 23 November 1887 and finishing on 28 February 1888. Charles Longman wrote to him on 4 August 1888; 'I think, too, that *Beatrice*, is your best piece of purely modern Nineteenth Century work.' He adds: 'We have sold 20,000 copies of *Maiwa* on the day of publication.' Lang also liked *Beatrice* and wrote to Rider on 8 May 1888: 'I have read *Beatrice* and if she interests the public as much as she does me, she'll do.'

Rider's first literary adviser, J. Cordy Jeaffreson, wrote:

> it [Beatrice] is a fine, stirring, effective story; but with all its power and dexterity it is not the book which will determine your eventual place in the annals of literature. You will write that book some ten years hence, when I shall be resting under the violets. . . .

That was not to be, for Rider had already written the two books that were to secure his literary fame.

Lady Florence Dixie, whom Rider had met in South Africa, wrote to Rider to rebuke him for what she saw as his prejudice towards women. Lady Florence was a keen supporter of women's rights.

> I have just finished reading your *Beatrice* and have put it
> down with a feeling that it is only another book in many
> ways which proclaims the rooted idea in men's minds that
> women are born to suffer and work for men, to hide all their
> natural gifts that man may rule alone. . . . Forgive
> me – but as you can write, why not set your pen to upraise
> woman, to bid her become a useful member of society – the
> true companion and co-mate of man, and they working
> together shall help to make impossible such miserable
> victims of a false and unnatural bringing up as Elizabeth
> and Lady Honoria?

At the same time as this, Rider was already working out yet another idea; this time it was for a novel about Helen of Troy, a sequel to the *Odyssey*. The idea of writing a sequel to the mightiest of all epics has been one that has attracted writers from every clime and country since Eugammon of Cyrene produced his sequel, *Telegonia,* around 568 BC. He made a tentative arrangment with Andrew Lang to produce the novel as a joint work and by January 1888 he had started work on a first draft which he entitled *The Song of the Bow*. He sent the manuscript to Andrew Lang who promptly lost it.

Somewhat annoyed and discouraged, Rider turned his fertile mind to another idea which had always fascinated him . . . the writing of an Icelandic saga. Lang greatly encouraged the idea and Rider had always found a strong affinity for Icelandic sagas. He decided to accompany a friend, A. G. Ross, who was visiting Iceland during the summer of that year, 1888. He would explore the country, gather 'local colour' and return to write his saga.

CHAPTER 8

ICELANDIC SAGA
AND MEXICAN GOLD

Before starting for Iceland Rider went to visit William Morris who was an expert on Icelandic folklore and culture. Morris (1834–96) was prominent in the crusade against the materialism and ugliness of Victorian England. He was editor of *The Commonweal*, a committed Marxist, a prolific poet and a writer who, it is generally agreed, revived the heroic fantasy genre. He was distinctly a man of genius – pioneer socialist, humanist, illuminator, poet, woodcarver, painter, architect, designer, writer and printer – such were his diverse activities. Some of his best works were based on Norse mythology and Icelandic saga and he had visited Iceland many times. Rider wanted to pick his brains and Morris was quite helpful, inviting him to his house for a meal and a talk. Rider recalled: 'I remember that when I departed I rather wished that Fate had made me a Socialist also.' Morris gave Rider letters of introduction by which he secured the services of Thorgrimmer Gudmunson, a school teacher, who acted as a guide during the summer.

Rider and his friend Ross reached Reykjavik on 19 June. It was, wrote Rider, 'a curious town built for the most part of wood and situated on stony and barren land on the shore of the bay'.[1] Two days later, with Thorgrimmer Gudmunson, and a string of shaggy Icelandic ponies, the two men set off to travel over the historic sites of the island. They went on a circular route, returning to Reykjavik on 2 July but, not stopping there, going on to Halsi, where they stayed a fortnight fishing for salmon. Already the saga of *Eric Brighteyes* was forming in Rider's mind.

On 20 July Rider and Ross set off for home in a ship called the *Copeland*. The ship put out from Reykjavik and immediately ran into a terrible gale which blew for three days without ceasing. From the night of 22 July *Copeland* lay to and, although the weather steadied on 24 July, a heavy fog came down thwarting an attempt to put about and run for shelter. The *Copeland* carried a cargo of Icelandic ponies and these now began to die. On the 25th the fog cleared and to the horror of the crew and passengers they saw they were right against the precipitous rocky cliffs of the island of Stroma, lying off Caithness, Scotland, in the Pentland Firth. The *Copeland* was being swept by the strong tides towards the crashing surf. The captain reversed his engines but the current was so strong that the ship continued forward and eventually crashed against the rocks.

> Orders were given to get out the boats, and it was attempted with the strangest results. My belief is that those boats had never been in the water since the day the ship was built. Some of them went down by the stern with their bows hanging in the air; some of them went down by the bows with their stern hanging in the air; or would not move. Also, in certain instances, the plugs could not be found. Not one of them was got into the water; at any rate at that time.

Rider, realizing that the position was serious, went to his cabin and packed what he could, calling to the steward to bring him a bottle of beer ('as I did not know when I should get another'). 'Whilst I was drinking the beer I felt the vessel slip back several feet; it was a most unpleasant sensation, one moreover that suggested to me that I might be better on deck.' The passengers gathered in an anxious group and Rider could see a boat putting out from Stroma. Rider went up to the *Copeland*'s captain and asked him if the passengers might hail this boat. 'Aye, Mr Haggard,' answered the distracted man, 'do anything you can to save your lives.' Rider had a powerful voice and it carried over the crashing waves. He asked if the boat could get near enough to take the passengers off. A voice answered that they dare not approach the ship in case they were dashed to pieces against its side. But Rider encouraged them and after one abortive attempt they came alongside. A man boarded and said to Rider: 'For God's sake get out of this, ye've five feet of water in your hold and sixty fathoms under your stern! Ye'll slip off the rock and sink.' Aided by the Stroma islanders, both passengers and crew were eventually evacuated.

They spent eight or ten hours on Stroma watching and waiting for the *Copeland* to go down. Stubbornly, it clung precariously to its rocky hold. The courageous Stroma islanders returned to the abandoned vessel and managed to save many of the ponies, but most of the poor beasts were either maimed or drowned. Rider recalls that as he stood on the shore with the rest of the passengers, an islander, on hearing his name, approached him and said: 'The author of *She*, I believe. I am verra glad to meet you.'

Eventually, with the seas relatively calm, the passengers hired a boat to take them to the mainland, John O'Groats being the nearest landfall. Their adventures were not over yet. As the boat was passing the wreck of the *Copeland* a man suddenly appeared on deck crying to be taken off. He was identified as a petty officer who had broken into the ship's liquor store and been overwhelmed by drink. There was a debate as to what to do. The *Copeland* could not survive another tide and unless they took the man off he was doomed. They eased the boat alongside the hull. 'We wondered from moment to moment whether she would not come off the point that held her and crush us into the deep.' But eventually the rescue was carried out. Finally, after a rough passage, the boat with the survivors made its way to the mainland.

> From wherever we landed we travelled in carts to Wick, where we slept at some inn. I remember that I did not sleep very well. During the shipwreck and its imminent dangers my nerves were not stirred, but afterwards of a sudden they gave out. I realised that I had been very near to death; also all that word means. For some days I did not recover my balance.

Rider turned the adventure to good account and wrote 'The Wreck of the *Copeland*' which appeared, with two illustrations, in the *Illustrated London News* on 18 August 1888. This account, with a piece called *My Fellow Labourer*, written especially for Collier's *Once a Week* in America, was put in book form by George Munro of New York as *My Fellow Labourer and The Wreck of the Copeland* and published on 30 November 1888. It was the only book by Haggard which was never published in Britain.

Rider had reached home on 27 July and, after resting and then writing about his adventures, he sat down to write his Icelandic saga, *Eric Brighteyes*, on 29 August. By 25 December 1888, he had finished 266 foolscap pages. Lang, to whom he first showed the manuscript, was ecstatic: 'I have read four chapters, including Golden Falls, I think it is the best thing you have done. . . .' Later, he wrote, 'I don't want to flatter but it literally surprises me that anyone should write such a story nowadays. Charles Kingsley would have spoiled it by maundering and philosophising. I have hardly seen a line which is not in keeping yet. . . . As literature I really think it is a masterpiece so far as I have gone. I'd almost as soon have expected more Homer as more saga.' In his study *Old Iceland Sources in the English Novel* (1935) Ralph Bergen Allen places *Eric Brighteyes* ahead of all other English novels of this type.

Rider dedicated the book to Victoria, Empress Frederick of Germany, for he had been told that the Empress and her husband, who had died shortly before, had read his books with enjoyment. The story came from Rider's brother, William, now First Secretary at the British Embassy in Athens. He wrote to Rider on 30 October 1889, telling him of a talk he had with the Empress in which 'she begged me to write to tell you'. Rider wrote asking whether he might dedicate *Eric Brighteyes* to her. The Empress was delighted and said she was 'anxiously looking forward to reading the book itself, which will now have a special interest for her'. *Eric Brighteyes* was serialized by the *People* in 1891 and published in a 10,000 edition on 13 May of that year by Charles Longman. The Prince of Wales announced that he preferred it to Rider's other tales.

In his correspondence to Victoria, Empress Frederick, Rider mentions the fact that he is leaving for Athens on 13 December 1889, presumably to visit his brother William. Whether he took Louie on this trip there is no record. He had already mentioned the idea of a trip to Greece to Louie in March 1887 when he said, 'it seems to me the trip would be better left to another year, when Will would be at Athens and when you and I might, perhaps, manage it together.'

It was while he was finishing *Eric Brighteyes* that Rider received a letter from Lang about the sequel to the *Odyssey* that they had tried to collaborate on. Rider had written a first draft, entitled *The Song of the Bow*, and sent it to Lang who had promptly lost it. Early in October Lang wrote: 'I've found your lost MS! I don't think it is a likely thing, style too Egyptian and all too unfamiliar to the B[ritish] P[ublic].' The two men decided to have another attempt at completing the sequel. Actually, in Lang, Rider had the perfect co-author for this type of book. Eight years before, with S. H. Butcher, he had written a prose translation of the *Odyssey* and was the author of a book-length poem entitled *Helen of Troy* which had appeared five years earlier. But, temperamentally, the co-authors were hardly suited. Rider wrote with his customary swiftness and disliked revision. Lang pondered and worried over detail, referring Rider on occasion to checking sources such as Euripides' account of Helen and so forth. It is in Euripides that the story of Helen hiding in Egypt was first told. Lang, however, was worried as to the development of the story. 'I fear it is too remote for this people [the British]. It isn't my idea how to do it (not that that matters) for I'd have begun with Odysseus in a plague stricken Ithaca and got on to Egypt. And I'd have written in modern English.'² The partnership was not an easy one and it was the first and last book that Rider was to write in collaboration. When the book finally emerged entitled *The World's Desire*, it was finished with Rider doing all the writing and Lang merely correcting Rider's drafts.

Lang was to write a preface to the volume which was never to be published:

> In *The World's Desire* we tell of the ending of that tale, we tell of the last seafaring of Odysseus, of his latest battle, of his latest love, and the death which came upon him from the sea. Back to the dawn of time we look with the dim eyes of the world's elder days, striving to see the sunlight gleam upon the golden helm and haubeck and the fire of burning citadels glitter on points and blades of bronze. Wistfully we listen for a word out of that eager time, for a fragment of an ancient song, a murmur of grey tradition, a woman's name cried aloud through the din of battles, the clash of sword on shield, the hurtling flight of the shafts of sorrow. We listen and we look, piecing together what we may tell of the ending of Odysseus![3]

The story concerned Odysseus' second voyage and the finding of Helen of Troy as a priestess of Egypt.

After a serialization in the *New Review* (April to December, 1890) *The World's Desire* was published on 5 November 1890 by Charles Longman. It was immediately savaged by the critics. One reviewer described it as 'a tortuous and ungodly jumble of anarchy and culture'[4] while the *Spectator* blamed Rider entirely for the production, adding 'we think so well of Mr Lang, that what would please us best would be to be told that his name on the title page is his principle contribution. . . .'[5] The *Athenaeum* was indigant: 'Why should Mr Lang lend himself and his genius to such unreal stuff?' it demanded.[6]

Lang sadly wrote his comment in verse.

> It did not set the Thames on fire,
> It is not quite *The World's Desire*!
> Much rather do the public scoff
>   And yell to Nature 'Take them off!'
> While critics constantly conspire
>   To slate the hapless *World's Desire*.[7]

'I brought you worse luck than you would have done alone',

wrote Lang to Rider. He was proved wrong, however, because *The World's Desire* has been in print almost continuously from the day it was published and it has influenced many writers, among them James Branch Cabell in his famous *Jurgen* and *Something About Eve*. Robert Louis Stevenson enjoyed the tale immensely and penned the following verses to Lang and Haggard:

1

Awdawcious Odyshes,
Your conduc' is vicious,
Your tale is suspicious
     An' queer.
Ye ancient sea-roamer,
Ye dour auld beach-comber,
Frae Haggard to Homer
     Ye veer.

2

Sic veerin' and steerin'!
What port are ye neerin'
As frae Egypt to Erin
     Ye gang?
Ye ancient auld blackguard
Just see whaur ye're staggered
From Homer to Haggard
     And Lang!

3

In stunt and in strife
To gang seeking a wife –
At your time o' life
     It was wrang.
An' see! Fresh afflictions
Into Haggard's descriptions
An' the plagues o' the Egyptians
     Ye sprang!

4

The folk ye're now in wi'
Are ill to begin wi'
Or to risk a hale skin wi'
    In breeks –
They're blacker and hetter
(Just ask your begetter)
And far frae bein' better
    Than Greeks.

5

There's your *Meriamun*:
She'll mebbe can gammon
That auld-furrand salmon
    Yoursel';
And *Moses* and *Aaron*
Will gie ye your fairin'
Wi' fire an' het airn
    In Hell.

I refuse to continue longer. I had an excellent half-verse there, but couldn't get the necessary pendant, and anyway there's no end to such truck.

Yours,
R.L.S.[8]

No sooner had he finished writing *The World's Desire* than Rider launched into a new saga. He had always wanted to write a specifically Zulu story and, on 27 June 1889, he sat down to write *Nada the Lily*. He finished the tale on 15 January 1890, and immediately sent the manuscript to Lang. On 20 April Lang replied 'it is admirable, the epic of a dying people, but it wants relief'. A few days later, Lang wrote again: 'I've finished *Nada*. If all the reviewers in the world denied it, you can do the best sagas that have been done yet. . . .' Charles Longman, writing on 14 May added his voice in praise.

Nada strikes me with wonder and awe. It is in some ways the greatest feat you have performed; I mean because you have constructed a story in which the dramatis personae are all savages and yet you have kept the interest going throughout. There will of course be a terrible outcry about gore. I never read such a book. It is frightful and the only justification for it is the fact that it is history, not imagination. Wherever it is possible I would tone down the effect rather than heighten it, so as to avoid the charge of wallowing or gloating as far as possible. The wolves and the wolf brethren are delightful; I wish you could have given us more of them. I was very glad to meet our old friend Umslopogaas as a boy.

Rider dedicated *Nada* to his old chief Sompseu, Sir Theophilus Shepstone:

Sompseu, my father, I have written a book that tells of men and matters of which you know the most of any who still look upon the light; therefore, I set your name within that book and, such as it is, I offer it to you.

On 13 July 1892 Shepstone wrote to thank Rider: 'I need not say how gratifying to me that gift was; nor how deeply touching the kind words of Dedication were. Indeed, you give me more credit than I am entitled to.' Shepstone does not pass by the opportunity of making another justification of his annexation of the Transvaal. Indeed, Rider had already made that justification in his dedication:

You did it because, had it not been done, the Zulus would have stamped out the Boers. Were not Cetywayo's impis gathered against the land, and was it not because it became the Queen's land that at your word he sent them murmuring to their kraals? To save bloodshed you annexed the country beyond the Vaal.

Shepstone's letter over *Nada* was the last letter that Rider received from Sompseu before his death on 23 June 1893.

'*Nada the Lily*,' wrote Rider in later years, 'has one claim on the gratitude of the world'. Writing from Vermont on 20 October 1895, Rudyard Kipling, whom Rider met for the first time during the year he wrote *Nada*, told him

> it was a chance sentence of yours in *Nada the Lily* that
> started me off on a track that ended in my writing a lot of
> wolf stories. You remember in your tale where the wolves
> leaped up at the feet of a dead man sitting on a rock?
> Somewhere on that page I got the notion. It's curious how
> things come back again, isn't it? I meant to tell you when
> we met; but I don't remember that I ever did.[9]

In *Something of Myself*, Kipling echoes this acknowledgment: 'a phrase in Haggard's *Nada the Lily* combined with the echo of this tale. After blocking out the main idea in my head, the pen took charge, and I watched it begin to write stories about Mowgli and animals which later grew into the *Jungle Books*.'

Rider had first been introduced to Kipling, then a 23-year-old journalist who had achieved some literary fame in India, at the Savile Club. Rider, in fact, supported Kipling's nomination for membership. It was immediately seen that Rider and Kipling appealed, more or less, to the same audiences and some predicted that Kipling would eclipse Rider's popularity. Instead of becoming bitter rivals, the two men soon became friends although they did not draw really close until the years of the First World War. 'Took to him at once,' wrote Kipling, 'he becoming the stamp adored by children and trusted by men at sight and he could tell tales, mainly about himself, that broke up the table.'[10] As early as 1891, F. K. Stephen had coupled their names together in a rather abusive doggerel which deplored the state of contemporary writing.

> Will there never come a season
> Which shall rid us from the curse
> Of a prose which knows no reason
> And an unmelodious verse:
> When the world shall cease to wonder

At the genius of an Ass
And a boy's eccentric blunder
Shall not bring success to pass.

When mankind shall be delivered
From the clash of magazines,
And the inkstands shall be shivered
Into countless smithereens:
When there stands a muzzled stripling,
Mute, beside a muzzled bore;
When the Rudyards cease from kipling
and the Haggards ride no more?[11]

Kipling attended several parties at Rider's town house and, after a few years, he and his American bride, Caroline, went to settle in Vermont, USA. They were there between 1892 and 1896 and Kipling kept up a desultory correspondence with Rider.

During 1889 Rider met another man who was to become a friend and to influence him to a great extent. This was John Gladwyn Jebb, fifteen years his senior and a rugged adventurer who was then Managing Director of the Santa Fé (Chiapas) Copper Mines in south-east Mexico. They met at a London dinner party and soon became close friends. Jebb was one of the typical intrepid Victorian adventurers who, oblivious to physical dangers, explored uncharted areas of the world. Soon, on Jebb's advice, Rider was investing in Mexican mining and was an eager audience to Jebb's tales of adventure in central America, in particular, his tales of the Aztecs. Jebb suggested that Rider should accompany him to Mexico to collect material for a book on Montezuma, the great Aztec leader. He also confided that a Cuban friend of his named Don Anselmo claimed to have found the burial place of a treasure buried by Montezuma's nephew, Gautemoc, on the shores of Lake Tezcuco. This treasure, eighteen large jars of gold, precious stones, gold armour and a great golden head of Montezuma himself, had been hidden from the Spanish conquistadors.

Jebb and his wife returned to Mexico in 1890 and, after spending Christmas 1890 at Ditchingham, Rider and Louie set off to join them. They decided to leave the children behind. Young Jock was packed off to stay with Edmund Gosse in London. Rider and Louie sailed in the *Etruria* which arrived in New York on 10 January. To Rider's surprise, he was immediately besieged by a dozen reporters who shouted such questions at him as 'What is your opinion of the elevated railroads?'; 'How do American reporters compare with reporters in England?' and 'Do you make your plots before you write your stories, or do you write your stories first?'[12] The *New York Times* described Rider as

> a tall man, probably six feet high, somewhat loosely put together, with a slight stoop of the shoulders. He has dark hair, but the delicate moustache which adorns his lip is quite light in colour. A long pointed nose gives his face a thinnish appearance but a careful look at him shows that he has a full forehead and that his eyes are well apart. He has an agreeable manner and a pleasant smile. When he shakes hands he gives a quick, nervous grip and he simultaneously gives a pull sufficiently strong to take a man who has not good understanding quite off his feet.[13]

Rider and Louie went on to New Orleans by train and finally reached Mexico City where the Jebbs owned a house. Louie and Mrs Jebb remained in the city while Rider and John Jebb set off to explore the wilds on horseback, travelling beyond Vera Cruz and deep among the Chiapas. Rider absorbed everything from the Aztec ruins to the native methods of farming. He was deeply interested in the flora and fauna and collected many samples of plants which he succeeded shipping back to Ditchingham where, in his greenhouses, they thrived for some decades.

Rider and Jebb made arrangements to leave Mexico City on 9 February to head for Lake Tezcuco to look for the buried treasure which Don Anselmo claimed was there. On Sunday, 8

February, a cablegram from England arrived as they were preparing to go to church.

> Mrs Jebb called us to their bedroom. She had a paper in her hand. 'Something is wrong with one of your children', she said brokenly. 'Which?' I asked, aware that this meant death, no less, and waited. 'Jock' was the reply, and the dreadful telegram, our first intimation of his illness was read. It said that he had 'passed away peacefully' some few hours before. There were no details or explanations.

They were later to learn that John had measles and this illness was followed by the complication of a perforating ulcer. Two hours later Rider wrote to his father.

> We have within the last two hours received the awful news of the death of our most beloved son, and I have telegraphed you asking you to represent me at the funeral. As you will readily understand, my dear wife and myself are utterly overwhelmed and can only say one thing – God's will be done. The boy has gone hence before sin and sorrow have touched him, leaving us to mourn his memory – to hope for reunion with him in God's own time. So it is – so it must be. With our feelings in this distant place, unable to stand at his graveside – you and all your kin, will understand and sympathize. We were starting for Chiapas and Palenque in the morning, but shall not go now – still we may stop here awhile before undertaking the journey home – for, alas, we cannot arrive in time to be of any use. I have given directions that he should be buried near the Chancel door at Ditchingham – where I hope to lie at his side one day.[14]

The death of his son Jock was the biggest blow that Rider was ever to receive. 'I did not know then', he wrote, 'what a man can endure and live.' At one time the Jebbs were worried and asked a visiting American doctor to examine Rider. The doctor found him suffering from nervous shock. For years afterwards he suffered 'acute mental depression', was constantly ill with psychosomatic disorders and began to sink into a deepening melancholy. Everything that reminded him of Jock was put out of sight and the family were never to mention Jock's name in Ditchingham House. His nephew, Sir Godfrey Haggard KCMG, was to write:

> There was . . . a super taboo – the subject of his son.
> Although it was assumed that Jock's memory was for ever in
> Rider's thoughts, years passed without his name being
> mentioned. It was unnatural so to bottle the thing up,
> especially in a talkative family like ours. . . . It should
> have been dragged out into the light as a measure of
> relief.[15]

Rider's youngest daughter, Lilias, wrote:

> Everything that Jock possessed was put away. His books on
> the highest shelf of the library – his toys in cupboards or
> hidden in the loft, his letters, every one he had ever written,
> locked away in his desk. Even his small sisters realised Jock's
> name must never pass their lips within their father's
> hearing.
> Those letters, together with Jock's school reports lay in
> the desk drawer for fifty years – a pathetic reminder of the
> permanence of perishable things.
> There they lay, more than forty of them, with the stamps
> and the crests and drawings of ships enclosed 'to be kept'
> still in the envelopes. So Jock's pathetic little shade, an
> unquiet ghost begging to be laid, dwelt on in the
> house – speaking though silent, ever present though never
> acknowledged, a shadow which lay on all the household.
> Should another child ask a question about the pictured face
> on the walls, Jock's sisters would start and turn pale and lay
> their fingers on their lips – dreading the mention of a name
> which once had meant so much love, and sweetness, and
> laughter in their lives.[16]

Writing twenty years later Rider was still blaming himself for being absent when his son died, recalling to mind real or

imagined presentiments with which he flagellated himself for
not paying close attention to.

> It is strange, but when I went to Mexico I knew, almost
> without doubt, that in this world he and I would never see
> each other more. Only I thought it was I who was doomed
> to die. Otherwise it is plain that I should never have started
> on that journey. With this surely in my heart – it was with
> me for weeks before we sailed – the parting was bitter
> indeed. The boy was to stay with friends, the Gosses. I bade
> him goodbye and tore myself away. I returned after some
> hours. A chance, I forget what, had prevented the servant, a
> tall dark woman whose name is lost to me, from starting
> with him to Delamere Crescent till later than was expected.
> He was still in my study – about to go. Once more I went
> through that agony of a separation of which I knew to be the
> last. With a cheerful face I kissed him. I remember how he
> flung his arms about my neck – in a cheerful voice I blessed
> him and bade him farewell, promising to write. Then he
> went through the door and it was finished. I think I wept.

Rider even recalled to mind that he had dedicated *Allan
Quatermain* to

> my son Arthur John Rider Haggard in the hope that in days
> to come he, and many other boys whom I shall never know,
> may in the acts and thoughts of Allan Quatermain and his
> companions, as herein recorded, find something to help
> him and them reach to what, with Sir Henry Curtis, I hold
> to be the highest rank we can attain, the stage and dignity
> of an English gentleman.

The tale, told by Allan Quatermain, starts off:

> I have just buried my boy, my poor handsome boy of whom
> I was so proud, and my heart is broken. It is very hard
> having only one son to lose him thus, but God's will be
> done. Who am I that I should complain?

Rider, in his melancholy, wondered if he had 'ill wished' the boy. On his tomb Rider had carved 'I shall go to him' and in later years he spent many an hour beside the grave deriving comfort from these words. Years later, when he finished his autobiography at midnight on Whit Sunday 1912 he wrote a dedication 'To my dear Wife, and to the memory of our son whom now I seek.'

With Rider almost indulging in his grief, there was no room for Louie to display her own grief for she had to support Rider in his. One of them had to be strong.

The distracted couple stayed in Mexico until April and then made their way home via New York and Liverpool. After a few weeks Rider decided to throw himself into his work and, on 5 June, he commenced to write a tale of Montezuma. By 3 September he had finished his manuscript, the last he was to write by his own hand, and he entitled it *Montezuma's Daughter*. It was published as a serial in the *Graphic* from 1 July to 11 November 1893 and, on 13 November, Charles Longman brought out a book edition. *Montezuma's Daughter* was overshadowed with an air of gloom, a depression which becomes clear when one knows the period during which Rider wrote it. In the tale the narrator looses his children and says:

> Ah! we think much of the sorrows of our youth, and should a sweetheart give us the go-by, we fill the world with moans and swear that it holds no comfort for us. But when we bend our heads before the shrouded shape of some lost child, then it is that for the first time we learn how terrible grief can be. Time, they tell us, will bring consolation; but it is false; for such sorrow time has no salves. I say it who am old – as they are so shall they be. There is no hope but faith, there is no comfort save in the truth that love which might have withered on earth grows fastest in the tomb, to flower gloriously in heaven; that no love indeed can be perfect till God sanctifies and completes it with His seal of death.

Even with this book, Rider did not escape controversy. In the story a character named Isabella de Siguenza is condemned to death by being buried alive because she broke her vows as a nun. Rider added a footnote in the book which implied that this was typical of the punishment meted out in the Catholic Church in the sixteenth century. The footnote caused a stir among leading Catholics and a considerable and somewhat heated correspondence took place in the *Pall Mall Gazette* under the general heading 'The Immuring of Nuns'.[17] This resulted in Rider withdrawing the footnote in the 1895 edition.

He dedicated this book to Jebb: 'Strange as were the adventures of Thomas Wingfield, once of this parish, whereof these pages tell, your own can almost equal them in these latter days.' Jebb wrote to Rider thanking him and saying

> Your letter of dedication reads charmingly, and only has one flaw – that it should have been addressed to one more worthy, but no one could appreciate it more than myself, and more than that, no man could value the expression of your friendship more deeply than I do.

Sadly, Jebb was never to see the publication of the book. He and his wife had returned to England, accompanying Rider and Louie, for a short period before returning to Mexico. Jebb found it hard to live in the gloomy atmosphere of London and, worried by financial losses, he risked his remaining money on a new Mexican mining scheme. It failed and they returned to London again with Jebb, aged fifty, broken in health and spirit. On 2 March 1893, he wrote to Rider: 'I may make another rally, but I confess my own notion is to the other way.' On 18 March Jebb died. Mrs Jebb wrote to Rider:

> He thought of you so often – his one great desire was to live until the book came out, he was so proud and pleased about it, but when, at last, the proofs came he was too ill to know. You who have suffered such a heavy loss will know what mine is. . . .

The following year Mrs Jebb wrote a book about her husband's adventurous life entitled *A Strange Career: Life and Adventures of John Gladwyn Jebb* and Rider wrote an introduction to the work.[18]

Adding to Rider's gloom in the early months of 1892 his father, old Squire Haggard, was taken ill. He went to Bradenham in March to visit him and was 'shocked to find him so much changed and shrunken'. Squire Haggard had been ill with jaundice but had recovered a little. Then in April his strength began to give out and on 21 April the old squire sent for Rider. The old man had a premonition that he would not last much longer. Rider, travelling up from Ditchingham, was unable to arrive until midnight and during the evening Squire Haggard told his servant, Hocking, to give Rider his gold watch and chain. About 9.40 p.m. he was overheard to say in a clear voice: 'If I am to get better God will be with me – if I die He will also be with me – God is always present, is He not? He is in this room.' He never spoke again and by the time Rider arrived he was dead. 'He looked fine and peaceful in death: he was a very handsome and in many ways a remarkable man. I never knew anyone who resembled him in the least or who was the possessor of half his energy. God rest him!' It was certainly the end of an era at Bradenham and within a few years, William, who inherited the estate as the eldest son, had to sell up. After close on a century and a half, the Haggard family severed their connection with the village.

Throughout this period Rider had mostly isolated himself in Ditchingham House, still indulging in his melancholy, much to Louie's growing resentment. After all, Jock had been *her* son as well as Rider's, a fact that Rider hardly ever acknowledged, for always his references were to 'my son' and never to 'our son'. In his autobiography, he dismissed Louie's grief in the words 'Of the suffering of the poor mother I will not speak. They belong to her alone.' But Louie wanted the problem shared, wanted to speak about it and release the tension and so her resentment grew. However, in the early summer of 1892 Louie discovered she was pregnant for the fourth time. The child was born on 9 December 1892, three years to the day of Rider's mother's death. Rider's cousin Lily Hildyard was with him when Dr

1 Sir Henry Rider Haggard, 1914

2 Squire William
Meybohm Rider Haggard
(1817–93), Rider's father

3 Five of Squire Haggard's son's: (l. to r.) Alfred Hinuber, Andrew
Charles Parker, Henry Rider, William Henry Doveton and John
George ('Jack'). The second eldest son, Bazett Michael, is not in the
photograph

4 Trekking through the Transvaal, 1877. W. and J. Sergeant with Rider's friend, Arthur Cochrane, whose Zulu name, Macumazahn, was to be bestowed on Allan Quatermain

5 The Annexation of the Transvaal. Taken in Pretoria, 24 May 1877, just before Rider formally hoisted the Union Jack (left of the picture) over the Boer capital. Back row (l. to r.) Lt. Phillips, Melmoth Osborn, Col. Brooke and Capt. James. Front row (l. to r.) Mr Morcom, Mr Henderson, Sir Theophilus Shepstone, Rider (seated on ground), Dr Lyle and Mr Fynney

6 The Boer camp near Pretoria in 1879 over which Rider, as a lieutenant in the Pretoria Horse, was ordered to keep watch

7 Majuba Hill, commanding the vital pass through the Drakensberg Mountains, the site of the last disastrous defeat of the British during the First Boer War on 27 February 1881. The British sustained 280 casualties out of a total force of 550, including the commanding officer, General Sir George Colley. The British were dug-in on top of the hill while the Boers, under Petrus Joubert and numbering only 100 men, attacked up the sides of the hill. Louie Haggard, sitting on the verandah at Hilldrop, could hear the guns firing all that morning

8 Signing of the First Boer War Peace Treaty, 1881. The peace
negotiations were conducted in Rider's farmhouse at Hilldrop but
the ceremonial signing of the peace treaty was carried out at
O'Neil's Farm, near Prospect Camp, on 21 March. (L. to r.) Swart
Dick Uys, Paul Kruger, Lt Hamilton, Maj. Clarke, Petrus Joubert,
Maj. Fraser, Capt. Crooper, Pres. Brand, Capt. Roberts, Gen. Sir
Evelyn Wood and Comdt Smidt

9 Umslopogaas, in real life the son of a king of Swaziland, was immortalized as a Zulu warrior in many of Rider's African tales

10 Umslopogaas just before his death

11 H. Rider Haggard on the steps of Ditchingham House soon after his return from Africa

12 Marianna Louisa Margitson ('Louie') who married Rider on 11 August 1880

13 Ditchingham House, Norfolk

14 H. Rider Haggard and family at Ditchingham House; Louie is seated with Sybil Dorothy Rider, Arthur John Rider ('Jock'), Agnes Angela Rider and Rider's mother, Ella Haggard

15 Andrew Lang (1844–1912), the noted Scottish author and editor who was one of the first to recognize Rider's literary talent and who became a close friend

16 Fame in the form of a cartoon which appeared in *Vanity Fair* after the publication of *She* in 1887. The artist was Spy (Sir Leslie Ward)

17 H. Rider Haggard, *c.* 1885

18 Arthur John Rider Haggard
('Jock') (1881–91), painted shortly
before he died. Rider was profoundly
affected by his only son's death

19 Family group on the steps at Ditchingham House. Rider is on the left in the back row while Louie is seated in foreground with her youngest child Lilias Margitson Rider. Each side of her are seated Dorothy and Angela

20 H. Rider Haggard, *c.* 1905

21 Rudyard Kipling (1865–1936) who was Rider's closest friend of later years

22 Theodore Roosevelt (1858–1919). He became President of the USA in 1901 when McKinlay was assassinated and was elected for a second term in 1904. Both Rudyard Kipling and Rider were among his friends. Rider first met him in 1905

23 Family group at Ditchingham House. Standing (l. to r.)
unknown, Lady ('Louie') Haggard, Lady Buchanan (Joan Haggard),
Rider, Dorothy (Rider's daughter) and Tom Haggard. Seated (l. to
r.) Lilias (Rider's youngest daughter), Miss Ida Hector (Rider's
secretary), Angela (Rider's eldest daughter and Tom Haggard's
wife); the boy and lady on the right are unknown

24 Sir Henry Rider Haggard during the war years

25 Sir Henry Rider Haggard, c. 1920, in his study at Ditchingham examining Nelson's pewter plate, one of a pair given to the Norfolk Norwich Club by Angela Rider Haggard

26 Sir Henry Rider Haggard in the Abydos Temple during his last visit to Egypt in 1924

27 Sir Henry Rider Haggard, *c.* 1920, in his study at Ditchingham House

Crowfoot announced the birth of a girl. She felt that Rider was bitterly disappointed that Louie had not given birth to a son to replace Jock and give him the male heir he so desired. The child, however, was named Lilias (after Lily Hildyard) Margitson Rider.

There was another addition to the Haggard household at the end of that year in the person of Miss Ida Hector whom Rider employed as his secretary. Ida Hector was the daughter of the Irish writer Annie French Hector (1825–1902), an extremely successful novelist publishing over forty books which were translated into many languages: among the best known were *Blind Fate* (1891), *A Choice of Evils* (1895) and *Kitty Costello* (1902). Ida became, in Rider's words, 'a very faithful friend and companion'. She was an efficient secretary and a good horsewoman who took her place easily within the family circle. A typewriter was bought (the first commercial machines were on the market in 1874) and an instructor came to Ditchingham House to show Ida how to use it. Rider immediately began work on a new romance *The People of the Mist* which was the first book he dictated to his new secretary. Rider, however, did not stick to one particular method of working. In an interview he said: 'Sometimes I write a first draft in my own hand, and then dictate to a typist; sometimes I dictate straight off, sometimes I write and don't dictate at all. I am not a slave to any one method.'[19]

By the end of 1892 Rider had reasserted enough interest in the outside world to publish a letter in *The Times* on 'A New Argument Against Cremation'[20] and was preparing an article on how he came to write his first novel, *Dawn*, for the *Idler*'s April issue (1893). This was part of a series from twenty-two writers to be collected into volume form as *My First Book*.

CHAPTER 9

THE AGRICULTURAL REFORMER

In 1892 Rider declined an offer from the local Conservative Party to stand as parliamentary candidate for the King's Lynn constituency. This had been quite an honour, for King's Lynn was a 'safe seat' for the Tories and Rider would have been certain of electoral success. But in 1892 Rider was still brooding on the death of his son, and had the additional shock of his father's death. In 1894, however, the Conservatives approached him again and asked him whether he would be willing to stand in East Norfolk. The East Norfolk constituency had once been 'safe' for the Conservatives in the person of Sir Edward Birkbeck but a new franchise act, increasing the number of people eligible to vote, had caused Sir Edward to lose the seat to the Liberals. The seat was won by R. J. Price (later to be knighted) with a 440 majority. Sir Edward decided not to contest the seat in the election of 1895 and the candidate to whom the seat was offered politely declined to stand. Therefore the Tories turned to Rider who agreed to fight the seat for them.

Taking a banner as a 'Unionist and Agricultural' candidate, Rider soon displayed that he was not of the stuff that Conservative politicians are made. He ruefully wrote afterwards:

> Now I understand that I never was a real Tory – that, in short, as a party man I am the most miserable failure. As a politician I should have been useless from any whip's point of view. He would – well, have struck me off his list as neither hot nor cold, as a dangerous undesirable individual who, refusing to swallow the shibboleths of his tribe with shut eyes, actually dared to think for himself and to possess that hateful thing 'a cross bench mind'.

In spite of the fact that he was representing what he later admitted was a 'somewhat fossilised creed', Rider toured the Broadlands of East Norfolk with his wife, Louie, and his friend of African days, Arthur Cochrane. His speeches were often accompanied by violent displays and the press began to follow his campaign with relish. Many of his ideas were contrary to the Conservative central policy and his suggestions of a tax on imported grain by which to protect farmers who could not compete with low-priced imported grain, was in line with the socialists' policies as indeed were his views on the institution of an old-age pension scheme.

During July 1895, as the campaign neared its climax, many of his meetings were broken up. At Horsford, his meeting ended in total disorder while at Walsham the meeting was broken up by politically inspired rowdies. At Sodham he was showered with mud and stones and at Stalham the meeting went down in local history as 'the battle of Stalham Bridge'. Rider had to seek refuge in the local Swan Hotel until a police escort was sent for and two men, one a local Conservative peer named Lord Wodehouse, were fined for common assault.[1] The constituency went to the polls on 19 July and Rider lost, but he had reduced his opponent's majority to 198 votes.[2]

Rider was rather bitter about losing. He had spent £2000 on his campaign and now he sat down and devoted a great deal of time in writing letters to newspapers in an endeavour to correct them on misquotations. The *New York Times* correspondent wrote from London:

> Rider Haggard's tempestuous boohooing about the way
> that the rustics chivied him and his swell turnout in Norfolk
> lanes might have been funny if it had not been angering to
> see a grown man so little able to take a beating with decent
> grace.[3]

Writing nearly twenty years later Rider still implied he had been cheated out of the seat and would have won had it not been for the carelessness of the constituency organization in that people who would have voted for him had not received their polling cards or were directed to the wrong polling stations. Nevertheless he added:

> Although I might have done so more than once, never again have I stood for Parliament. To tell the truth, the whole business disgusts me with its atmosphere of falsehood, or at the least of prevarication, and its humiliating quest of falsehood. In such struggles in Britain there is, it is true, little actual corruption, but of indirect corruption there is still a great deal.

In retrospect he was able to say:

> Mercifully the thing miscarried, for had it been otherwise I might have had to bear upon my shoulders much of the burden of the Parliamentary defence of the inspirers and perpetrators of the Jameson Raid, which would have been neither a pleasant nor an easy task.

On 29 December 1895, Dr L. S. Jameson, a close friend and confidant of Cecil Rhodes, the Premier of Cape Colony, had led an armed force of 600 men into the Transvaal Republic from Mafeking. The invading force expected the British residents in the Transvaal to rise up in an armed struggle against the Boer government and force Britain to intervene and annex the country once more. It was a stupid and ill-advised plan. The British in the Transvaal made no attempt at insurrection and the Boers quickly surrounded and defeated Jameson's men. In January 1896 the German Kaiser sent President Paul Kruger a telegram of congratulations on the successful defeat of the invading force. For the Boers it was a splendid propaganda victory. It also alienated the Cape Boers led by J. H. Hofmeyr. Cecil Rhodes, who had been in the conspiracy to overthrow Kruger and put the Transvaal under British control once again, was forced to resign from office. By now, however, both the Boers and British knew that confrontation would not be long in coming. Kruger realized that the British would not rest until they had seized control of the minerally wealthy Transvaal. War was imminent. The Boers of southern Africa began to join forces and Kruger concluded an offensive and defensive treaty with the Orange Free State and both Boer republics started to arm. The Transvaal Volksraad also passed an Aliens Immigration Restriction Act in September 1896, in an attempt to stop the flow of British migrants into the republic. Hofmeyr's Cape Boers were now fully behind the Boer republics and began to agitate for more freedoms for themselves.

Cecil Rhodes was in England just before the Jameson Raid and Rider met him several times. He had not known Rhodes in Africa, Rhodes only arriving there shortly before Rider returned home, but the two men had been introduced in 1888 at the National Liberal Club. Just before the 'raid' Rider breakfasted with Rhodes at the Burlington Hotel. Rhodes was then at the height of his power. Rider last saw him a year later at the same London hotel: 'He paced restlessly up and down the long room like a lion in a cage, throwing out his words in jerky, isolated sentences, and in a curious high voice that sometimes almost attained to a falsetto.' Although Rider felt that Rhodes had a love of country 'he was personally very ambitious'. Rhodes was greedy for territory and wealth and carved his own personal empire in southern Africa, the results of which are still being felt today. Rhodes reminded Rider of Alexander, Caesar, Napoleon and Chaka. He had wanted to seize the Transvaal but had 'miscalculated'. Rider had also known Jameson 'who possesses, I think, in some ways a higher nature than did Rhodes'.

Thus the South African tragedy continued to be played out developing towards that Second Boer War which Rider had predicted, though for the wrong reasons. The Boers, having armed, had demanded the withdrawal of British troops from the borders of the Boer republics. The Boer ultimatum expired on 11 October 1899, with Britain ignoring it. The Second Boer War had become a reality. Rider was still an interested spectator of events and continued to write on southern Africa, including several letters to *The Times* on the Jameson raid. He also spoke on the subject to the March 1896 dinner of the New Vagabonds Club held at the Holborn Restaurant on 5 March.[4] On 23 July he attended the South African Association Inaugural Banquet and replied to a toast 'Prosperity to South Africa' given by the Marquis of Lorne.[5]

During this period Rider's interest in southern Africa was also increased by the settling of the new territory called after Rhodes, Rhodesia. The white settlers moving into the territory following the discovery of gold in Mashonaland, had, in 1894, come into conflict with its inhabitants, the Matabele nation, a Zulu offshoot, led by their king Lobengula. Rider had learnt that the baby daughter of a friend of his had died in the hardships of the war. The friend was an American adventurer, Major Frederick Russell Burnham DSO, who had named his daughter Nada in Rider's honour. Burnham had been born in Minnesota in 1861 and his first recollection was, at the age of three, hiding in a shock of maize during an Indian attack. Nada, born in Buluwayo, died on 22 May 1896, when Burnham was fighting the Ingubu regiment of the Matabele. Burnham was one of two men who survived when a force commanded by Wilson was annihilated on the banks of the Shangiani by a Matabele regiment: Burnham and his brother-in-law, a man named Ingram, had been sent back to base to get reinforcements. Rider was to tell this gripping tale in an article 'Wilson's Last Fight'.[6] Burnham had frequently stayed at Ditchingham House where he used to recount his adventures which were, recalled Rider, 'far more marvellous than those of Allan Quatermain'.

It was a busy period for Rider. He had been elected chairman of the Society of Authors, which he held until 1898, was also a member of the Athenaeum Club, chairman of the Anglo-African Writers' Club, a dining society, and co-director of a weekly newspaper called the *African* which he also helped to edit. His co-director in this venture was a financier in African goods. Rider decided to go into partnership with him to buy and sell imports on the open market. His family tried to dissuade him and his elder brother William urged him to consider his 'ignorance and distaste for business detail'. Rider was not to be dissuaded and became the traditional city business man for nine months with the African Trust Limited.

> My City labours endured but for nine months, after which time I was delivered. During those tumultuous days I toiled in a fine office in London, where thousands were talked of as no account. It was the period of the great African boom, and the business machine hummed merrily. We made money, I remember; also we lost money. But it was all much too speculative and nerve racking for me, while the burden of those companies weighed upon my mind heavily. The true-bred City man cares little for such things, which to him are all part of the day's work, as writing a chapter of a book might be to me. He is accustomed to take risks, and an adept at getting out of difficult situations.

Rider's partner then announced that he was going to live in South Africa for a year and would be leaving the running of the business entirely in Rider's hands. It was too much for him and he resigned. He returned to Ditchingham and was promptly seized with a new subject of interest, and a new phase of his life opened at the end of 1895. His new interest was the land.

He had returned to his estate determined to devote his time to becoming the squire-writer of Ditchingham. He had been elected to the chairmanship of the local magistrate's bench, a position he held until shortly before his death. He was resolved, therefore, to carry out his civic duties and return to romance writing.

> Oddly enough, I found that the thorough change of thought seemed to have rested my mind, with the result that my imagination was fresher than it had been for some years. Also the work itself was and has remained less irksome to me than during the years 1891 to 1895. Still the desire haunted me to do something in my day more practical than the invention of romance upon romance. By degrees it came home to me that a great subject lay to my hand, that of the

state of English agriculture and of our rural population, also of all the questions thereto pertaining.

Rural life in England was undergoing a definite revolution. In the early part of the later nineteenth century, English farming had enjoyed one of the most prosperous periods in its history. Farm wages were higher than anywhere else in Europe. Rider had grown up in this agricultural prosperity, a period of high profits and rents, a time when the old squire of Bradenham could afford to invest in buying new farm lands and expanding his rural empire. But from the mid-1870s there began a slump. The decline began with the increased competition from America, followed by a series of bad crops between 1875 and 1879. Rinderpest had followed in 1879, a sheep-liver rot in 1882 and outbreaks of foot and mouth disease. One million rural workers, half the work force at the time, and their families, emigrated to the cities.

As early as 28 April 1886, Rider had written to *The Times* on 'The Land Question' voicing his dismay at the state of the agricultural economy. During 1895 he wrote several letters to *The Times* on 'the decrepit and even dangerous state of the farming industry in Eastern England'.[7] Now he flung himself into farming, taking a personal interest in the Ditchingham estate and not merely leaving things to his farm manager, as had previously been the case. On 2 October 1899, Longman published the first result of his new interest, a book called *A Farmer's Year, Being His Commonplace Book for 1898*. The work was first serialized in *Longman's Magazine* from September 1898 to October 1899. It was not merely a journal of a year of farming but an informative handbook on farming technique. It presented a way of life deteriorating before the onslaught of 'change', and turned into an impassioned plea to British farmers to change their attitudes and techniques. It contained many remarkable prophecies which the next half-century was to see grimly fulfilled. Rider passionately believed in stopping the rural exodus to the cities.

I am sure that one of the worst fates which can befall
England is that her land should become either a plaything
or a waste, and that her greatest safeguard lies in the
recreation of a yeoman class, rooted in the soil and
supported by the soil.[8]

A Farmer's Year did not merely show the degradation of
English farming but Rider made some general recommenda-
tions to the effect that the government should give financial aid
to agriculture, revise the various land taxes, alter ratings, take
stronger measures against the adulteration of farm produce and
devise cheaper transport to enable the farmer to get his produce
to market more efficiently.

The book was well received by the critics. The *Literary World*
felt that it was 'of permanent value as portraying the
agricultural life of the times'.[9] Even American reviewers were
interested and the *New York Times* said 'you understand old
England better as Mr Haggard sees it'.[10] Rider followed up the
impact which his book created by addressing the Norfolk
Chamber of Agriculture on 6 May 1899, on the subject of the
rural exodus. The Chamber passed a resolution asking the
government to set up a national inquiry on what was described
as a matter which would have 'grave and obvious conse-
quences'.[11] On 30 May Rider moved a similar resolution before
the Central and Associated Chambers of Agriculture in London
where it was also unanimously carried.[12]

Rudyard Kipling wrote from Rottingdean, Sussex, on 12
November 1899:

I wish you knew how much the wife and I enjoyed your
Farmer's Year. In our tiny way we also have made
experiments with land: and your figures made us groan
sympathetically over and about the cruel facts. I don't think
there has ever been a better book of the same, common
(which is uncommon) quiet humorous real country life of
England. I've been going back and rereading it slowly and
leisurely: for the mere taste of it.[13]

The Kiplings had returned to England in 1896 when Kipling fell out with his wife's brother, Beatty, and a court case ensued. Life in America became unbearable and Rudyard and Carrie (Caroline) moved to Torquay. From there they settled for a time in Rottingdean. Kipling respected Rider's opinion very much and he sent him the draft of a poem which *The Times* had commissioned him to write for Queen Victoria's Jubilee on 22 June of that year. Writing on 10 July, Kipling expressed gratitude for Rider's advice and informed him that he and Carrie were going to South Africa for a while, asking him about domestic information. They left in January 1898, and were back in April the same year. Rider invited Kipling to speak at the Anglo-African Writers' Club at the Grand Hotel, London, on 20 May. There was an unusually large turnout and another room had to be set up to accommodate all the guests.[14]

In introducing Kipling, Rider said he did not believe in the divine right of kings but 'in a divine right of a great civilising people – that is, in their divine mission'.[15] Kipling praised the Englishmen who were bringing civilization to southern Africa and launched an attack against the Boers who objected to the 'elementary rudiments of civilisation'. But, Kipling insisted, the English should leave the Transvaal Republic alone and have patience. He could not advocate, as some did, claiming 'our rights by force'. Only if the Boers themselves attacked would England be justified in taking up arms against them. The meeting wound up with Kipling being nominated as vice-president of the club.

As the Boers and the British drew further and further apart, President Kruger decided to dismiss Rider's old chief, Mr Justice John G. Kotzé of the Transvaal High Court. Kotzé had held the position since the British annexation of 1877 and was retained by Kruger after the Transvaal had re-established its independence. Kotzé was dismissed on 17 February 1898, and Rider was instrumental in asking him to come to London and address the Anglo-African Writers' Club at the Grand Hotel on 20 June.[16]

Now Rider turned his talents to a crusading novel entitled *Doctor Therne*, which Longman published on 28 November

1898. It concerned the problem of smallpox vaccination and the narrow attitude of the people who were against vaccinations. Instead of making the vaccination mandatory, the government of the day had given way to the powerful anti-vaccination lobby and Rider ('as a person who in other lands has seen and learned something of the ravages of smallpox among the unvaccinated'[17]) wrote a moralistic tale.

> The importance of the issue to those helpless children from whom the State has thus withdrawn its shield, is this writer's excuse for inviting the public to interest itself in a medical tale. As for the moral, each reader can fashion it to his fancy.

Rider presented copies to his friend Edmund Gosse and to Thomas Hardy, an acquaintance of his from the Savile Club. *Doctor Therne* did not sell well but the Executive Committee of the Jenner Society at Gloucester, passed a resolution on 22 December 1898, expressing

> their appreciation of the recognition of the work of the Society by Mr Rider Haggard in the dedication to its members of his powerful story *Doctor Therne* . . . and desire to assure Mr Rider Haggard of their warm sympathy with his just and vigorous protest against the dangerous agitation carried on against vaccination.

The *Lancet* also commented:

> In conclusion we must commend Mr Haggard's courage in thus entering the lists against the Anti-Vaccination party. As a novelist and a politician alike it is evidently to his advantage to take no step that would be likely to alienate from him any large body of possible supporters. Yet he has risked losing many readers and creating a fanatical opposition to whatever he may do in a public or private capacity for the sake of telling the truth.[18]

Another African tale, a story of the Great Trek, entitled *Swallow*, was published serially in the *Graphic* from July to

October, 1898 and then published in book form on 1 March 1899. It was dedicated to Lieutenant-Colonel Sir Marshal Clarke. This piece of Boer history had a timely publication, with the start of the Second Boer War. Kegan Paul, Trench and Trübner had also decided to reissue, in a paperback format, 'The Transvaal' section of *Cetywayo and His White Neighbours* under the title *The Last Boer War* on 20 October 1899. Due to the timely publication over 30,000 copies were sold as well as an American edition.

The year 1899 had its share of unhappiness for Rider. In May 1899 his brother Bazett died. Following the break up of his marriage to Julia Barker, from which there were four sons, Bazett had become Her Britannic Majesty's Commissioner to the Island of Samoa in 1892. It was on Samoa that Robert Louis Stevenson and his wife Fanny had settled and Bazett became a close friend of the couple. Fanny Stevenson wrote that Bazett was a 'determinedly patriotic Englishman'. In 1893 the Stevensons and their friends concocted a community romance with Bazett as its hero and which they had printed as *An Object of Pity; or, The Man Haggard. A Romance by Many Competent Hands.* Bazett had spiritedly replied with a second volume *Objects of Pity: or, Self and Company. By A Gentleman of Quality.* Stevenson sent both volumes to Rider in which he confessed that 'your brother and I have been indulging in the juvenile sport of shying bricks at each other'. But now, in 1899, Bazett had returned from Samoa broken in health and spirits. Rider went to see him at Parkstone just a few days before he died.

The new year of 1900 started with *The Times* offering Rider a job to go to South Africa as their war correspondent 'but this did not strike me as an attractive business at my age'. Then came an offer from Arthur Pearson, whose publishing empire included the *Daily Express*, asking whether Rider would be prepared to write a series of articles on 'The New South Africa' after the war was concluded. Rider agreed.

In January 1900, he decided to take his family to Florence to stay with his sister-in-law, Agnes, the wife of his brother John

George who was now British Consul in Trieste. John had to go to Noumea and had left Agnes and their three children in a house in Florence which was big and rambling and which had once been a convent. The Haggards arrived, exhausted and ill, to find Florence in the middle of one of its coldest winters, with gales, fogs and torrential rain. Rider wrote:

> When the *tramonane* (sic) [north wind] in its glory leaps
> and howls along the dusky streets of Florence, then indeed
> does the traveller think with repentant affection of the very
> bleakest spot he knows upon England's eastern shores, even
> on the bitterest day in March.

Added to this, a virulent influenza epidemic raged in the city and the chapel opposite Agnes' house never ceased tolling its bells for the dead. The worry heightened when Lilias, Rider's youngest, caught the bug. Rider nearly went mad with worry. According to Lilias:

> He cursed the day he ever came to Florence. He was
> convinced his small daughter was going to die, and worked
> himself into such a state that Louie decided the only hope
> for his peace of mind was to get him off on the proposed
> trip as soon as possible. The moment Lilias began to get
> well, Rider was bundled off to Cyprus with his eldest sister,
> Ella's boy, Arthur, as his secretary.[19]

Rider had decided to visit Cyprus and Palestine and take with him Ella's son, Arthur Maddison Green, who had just left school. Rider found the boy had his shortcomings; he lost the luggage on the Italian railway and although the boy took along a typewriter to work 'all he did with it was to drop it on my toes out of the rack of the railway train'. Mishaps aside, Rider and Arthur spent some pleasant weeks in Cyprus staying with John Jebb's daughter and her mining-engineer husband. They then went on to Palestine, a country which greatly intrigued Rider, visiting the Dead Sea, Bethlehem, Nazareth, Jericho, Golgotha and Jerusalem. 'I was not disappointed,' wrote Rider, 'its living and perpetual interest came home to me more closely than I had dared hope.'[20] He had agreed with Moberly Bell of *The Times* to write a series of articles on Palestine but, though he made copious notes, he did not write them. Instead, he used the information he gathered to fashion two historical romances: *Pearl Maiden*, about the fall of Jerusalem, published in 1903, and *The Brethren*, about Saladin and the crusaders, published in 1904. On returning to England, Rider also wrote an account of his travels under the title *A Winter Pilgrimage* which was serialized in the *Queen* from 5 January to 29 June 1901, and then by Longman in book form on 7 October 1901.

Towards the end of the year Rider began to think seriously about his agreement with the *Daily Express* to write about the Boer War. Kipling had given his talents to a British army news-sheet called *Friend* and also devoted his energies to recruiting a volunteer company to fight the Boers. In March, while Rider was in Palestine, Kipling was watching the Britons and Boers in battle at Karee Siding. In April he was back in England but returned to South Africa during the winters of 1901 and 1902, staying as the guest of Cecil Rhodes at The Woolsack, from where he corresponded with Rider. Kipling's verses became intensely imperialistic, full of jingoist tirades against the Boers. His imperialism even began to alienate his relatives, friends and readers and his reputation as an artist suffered considerably. Nevertheless, Kipling saw it as his patriotic duty to rouse the 'soldiers of the empire'.

By comparison, Rider was sickened with the whole war. It was growing clear that the British public was trying hard to forget the problems of South Africa. After their initial successes, the Boer field armies had suffered defeat after defeat but they refused to surrender. The initial phase of 'imperialistic patriotism' quickly wore off and most of the Liberal Party deplored the war. There was a strong lobby to get negotiations under way with the Boers. Sir Alfred Milner, in command in South Africa, refused to make any attempt at reconciliation or compromise. To him the Boers must first surrender uncon- ditionally and hand the Boer republics over to Britain. One of the blackest periods in British imperial history began; Milner built a system of blockhouses across the Boer republics; Boer families were turned out of their homes and farms which were then burnt to the ground; livestock was confiscated and grain and produce either taken away to feed the British soldiers or destroyed. The women and children were herded into special camps, concentration camps as the British called them. In these camps, according to British records, some 18,000 Boers, mostly women and children, died of disease and starvation. According to Boer sources, the figure reached 25,000. Out of a small population, it was a terrifying figure. The revelation of the terrible condition of these camps caused a great outcry among the anti-war faction in Britain and throughout the world. The camps also strengthened the deepening hate between the Boers and the British, and earned Britain an unenviable place in history as the country which invented the concentration camp. It was not until 31 May 1902 that the surviving Boer commandos, no more than a few thousand men, were finally worn down by a British army of 300,000 troops. Starving and with few arms to carry on the fight, their will sapped by the suffering of the civilians and the deaths of their women and children in the camps, the Boer leaders came to Vereeniging and submitted to Milner. The two Boer republics of the Transvaal and Orange Free State became part of Britain's South African territories. It was a hollow victory.

Arthur Pearson had to agree with Rider that the British public wanted to forget about South Africa as quickly as possible.

It was while Rider was in his bath one day that he was struck by an idea. 'It was to the effect that I should like to emulate Arthur Young, who more than a century before, had travelled through and written of the state of agriculture in the majority of the English counties.' Arthur Young (1741–1820) was an agricultural pioneer who had set out on his tour in 1767. Rider asked his agent, A. P. Watt, to negotiate with the *Daily Express* that instead of a series on South Africa they would publish a series on rural England. The *Daily Express* promised to publish fifty articles on the state of rural England and Rider set off in the early spring of 1901, making Wiltshire as his starting point.

With him, as a companion and secretary, went Arthur Cochrane. The idea was to get a picture of the overall state of agriculture in England and the position of the rural population. The articles appeared between April and October 1901 and then were rewritten to form a great two-volume work entitled *Rural England*, which Longman published on 28 November 1902. According to Morton Cohen 'Anyone who ventures to read *Rural England* will be shocked by the condition of English farmers and farmland at the beginning of the century.'[21]

So disturbing were the facts that he had uncovered, Rider decided to devise a detailed programme for the reform of agricultural England. He saw two root causes of the problem: the rural exodus, and the way that agriculture was practised. Census figures showed that even with a rising population the number of agricultural workers was declining with the number of acres under cultivation. One way to stop the flow of farm labourers to city industry was to make life on the land more profitable, more comfortable and more alluring. But the propositions that Rider put forward for a rural rejuvenation were thirty-five years in advance of total acceptance in a conservative England.

Rider saw salvation in the hands of government. He called upon parliament to enact legislation to bring about two major reforms: the first to give active and generous support to a system of small holdings, to enable people to farm them adequately; the second to aid farmers in getting their produce to market efficiently and cheaply. The small holdings proposal was nothing new. There had been a Small Holdings Act in 1892. However, what Rider was asking for was a revivified act with the government giving small holders loans at low interest, direct from the treasury, to help build up the system. In addition, Rider wanted the tax laws revised, the copyhold system abolished, a strengthened and powerful Board of Agriculture, a better railway system for shipping produce, a law requiring all foreign imported meats to be branded as such and the promotion of co-operative societies for butter manufacture. In addition, he wanted a complete review of rural education.

In 1902 Rudyard Kipling had bought a seventeenth-century house at Burwash in Sussex called Batemans. From here, on 22 December 1902, Kipling wrote to Rider addressing him as 'Dear Cobbett-Young-Haggard':

> For the last week or more the wife and I have been reading *Rural England* with deep joy (I don't mean on account of the state of things revealed) and admiration. I bought it lawfully in market overt and it stands with your *Farmer's Year* between Young's *Agriculture of Sussex* and *Selbourne* (Gilbert White). I take off my hat to you deeply and profoundly because it's a *magnum opus* and altogether fascinating and warning and chock full of instruction.[22]

Joseph Chamberlain also wrote to Rider saying that he entirely agreed with his views and Rider found sympathy with Thomas Hardy, from whose article 'The Dorsetshire Labourer' he had quoted.

The *Quarterly Review*, however, felt that 'his gospel of dependence on the government is a confession of failure'[23] and indeed, most of the conservative press were outraged by Rider's radical proposals pointing out that they bordered on socialism! Rider was not daunted by the apathetic and hostile response from parliamentary circles and continued to propound his theories by writing letters, articles and making public speeches until the *Literary World* noticed that 'Mr Haggard's position as a social reformer had become almost apostolic'.[24] But Rider's ideas were generally ignored. In a preface to a new edition of *Rural England* in January 1906 he wrote 'after four years are gone by I must with humiliation report that nothing of consequence has happened'.

The same year he wrote:

> It will be admitted that such a record of progress or rather the utter lack of it, is not very encouraging to a private person who has devoted years of his life and the best labour of his brain, every hour that can be spared of both of them from the actual task of earning his living indeed, to the

furtherance of what we acknowledge to be national needs by
the most reflective and able minds in all the political
parties. At times, I confess, I have been tempted to
abandon the crusade in despair.

Through 1903 he busied himself with his garden at
Ditchingham and wrote *A Gardener's Year* on the same lines as
he had written *A Farmer's Year*. It was serialized in the *Queen*
from 9 January to 3 December 1904 and then published on 13
January 1905. The garden at Ditchingham had become his
hobby as the farm lands had been his passion. His daughter
Lilias wrote:

> No corner of that garden was, however, too humble for his
> interest. He drained and double dug, planted fences for
> shelter and built walls to shut out the north easters, whose
> cutting sharpness in spring would send his sun-loving
> person shivering below the Vineyard Hills for a little
> warmth. He was a practical as well as an imaginative
> gardener, and realising only too well that the tropical and
> semi-tropical plants gathered on his travels, and sent by his
> many friends, might have a short life, he did not neglect
> hardy flowering shrubs, roses, primroses, periwinkles and
> the daffodil.[25]

Having read *A Gardener's Year*, Kipling wrote to Rider:
'Everything in the book delights my sympathetic soul except
your orchids!'[26]

CHAPTER 10

ROYAL COMMISSIONER

In the spring of 1904 Rider, with his eldest daughter Angela, went on holiday to Egypt. They went out on a P & O ship which was making its maiden voyage, a voyage which turned into a nightmare. First they were grounded in the Thames, then a crewman died and had to be buried at sea. In the Channel they encountered a terrific gale and when, on reaching the Mediterranean, they expected calm seas, a sandstorm blew from Africa and nearly swamped the ship. On top of this the engines overheated, the ship nearly ran aground and at Marseilles many passengers left with grim warnings to the remaining group that the ship would surely sink. Finally, as they reached Port Said, the chief engineer had to be carried ashore raving, and he died not long afterwards.

Once in Egypt, Rider settled down to enjoy himself. It was his second visit and this time he bought a new camera and set out to explore the ancient tombs. He went as far as the rock temple at Abu Simbel, near to the second Cataract of the Nile, and to the tomb of Queen Nefer-tari. He filled copious notebooks and used much of the material to write a series of six articles on Egypt for the *Daily Mail*.[1] In two of the articles – 'The Debris of Majesty' and 'The Trade in the Dead' – he wrote of the wholesale robbery of the ancient tombs which was a theme he was to emphasize in his tale *Smith and the Pharaohs*, which was serialized in the *Strand Magazine* between December 1912 and February 1913. With a collection of other stories, *Smith and the Pharaohs* appeared in book form in 1920. Rider was fascinated by Egypt.

Egypt, with all its history and problems, which, whenever I

can find time, it is my greatest recreation to study. Truly its old inhabitants were a mysterious and fascinating folk and, across the gulf of ages – largely, it must be admitted, through these very excavations – they have come very near to us again. I confess I know more of her kings, her queens, and her social conditions than I do of those of early England.

In his notebook he recorded that he

rode to the tombs of the Kings and saw those of Seti, Rameses III, and Amenhotep III, all lit now with electricity. The unwrapped body of Amenhotep lies in its sarcophagus, calmly sleeping with the electric light blazing full upon his still majestic face. Such is the end of royalty – a poor, hideous, dishevelled corpse. . . .

A wonderful and weird place this Valley of the Kings, with its rugged, naked cliffs, shattered by sun and time. Another proof of the genius of the Egyptians that they should have chosen such a spot, so strangely suitable for the burial of the great. But the hideous mockery of it all – the royal bodies torn, carted away – stripped – made a show of even in their everlasting habitations, or grinning from the glass cases of museums – Farewell, O King![2]

This Egyptian trip inspired Rider to write two books on his return. The first was a 'straight' novel, *The Way of the Spirit*, and the second was a romance, *Morning Star*. *The Way of the Spirit* was originally entitled *Renunciation* but it was changed when a book of the same title written by Dorothy Summers was published by T. Fisher Unwin in October 1905. Rider's agent, A. P. Watt, was delighted with the novel and proposed to ask for £2500 advance against royalties for the British book rights alone. 'I cannot resist telling you', he wrote to Rider, 'how much I admire *The Way of the Spirit*; it is, perhaps, one of your best and finest books, causing one to wonder if renunciation is not, perhaps, the more excellent way.' Kipling also thought well of the story and Rider dedicated the volume to him.

Charles Longman was not so keen on the book and refused to run it in *Longman's Magazine*:

> The basis of the book is sexual relationship and renunciation – it cannot be put in the background, and it is this particular relation which I think it better not to discuss in magazines. I have been a good deal tempted – but there it is – we all have our cranks, and that, I suppose is mine.

Watt tried *Cassell's Magazine* but they, too, were dubious about the merits of the story. Watt eventually had to give up on getting a serialization and even had to find an entirely new publisher, Hutchinson, to issue the book in March 1906. The book was not successful and did not even sell an American edition. *Morning Star*, a more traditional Rider romance, was serialized in the *Christian World News of the Week* before being published by Cassell in March 1910.

From Egypt Rider and Angela returned via Naples and southern Spain.

> At Granada we saw that wondrous building, the Alhambra, and in the cathedral the tomb of Ferdinand and Isabella the Catholic. I descended into a vault and was shown the coffins of those great people; also those of Philip le Bel and his wife Joanna. Readers of Prescott will remember that the mad Joanna insisted upon opening the coffin of her husband after he had been some while dead. I procured a candle and examined it, and there I could see the line where the lead had been cut through and soldered together again.
>
> Of all the buildings that I saw upon this journey I think the mosque at Cordova, with its marvellous shrine and its forest of pillars of many multi-coloured marbles struck me as the most impressive. The great cathedral at Seville, however, with its vast cold spaces runs it hard in majesty.

Spain also inspired Rider. The result was the romance entitled *Fair Margaret* which Hutchinson published in September 1907 after it had run serially in the *Lady's Realm* between November 1906, and October 1907.

Back at Ditchingham, Rider had an experience which was to alter his life-style. As a young man he had attended some séances and had decided that 'spiritualism should be left to the expert and earnest investigator'. But in July 1904 an incident occurred which sent Rider writing letters to *The Times* and the Society for Psychical Research.[3]

> On the night of Saturday, July 9, I went to bed about 12.30 and suffered from what I took to be a nightmare. I was awakened by my wife's voice calling to me from her own bed upon the other side of the room. I dreamed that a black retriever dog, a most amiable and intelligent beast named Bob, which was the property of my eldest daughter, was lying on its side among brushwood, or rough growth of some sort, by water. In my vision the dog was trying to speak to me in words, and, failing, transmitted to my mind in an undefined fashion the knowledge that it was dying. Then everything vanished, and I woke to hear my wife asking me why on earth I was making those horrible and weird noises. I replied I had had a nightmare about a fearful struggle, and that I had dreamed that old Bob was in a dreadful way, and was trying to talk to me and tell me about it.[4]

At breakfast the next day, Sunday, Louie recounted the story but in spite of that it was not until Sunday evening that Angela reported that Bob, her dog, was missing. On Thursday, 14 July, Rider and a servant named Charles Bedingfield discovered Bob's body in a river, the Waveney, against a weir about a mile and a quarter from the house. It was eventually discovered that Bob had been struck by a train, the last to run by Ditchingham, some time after 11 p.m. that Saturday night. Rider wrote:

> I am forced to conclude that the dog Bob, between whom and myself there existed a mutual attachment, either at the moment of his death, if his existence can conceivably have been prolonged till after one in the morning, or, as seems more probable, about three hours after the event, did

succeed in calling my attention to its actual or recent plight by placing whatever portion of my being is capable of receiving such impulses when enchained by sleep, into its own terrible position.[5]

The experience had a profound effect on Rider.

This experience produced a great effect upon me, and at first frightened and upset me somewhat, for without doubt it has a very uncanny side. By degrees, however, I came to see that it also has its lessons, notably one lesson – that of the kinship, I might almost say the oneness, of all animal life. I have always been fond of every creature, and especially of dogs, some of which have been and are as very dear friends to me. But up to this date I had also been a sportsman. Shooting was my principal recreation, and one of which I was, and indeed still am, extremely fond. Greatly did I love a high pheasant, at which sometimes I made good marksmanship. But now, alas! I only bring them down in imagination with an umbrella or a walking stick. From that day forward, except noxious insects and so forth, I have killed nothing, and, although I should not hesitate to shoot again for food or for protection, I am by no means certain that the act would not make me feel unwell.

In 1905 Rider's career took a new turn. In mid-January he received a letter from Alfred Lyttelton, the Colonial Secretary, asking him whether he would be prepared to go to the USA as a commissioner to report on the labour colonies established by the Salvation Army for the poor and slum refugees from the big cities. These colonies had been very successful and the government thought that they might copy the system and model upon it some scheme of emigration from the United Kingdom to the colonies. The Rhodes Trust had subscribed £300 to defray the expenses of the commissioner but it was obvious that, with a return trip of six thousand miles, loss of three months work, the investigation and the writing of a lengthy report, the commissioner would have to pay substantially out of his own pocket for the privilege of working for the government.

> I should be very glad if you would consent to do the work for which your experience as an observer both of men and agricultural affairs so eminently qualifies you. The remuneration is not very great, but the interest of the question to which the inquiry will relate and the public service which the Commissioner will be able to do, may induce you, I hope, to undertake it.

Rider did not need long to think about the proposition and accepted. He immediately arranged an interview with the leader and founder of the Salvation Army, General William Booth (1829–1912). He had already become acquainted with Booth in November 1901, when he interviewed him for his book on *Rural England*, publishing a verbatim report of the interview in the book. Booth took him to see the Salvation Army colony at Hadleigh.

On 22 February 1905, Rider, with his daughter Angela acting as his secretary, sailed for New York. They stayed at the Waldorf-Astoria where Rider found, as before, he was besieged by pressmen. A reporter from the *New York Herald* observed that 'the Rider Haggard of the new crusade is another man from the jaunty romancer of a decade ago'.[6] Rider and Angela found that there were so many people trying to contact them with all manner of queries that they, at last, took their telephone receivers off the hook each night in order to ensure an uninterrupted sleep. 'Every room in an American hotel has a telephone', observed Rider.

During the two months he spent in America, Rider visited the colonies at Fort Romie, near San Francisco, Fort Amity, in Colorado, and Fort Herrick, which specialized in rehabilitating alcoholics, in Ohio. Rider, with Angela, was entertained at various functions from a Franklin Club luncheon in Philadelphia, to a private luncheon in Washington with Secretary of State, Hay, who was a friend of his brother William. On 9 March Rider was invited to meet the newly inaugurated president, Theodore Roosevelt. Roosevelt was a great believer in the Victorian 'imperial' concept. Mark Twain disgustedly called him 'our native American imperialist'. He talked to Rider at length about the South African situation and finally

> expressed his hope that the Boers in South Africa, with whom he had great sympathy, would settle down, learn English, and become a dominant factor in that country under the British flag and rule. He added that he had expressed these views strongly to those of their leaders who had visited him in America, which shows that he, at least, was not working against us in the South African war.

A few days later Roosevelt entertained Rider and Angela to a private luncheon at the White House. There was a complete rapport between the two men.

> 'It is an odd thing, Mr Haggard,' said the President at that luncheon, 'that you and I, brought up in different countries and following such different pursuits, should have identical ideas and aims. I have been reading your book *Rural England* and I tell you that what you think, I think, and what you want to do, I want to do. We are one man in the matter.'[7]

Roosevelt and Rider were to correspond until Roosevelt's death. They were, in fact, to meet only once more and Rider observed they were 'men who are in deep and almost mysterious sympathy with one another'.[8]

Rider and Angela continued their journey and one pleasant interlude was visiting his old friends the Burnhams who had returned from South Africa in 1903 to settle in Pasadena. Burnham now had two sons whom he wanted to go into the army which, he told Rider, was 'that branch of the human organisation which is the last to decay in a too luxurious nation'.[9] Rider wrote to Lyttelton that

> our journey was very long and arduous, and towards the end of it my daughter developed influenza in the train which, as

I did not know what it was, frightened me. Also we had a
great escape of being drowned in the Colorado River.[10]

They also visited Canada and saw the Governor General, Earl
Grey, who made an official commitment on behalf of the
Canadian Government for a plot of 240,000 acres of land to be
used in settling British migrants.

The saddest part of the trip, however, was when Rider went to
see his brother Andrew who was then living in Maine. Andrew,
having left Winchester, had gone into the army and
distinguished himself as a soldier of unusual ability rising to
command the Egyptian Battalion as a lieutenant-colonel and
winning the DSO. General Sir Lyon Freemantle, once his
commanding officer, told his brother William 'Your brother
Andrew was a brave man – the bravest I ever knew – but I also
knew he would never succeed – he had no patience.'[11] Andrew
began writing quite early, and it was Andrew who first
encouraged Rider to start writing. Although Andrew had
written several works, such as *Ada Triscott*, by the early 1880s, it
was not until 1889 that his first novel *Dodo and I* was published
by Blackwoods. He wrote many novels and several books on
French history. Success, however, was to come later when he
specialized in works on the French revolutionary period. One of
his last works, *Madame de Staël* (Hutchinson, 1922), was
dedicated to Rider. But when Rider saw him in America in
1905, Andrew had fallen on hard times. He had given up the
army to devote himself to writing, certain he would be able to
emulate his younger brother's success. Now he was almost
penniless and his marriage to Emily Isabella Chirnside was
going through a very difficult period. When Rider and Angela
sailed for England, late in April on the RMS *Majestic*, Andrew
wrote Rider a very bitter letter.

> As to coming down to New York to see you sailing away
> home again, after your rapid and triumphant progress – and
> leaving me behind, well, my dear Rider, it would be too
> absolutely distressing and I could not stand it. To be alone
> on the wharf in New York, with no friends, no glory, no

excitement, no money, while seeing the smoke from your
funnels disappearing. And then all the headlines in the
papers – 'Departure of Rider Haggard' – 'Distinguished
Novelist Leaves for Europe' – That sort of thing greeting me
everywhere would be too much altogether – I know our
positions are very different – and the cry is why did I ever
leave the Army? Did I blame you for leaving Sir Henry
Bulwer for Shepstone, Shepstone for the High Court, the
High Court for Ostriches, Ostriches for the Bar and the
Divorce Courts, the Bar for Literature? I left the Army
because I did not choose to serve in subordinate positions
under Kitchener etc., who had served under me. Also I got
two thousand pounds – gone now! Because I have been less
fortunate than my rich and successful brother in my change
of occupation, *I* must be reproached for leaving the Army.[12]

Rider was moved to send Andrew some money for which
Andrew was grateful and replied in a more conciliatory tone:

It has a great deal more significance than the actual gift, old
fellow. . . . . It has shown me that the love which still exists
between us is the love that has always existed, that you want
to help me, above all that you are not careless of my fate.[13]

Rider was always being insulted by jealous relations, according
to his daughter Lilias.

Rider's family did and said the most outrageous and
unforgivable things. They bit the hand that fed them with
the utmost regularity, they were jealous of him, abused
him, and even insulted him in their astonishing letters,
having no control over their pens and over their tongues.
They landed their children on him to look after, then basely
sheltered behind their wives' skirts when domestic
differences of opinion arose over doctors, health, education
and interfering grandmothers and mothers-in-law or
accused him of abusing their confidence.[14]

Rider and Angela returned home and in May Rider set to

work to produce his *Report on the Salvation Army Colonies* which was published as a Blue Book by HMSO in June. At the same time he revised the work for a more popular version, *The Poor and the Land*, which was published by Longman on 18 August 1905. Rider reported in great detail on the project and thoroughly recommended the British Government to copy the scheme which he predicted would infinitely benefit the depressed industrial cities. His report had an excellent reception in *The Times*, *Morning Post*, *Daily Telegraph*, *Daily News* and *Standard*. Even the *Daily Express* said that the scheme was so excellent that the Conservative government should have no difficulty in finding financial support for it and the *Daily Mirror* urged 'the great thing is to get it started, and to realise that we are laying great bases for the future . . . the sooner we begin the better'.[15]

The government, however, was cold towards the report. Lyttelton gave Rider less than half an hour in which to explain his findings and then dismissed him saying that although he hoped the government would act on Rider's report, he felt that Arthur Balfour, the Prime Minister, would not even bother to read it. When the report came before the House of Commons in June 1905, it was voted into committee. Rider met a Conservative agent at a public dinner in London who told him that 'he had just been speaking to a Minister, who had told him that my Report was to be sent to a committee which would "knock the bottom out of it". Then I knew that all was finished.' The Conservative Party were, of course, in their last year of office and would not take power as a party again until 1922. They did, however, share power during the Conservative–Liberal–Labour Coalition from 1915 during the war years. Rider commented afterwards:

> The Conservative Party was already a mere corpse galvanised into a semblance of its lost life, and standing on the edge of an open grave, it pretended not to see, its pale eyes fixed upon those thunder-clouds which, after ten years, had become so very large and definite.

Little wonder they were not interested in 'reports on matters dealing with the transference of our superabundant city poor to colonial settlements'. Party politics apart, Rider was annoyed by the lack of response to his report.

> For me personally this issue was painful, I had worked hard and in all honestness, and, like many better men, I found myself thrown over. After all the Colonial Secretary's declarations as to the value of my work etc. I never even received a letter of thanks from the Government, or, for the matter of that, a copy of the Report and Evidence of the Committee, which I had to buy like any other member of the public. All that I got was the privilege of paying the bill for, of course, the small sum allowed by the Rhodes Trustees did not suffice to meet the expenses of my tour in a high official position through that very expensive country, the United States.

Rider did receive a letter of thanks from W. Bramwell Booth, General Booth's son, who wrote on behalf of his father to thank Rider for the 'important service you have rendered the community'. He added: 'My own feeling is that Government has really ceased any serious intention in this matter – they are practically in a state of suspended animation.' Within a few months the Conservatives were forced to declare a general election at which they were overwhelmingly defeated by the Liberals.

Rider returned to his work again. On 6 October 1905 the sequel to *She* was published as *Ayesha – The Return of She*. At the time of its publication Rider was in a nursing home undergoing an operation. He had never taken a major anaesthetic before and he did not find it pleasant. 'It was like death, only I hope that death is not quite so dark!' he wrote afterwards. He recalled coming round and finding himself surrounded by nurses who only wanted his autograph. 'However, of one of these nurses at any rate, a widow, I have grateful recollections. I amused myself, and, I trust, her, by reading *Ayesha* aloud to her during my long wakeful hours – for she was a night nurse.'

Rider had deliberately waited twenty years before undertaking his sequel, although the plot had been stirring in his mind for some years. He had first submitted an outline of the plot to Charles Longman in November 1898. He wrote:

> as we are on the subject, perhaps you would like to have my plot of the continuation of *She*, which I have always intended to write if I live. If only I can carry it out as I conceive it, it ought to be one of the most majestic romances in the world. Here it is – pretty good, I think, – what offers for that romance, my boy?

It would appear that Longman did not share Rider's enthusiasm for the sequel because it was Ward Lock who finally bought the book for a £1,000 advance against a 25 per cent royalty. It was first serialized in the *Windsor Magazine* between December 1904 and October 1905. Rider's original title was *Hes – The Further History of She-Who-Must-Be-Obeyed* but the publishers raised some objections and Rider submitted *The Goddess or the Return of She-Who-Must-Be-Obeyed*. Again, Ward Lock did not like the title and made a counter suggestion of *The Priestess*. Rider replied with *The Oracle* and both parties settled on *Ayesha – The Return of She* on 19 October 1904 as the title for publication.

Rider dedicated this sequel, as he had done the original, to his friend Andrew Lang. In recent years he had seen little of Lang, although the two men maintained an irregular correspondence. Rider sent the book to him not without apprehension for he considered Lang's opinion on fiction 'the soundest of any man of his time'. There was relief therefore when Lang replied: 'It is all right. I am thrilled; so much obliged. I thought I was too Old, but the Eternal Boy is still on the job.' He added: 'Unluckily I think the dam[n] reviewers never were boys – most of them the Editor's nieces.' Another friend of Rider's, the expert on malaria Sir Ronald Ross, was also delighted with *Ayesha* and wrote to him: 'It is really a very great romance because I think it has some very high allegorical meaning.'

It was about this time that Rider's first love, Lilith, the girl he would have married except for his father's interference, came into his life again. While Rider had been in South Africa, Lilith, tired of waiting for him, had married someone else. The marriage had ended in disaster and her husband had finally gone abroad leaving her with her children. She was penniless and her relatives were unable to help her. In desperation she turned to Rider for help. He secured her a cottage a mere stone's throw from Ditchingham House. Louie undertook to see to all the domestic arrangements. According to Lilias: 'only a woman of Louie's straightforward and unemotional temperament could have made a success of this risky experiment. As far as her husband was concerned, the past was dead and done with; she trusted him absolutely and what he wished she would do.'[16] Lilith stayed at Ditchingham for a year or two and then received a letter from her husband who said he was now 'making good' in South Africa and wished for another chance to mend the marriage. He begged Lilith to take her youngest boy with her and join him. Against Rider's advice, she went. From Madeira she wrote to say good-bye to Rider:

> I received safely your kind note of farewell – also the
> photograph, which I indeed greatly value. I hope and trust
> we may meet again and in (for me) happier circumstances!
> For all your generous help in the time of need, for your
> friendship and never failing kindness I shall all my life feel
> the deepest gratitude.

Rider picked up his pen and wrote one word, *Finis*, under her name and laid it aside with other letters belonging to the past.

But Rider and Lilith were to meet once more and not in 'happier circumstances'. As Rider had foretold, Lilith's return to her husband was a disastrous one. After a while her husband had died and she herself was stricken with a fatal disease. She returned to Ditchingham and, in the spring of 1909, she died. 'Almost in a dream', Rider followed the coffin to the grave.

Louie, dispassionate and efficient as ever, was there with him. His daughter wrote:

> He was not a middle-aged man who followed a coffin down the aisle of a church, but a fair-headed boy of nineteen walking down the red carpeted path of a garden in Richmond one spring night some thirty-five years ago. 'The girl with the golden hair and violets in her hand' whom he had seen for the first time that night, was in front of him. . . . Rider turned, and left the dead to their sleep.[17]

CHAPTER 11

PUBLIC SERVANT

Rider was now at the peak of his career. His popularity as a writer was reflected in the phenomenal print runs of the first editions of his romances and novels. Until 1905 average print runs had consisted of 10,000 copies except with a book like *Ayesha* which went to a staggering 25,000 copies. From 1906 first edition print runs were increased to an average 15,000. Rider's works were also appearing in superb illustrated editions. The illustrated novel today is a thing of the past but at this time it was a highly popular art form. Rider was lucky in the artists who illustrated his works for they succeeded in grasping his idea of characters and portraying them. The first artist to extensively illustrate Rider's works, beginning with the first illustrated edition of *She* in 1889, was, in fact, a personal friend of Rider's named Maurice William Greiffenhagen. Greiffenhagen had been born in London on 15 December 1862, won a scholarship to a Royal Academy school when he was only sixteen and had his first exhibition at the Royal Academy when he was in his early twenties. Greiffenhagen was forced to become an illustrator for financial reasons. He first met Rider while he was at Lincoln's Inn practising law and later Rider tried to make Greiffenhagen set up his home in Norfolk. The Greiffenhagens often stayed at Ditchingham. It was on one of these visits that Greiffenhagen showed Rider sketches for a picture he was working on and Rider, expressing his admiration for the work, asked what title he had given it. Greiffenhagen confessed he had not thought of a title whereupon Rider said 'Well, it ought to be called "The sons of God saw the daughters of man that they were fair".' Greiffenhagen adopted the suggestion and the painting was purchased by the Muncipal Gallery at Ghent.[1]

Rider's bibliographer, J. E. Scott, has written:

> When one looks at the illustrations done by Greiffenhagen,
> it is difficult to realise that he disliked doing
> black-and-white work; but this statement is true enough.
> From the beginning of his career, Greiffenhagen knew
> where his real talent lay – in oil painting – but like many
> another famous artist, his early life was a hard struggle;
> necessity made it imperative that he should earn some
> money in order to prepare himself for the long and
> expensive task of gaining recognition, and yet, during the
> time he was thus forced to augment his income, he never
> lost his sense of colour or decorative power. His early
> contributions to periodicals and books were executed in pen
> and ink, but he soon forsook this medium for wash which
> gave him scope for his sense of light and shade. Long before
> he achieved success with his paintings, Greiffenhagen had
> become well-known for his periodical illustrations, and it
> would have been easy for him to continue in this line of
> work. He was strong enough, however, to resist the
> temptation to take the easier of the two roads and preferred
> to work for his goal.[2]

The illustrations in *Ayesha* showed Greiffenhagen at his best.
He succeeds in portraying the immortal beauty of She exactly as
Rider envisaged her. Greiffenhagen was to paint Rider's portrait
(which still hangs in Ditchingham House at the time of writing)
and believed it to be one of the best things that he had done. It
was exhibited at the Royal Academy and two onlookers were
overheard discussing it:

> 'Who's that?'
> 'Oh, don't you know – it's that awful man who writes
> those awful books.'[3]

Greiffenhagen, indeed, caught Rider's image during the period
of the war years. His long, thin figure is sunk deeply into a chair
and there is a great air of weariness and suffering in it. Rider,
joking, thought the picture should be called 'Wrinkles' and his

family were rather unhappy at his portrayal. But his sister-in-law, Agnes, wrote to him:

> I went to the Academy the other day to see your portrait! Now that really is a portrait. Of course, it has got your The-end-of-all-things-is-at-hand-and-on-the-whole-it-is-better-so expression, but you sometimes do look like that, whereas never, never, thank heaven, did you look like any of the other presentments of you, except the 'Don Ridero' one in the shooting cape which Griffy did of you before. Do buy this picture if it is for sale, and make presents of all the other horrors to County Institutions. Joking apart, I do like the thing awfully. Also Griffy has got that odd glint in your eye which you got from your father.[4]

Greiffenhagen was elected a member of the Royal Academy in 1922 and died on 26 December 1931.

About this time another illustrator was working on Rider's books, a Welshman named Arthur C. Michael who studied at Swansea and in Paris. Rider took a great deal of interest in his work and corresponded with him, and at times lent him volumes from his library in order that he might obtain local colour and detail. In the same way as Greiffenhagen, Michael also managed to obtain a complete understanding of Rider's characters and he was particularly adept at portraying Rider's concepts of native characters. A third artist, Richard Caton-Woodville, also worked on Rider's books. Woodville, who was called the 'English Meissionier' was born in London on 7 January 1856, and studied art in Düsseldorf. His best work was the illustrations for *Nada the Lily*. He was a moody man, given to melancholia, and his health was deteriorating due to a wound he had received in the Egyptian War of 1882. He was found shot in his studio on 17 April 1927.

The appearance of Rider's works was greatly enhanced by the illustrations of these artists.

It was in December 1905 that Balfour's Conservative government lost the general election and was replaced by the Liberals under Campbell Bannerman. One of their announcements was on the establishment of a Royal Commission on Coast Erosion. This was a subject that Rider was particularly interested in and he wrote a letter to David Lloyd George, then President of the Board of Trade, describing his success in stopping erosion at his estate at Kessingland Grange with marram grass. Kessingland was a property on the east coast he had bought a few years before. Lloyd George responded by asking Rider to call and see him, then offering him a seat on the commission. Delighted, Rider accepted. Lord Ashby St Ledgers was the first chairman of the commission, to be followed by Ivor Guest. For about a year the commission conducted its inquiries and Rider noted: 'I do not suppose there is a groin or an eroded beach on the shores of the United Kingdom that I have not seen and thoughtfully considered.'

But after a year of careful study, the commission had come to the conclusion that coast erosion was not really a pressing problem. Rider, the agricultural reformer and conservationist, suddenly saw a way to utilize the commission in a positive way instead of merely returning a negative report to parliament. One night, at a dinner party, Lord Ashby St Ledgers and Rider approached Lloyd George and asked him if the question of afforestation could be added to the reference of the commission. It was agreed and the commission assumed the title of the Royal Commission on Coast Erosion and Afforestation. Rider recorded:

> I worked hard on that Royal Commission. During the five years of its life, indeed, I only missed one day's sitting, and that was because the steamer from Denmark could not get me there in time. Shortly after the commencement of its labours I was nominated the chairman of the Unemployed Labour and Reclamation Committee, which involved a good deal of extra but important and interesting business. Also I was the chairman of two of the tours that were made by the committees of the Commission to inspect the coasts of Great Britain and Ireland, during which tours I am glad to say

there were no differences of opinion or other troubles, such as have been known to arise on similar occasions.

The commission was to sit from 1906 to 1911. An interim report was drafted by Rider and Professor Somerville, with the assistance of the commission's secretary, a Mr Grimshaw. The commission presented a scheme under which enormous areas of waste or poor land in the United Kingdom would be planted and become forests of great value. The commission concluded that England's forests, in particular, were in danger of extinction and that wood would be of great commercial value in the future. The report was ignored and Rider wrote rather bitterly:

> The fact is that the venture was too sound and quiet to be undertaken by a Government of party men who look for immediate political reward rather than to the welfare of the country forty or fifty years hence, especially when, as was likewise the case in my Land Settlement Report, the immediate finding of large sums of money is involved.

In September 1907, an important event occurred at Ditchingham. Rider's eldest daughter, Angela, then twenty-four years old, married Thomas Barker Amyand Haggard, who was then thirty-two. Tom Haggard, a young officer in the Royal Army Medical Corps, was the eldest son of Rider's brother Bazett, who had died in 1899. Bazett's widow, Julia, and her children had been estranged from Rider's family for some years because of the resulting animosity when Bazett and Julia separated. Rider was pleased by the 'very posh affair with half the county there'. Champagne was drunk on the lawn of Ditchingham. Rider was extremely happy when, on 15 July of the following year, his daughter gave birth to a child – Diana Dorothea Rider. Tragically the child died on 11 February 1909. After Rider's death Angela decided to adopt a baby. Tom, her husband, had died on 18 October 1925, but Angela officially adopted a little girl, which she named Nada Helen Angela

Haggard on 15 April 1926. Nada had been born on 31 August 1925.

Nearly two years after Angela's marriage to Tom Haggard, Rider's second daughter Sybil Dorothy Rider married, in July 1909, a young Indian army officer named Reginald Edmonstone Cheyne. Cheyne was a brevet major in the 8th Indian Cavalry, who had fought in the Second Boer War during which he had been captured by the Boers after being wounded in the head. Placed on a wagon of wounded, Cheyne had waited until nightfall when, in spite of his wound, he escaped. Rider noted:

> I hope I have the details right, but Cheyne . . . is not given to talking of such things. It was only after much urging on the part of my daughter that he told me the story of which I had heard rumours from a brother officer, who spoke of him as 'a hero'. He was recommended, together with his Colonel, for a VC or DSO – I forget which – but, unfortunately for him, the Boers captured and burnt the despatch, so that nothing was known at home of his service until too late.

Reginald Cheyne was to reach the rank of a colonel.

On Friday, 7 May 1909 Rider bumped into Lloyd George, now Chancellor of the Exchequer, in Parliament Street. Lloyd George invited him to breakfast on the following Tuesday. After this appointment, returning to Ditchingham on the train, Rider made detailed notes about the conversation which he had Ida Hector type out and witness.[5] Over the breakfast Rider had started pressing Lloyd George to adopt the commission's interim report on planting forests and that such a scheme should be put into the hands of a permanent royal commission. Lloyd George, 'the Welsh wizard', ran true to form. He began by flattering Rider, telling him that he supported the scheme largely because Rider had personally interested him in it when they had met and stayed at Carrow Abbey in 1908. Then, with his typical egocentricity, Lloyd George added:

> The advocates of Afforestation were, he considered, very

fortunate in having to deal with *him*, since he was sure that no Chancellor who went before him, and none who were in the least likely to follow after him, would listen to them for a moment. As it was he had but one earnest supporter in this matter in the Cabinet – Winston Churchill.[6]

Lloyd George admitted that it was only from the Labour Party that he would receive any support for the scheme Rider envisaged. The Conservatives were totally opposed to it and the Liberals, in the main, were indifferent. This apart, Lloyd George was interested in the idea of a development board but pointed out that such a board could not be brought into being merely to supervise afforestation alone. The development board would have to look after agricultural development in the United Kingdom generally. This was precisely the sort of thing Rider had advocated in *Rural England*. He was naturally excited by the prospect. Lloyd George asked him what sort of people would serve the board well. After discussing several prominent figures, Rider suggested Lord Rosebery as chairman. 'Rosebery! The very man!' cried Lloyd George. 'Politically detached, universally known, beyond suspicion, and a master of the subject. The very man – that's a stroke of genius of yours – if he will serve.'[7] Rider then mentioned that he, too, would like a chance to serve on such a board. 'I was anxious to serve on the Development Board in the interests of Afforestation, and also I felt that it had its roots, or at any rate some of them, planted in the soil of my book.' Lloyd George raised no objection and told Rider to leave matters with him. Rider wrote in his notes on the meeting:

> The general impression left upon my mind is that Mr Lloyd George means to put this business through if he can, but owing to the great forces, secret and open, ranged against him and it, that he is not quite certain of his ability to do so.[8]

The proposals for a development board were incorporated in a Development Bill which went through parliament on

Christmas Day, 1909. The Bill authorized the Treasury to make grants and loans for forestry, agriculture, rural industries and transport. It laid the groundwork for the birth of a system of small holdings to develop in England. Rider had the satisfaction of seeing many of his proposals from *A Farmer's Year* and *Rural England* come into being. What was personally disappointing to Rider was the fact that he was not appointed to serve on the board. Before the passage of the Bill he received a letter from Lord Ashby St Ledgers: 'I had a conversation with Lloyd George and he intimated that he intended to offer you a post as Commissioner under the Development Board.' However, the Bill received a stormy passage from the Conservatives and one of the Tory MPs, Sir Frederick Banbury, threatened to sabotage the whole idea unless the number of proposed commissioners were reduced. Rider's name had been last on the list and was therefore the first to go. Rider was justifiably bitter when he wrote: 'Thus it came about that I, who directly and indirectly, had played a considerable part in connection with this beneficient measure, was prevented from having any share in its administration'. In spite of this personal disappointment, the Bill gave him a sense of fulfilment and it was with enthusiasm that he addressed the Bungay Farmer's Club on 25 November of the following year and announced that 'British agriculture has turned the corner'.[9]

The Commission on Coast Erosion and Afforestation still kept him busy and in 1910 Rider found himself in Ireland. 'I found the Irish the most charming and attractive people that I have ever met,' he wrote like many an Englishman before him, 'and the most incomprehensible'. He found the Irish had a 'mendicant attitude of mind' towards the British Government. Rider failed to understand that what was, to him, the great civilizing benefits of the Empire was, to Irish eyes, the crushing, heavy-handed interference of imperialism. Why, then, should not the Irish exploit to the full the crumbs that were thrown their way? As Rider records, he told one man: 'The fact is, sir, that after the British government has given you the horse, you expect that they should feed it also.' 'Shure, your Honour!' he

answered, quite unperturbed, or words to that effect.' Rider
seems to have failed to grasp the political situation in Ireland or
judged the degree of resentment the people felt towards the
British domination of their island with all its attendant
symbolism. This lack of understanding is shown when he
recorded:

> As I was dressing one morning at a Cork hotel, I received a
> telegram informing me that King Edward had died during
> the night. We did not leave Cork till ten or eleven o'clock,
> but up to that hour, although the news was well known, I
> saw no indication of public mourning. No bells were rung,
> and no flags flew at half-mast. This may have been mere
> carelessness, or it may have been – something else.

After visiting Connemara, Rider returned to London in time
to see King Edward's body lying in state in Westminster Hall.
With Thomas Hardy, he watched the funeral procession from
the upper balcony of the Athenaeum Club. It reminded him
that only nine years before he had witnessed a similar procession
for the funeral of Queen Victoria from a house which stood
opposite to the steps of the chapel at Windsor. A few days after
Edward VII's funeral he met one of the King's physicians at
dinner who told him that the man had 'died because his heart
was worn out, for he had warmed both hands at the fire of life'.
No one informed the king he was dying and on the very day he
died, he had smoked a cigar.

The Royal Commission on Coast Erosion and Afforestation
adjourned in September 1910 and Rider seized the opportunity
to go to Denmark to make a study of agriculture there. With
him went his sister-in-law, Agnes, and his youngest daughter,
19-year-old Lilias. They sailed from Harwich to Esberj and spent
two months travelling around the country collecting information and interviewing farmers. Rider firmly believed that the
Danish rural situation applied to England, and the application
of Danish methods would revive farming from its recurring
depression. But the Danish system depended entirely on

co-operation between small farmers – a system of collective farming.

Rider, Agnes and Lilias travelled to the wild, desolate moorland of north-west Jutland where he found the village of Aagaard, 'the place of the stream', where his ancestor was reputed to have come from. He was greatly impressed with the setting and used it as his inspiration in his tale of Olaf the Northman in *The Wanderer's Necklace*, published by Cassell on 29 January 1914. The group also travelled to see Hamlet's reputed grave at Helsingör (Elsinore).

In November, Rider was back at Ditchingham working on a new agricultural book. He entitled it *Rural Denmark and its Lessons* and it was published by Longman on 6 April 1911, in a limited edition of 1500 copies. Four articles from the work appeared in *The Times* between 22 February and 13 March. Rider dedicated the work to

> The farmers of Denmark in token of the admiration of a foreign agriculturalist for the wisdom and brotherly understanding that have enabled them to triumph over the difficulties of soil, climate and low prices, and, by the practice of general co-operation, to achieve individual and national success.

Rider had discovered that Denmark not only fed itself agriculturally, but even managed to export agricultural goods worth over £20 million a year, chiefly to Britain. What Denmark could do, he argued, England could do. In his final chapter he concluded that there were three lessons to be learnt from the Danish example: 1 Co-operative farming would solve many pressing problems; 2 farmers would join co-operatives only when they were freeholders; 3 an economic and social structure encouraging the accumulation of estates by passing them down from generation to generation does not permit small holdings to flourish. He therefore advocated nationalizing the land. As if realizing how radical such a proposal was, he added: 'These are the main lessons but there does not seem to be much prospect that they will be applied in Great Britain.' As he emphasized: 'We might change our system if we wished. The will is lacking, not the way.' While British farmers ignored the work, *Rural Denmark* was translated into Danish soon after publication, appearing first serially and then in book form, and is still regarded as one of the most important works on Danish agriculture today.

Early in 1910 a book was published entitled *The Salvation Army* by John Manson, showing the movement in an extremely unfavourable light. Later that year General William Booth wrote to Rider asking whether he would, as an impartial observer, undertake to write a history of the movement. Rider at first refused but, because of his admiration for Booth and what his movement was trying to achieve he finally agreed. Arthur Conan Doyle, who had been friendly with Rider since the 1890s, tried to dissuade him. When writing in March 1910, he said:

> I think it is splendid of you to do it, but is it right or logical to take no notice of an indictment which is backed up by figures, facts and most temperate reasoning? By lending your honoured name to it you are inducing very many people to support what, if this book of Manson's is true, is in many ways (or has become) an evil organisation so that the matter goes very far beyond yourself. Whereas if the heads of the Army found they were losing public support they would be forced to set their house in order and return to their pristine purity.[10]

Regeneration: Being an account of the social work of the Salvation Army in Great Britain was published by Longman on 16 December 1910. While taking his out-of-pocket expenses, Rider presented the copyright of the book to the Salvation Army and refused any fee. *Regeneration* received favourable reviews and was even noticed in a leader of *The Times*. Theodore Roosevelt also reviewed the book in *Outlook* on 1 July 1911, and was very fulsome in his praise of it: 'Few people who read this book can fail to be almost as much impressed as Mr Haggard acknowledges himself to have been by what he witnesses'. On 10 December 1910 William Booth wrote from his London headquarters:

> My dear Rider Haggard, I have just read *Regeneration*. It is admirable. You have not only seen into the character and purpose of the work we are trying to do, with the insight of a true genius, but with the sympathy of a big and generous soul. From my heart I thank you.
>
> May the blessing of the living God rest upon you, and on Mrs Haggard and on your daughters, both for this life and the life to come.

Rider remained on friendly terms with Booth until 21 August 1912, when he received a telegram from Booth's son Bramwell: 'With deepest sorrow I have to announce the General laid down his sword at 10.15 last night. Pray for us.'

Regeneration was not the first work in which Rider expounded the virtues of a religious body. In March 1895 he had published a pamphlet entitled *Church and State* which supported the Established (Anglican) Church in Wales. The Church of England in Wales was a minority denomination, the Welsh being almost entirely composed of Dissenting sects such as Methodists. Yet the Anglican Church, because of its establishment as the State Church, drew tithes and taxes for its upkeep from the Welsh. With the rise of political nationalism in Wales during the mid-nineteenth century. Disestablishment became a burning question and, indeed, by the 1890s Welsh Dissenters were refusing to pay tithes to the Anglican Church on religious and national grounds. In 1889 parliament passed a 'Tithe Rent Charge Recovering Bill' which allowed the Church to claim their tithes by the use of bailiffs, the police and the army. No less a personage than Edward Benson, Archbishop of Canterbury, wrote to Rider in August 1894, asking him if he would write a pamphlet presenting the Anglican Church's point of view and listing the various points on which he thought stress should be laid. The Church of England was delighted by Rider's effort and the Archbishop wrote to thank him. It is difficult to believe that Rider, had he fully understood the system he was defending as it applied to Wales, would have lent his name to this unfortunate piece of propaganda.

During the years he worked on the Royal Commission on Coast Erosion and Afforestation, Rider continued to work hard and his public addresses increased rather than declined. From 'Our Falling Birth Rate' to the Lowestoft, Great Yarmouth and District branch of the NSPCC,[11] his speeches ranged on Rural Depopulation, Neglected Land, the Transvaal Constitution, On War, Co-Operative Small Holdings, The Housing of the Poor, Children's Legislation, Radium, Modern Education and many other topics. His main interests continued to be agriculture and rural reform: *Cassell's Magazine* described him as 'a leader of the Back-to-the-Land movement'.[12] In addition to his speeches, articles and letters continued to pour from his pen on those subjects that were close to his heart.

His output of books was also prodigous, even for a writer with his extraordinary gift of fast writing. There were African tales such as *Benita* (1906), *The Yellow God* (1909), *Queen Sheba's Ring* (1910) and *Marie* (1912); historical romances such as *Fair Margaret* (1907), *The Lady of Blossholme* (1909), *Red Eve* (1911) and a tale of ancient Egypt in *Morning Star* (1910). There was also the publication of a story which was somewhat of a new departure. Rider called it 'a dream story'. Its title was *The Mahatma and the Hare* (1911).

In 1911 the Royal Commission on Coast Erosion and Afforestation made its final report. Three volumes of reports had been published in 1907, 1909 and 1911. As a positive reaction, following the final report, the government set up an Office of Woods which began sowing experimental forests at Inverleiver, Scotland, Hafod Fawr in Wales, and on the Isle of Man. From 1916–17 another government committee was established called the Acland Committee and, in 1919, a Forestry Commission was set up which at once commenced planting forests on the scale that Rider had advocated for over twenty years. With the commission ended, Rider felt somewhat at a loss. 'I missed that Commission very much,' he wrote, 'since its sittings took me to London from time to time and gave me a change of mental occupation and interests.' Now there seemed nothing to look forward to, 'nothing to do except the daily grind of romance-writing, relieved only by Bench business, my affairs.' He began to feel lonely and realized he was fifty-five years old. 'Indeed, I do not remember ever being more consistently depressed than I was during the first part of the following winter', he recalled. The summer of 1911 was very hot and dry and during the next autumn and winter, Rider was troubled by bronchitis. 'It really seemed as if everything had come to an end; then of a sudden things changed as they have a way of doing in life.' It was in this depressed state of mind that Rider started to write his autobiography. He wrote the dedication at midnight on Whit Sunday, 1912, 'to my dear Wife and to the memory of our son whom now I seek'. He finished the work on 25 September 1912 and sent the manuscript to his friend Charles Longman with instructions that the manuscript be sealed and locked in his safe and only opened and published after his death.

But, in the midst of his depression, things changed. In the New Year's Honours List of 1912 Rider was made a Knight Bachelor. He wrote:

> I took the knighthood when it was definitely offered, on the ground that it is a mistake to refuse anything in this world; also that a title is useful in the public service, and especially so abroad. Moreover, it was Recognition, for which I felt grateful; for who is there that does not appreciate recognition particularly after long years of, I hope, disinterested toil?

The knighthood was in reward for his public services. Within a week of the announcement, the Colonial Secretary, Lewis Vernon Harcourt, wrote to ask Rider whether he would accept an appointment to serve on a royal commission which was to visit the various dominions and report on them. Harcourt added:

> I greatly hope that you will be able to accept, and I trust for

the sake of the reading public that the Commission will not
prevent you from pursuing a good deal of your usual
avocations and might even incidentally provide materials!

Rider commented: 'I need scarcely say that to my mind this was
recognition – with a vengeance.'

Before undertaking his duties as commissioner, Rider went on
a short tour of Egypt with Angela. The climate put new vigour
in him and he set to work on his return to write a new Allan
Quatermain tale, *Marie*, and to put the finishing touches to his
autobiography. While he was sitting down to work on 'chapter
fifteen' of the autobiography, on 22 July 1912, he saw in the
newspapers that his old friend of thirty years' standing, Andrew
Lang, had died suddenly of angina. Lang was sixty-eight years
old. Rider made that chapter a memorial to Lang. Strangely, a
few days before, Rider had been in London and 'some vague
anxiety concerning him' had prompted him to go to Marloes
Road where Lang had his London house. The house was shut up
and a Scottish maid told Rider that Mr and Mrs Lang had left for
Scotland two days before.

> I have not seen much of Andrew Lang of late years for the
> reason that we lived totally different lives in totally different
> localities. The last time we met was about a year ago at a
> meeting of the Dickens Centenary Fund Committee, after
> which I walked far with him on his homeward way, and we
> talked as we used to talk in the days when we were so much
> together. The time before that was about two years ago,
> when I dined alone with him and Mrs Lang at Marloes Road,
> and we passed a delightful evening.

Letters, too, had been scarce between the two men for some
years. Lang and Kipling made it a policy to destroy incoming
letters. 'Why on earth do you keep letters?' asked Lang in a
letter of October 1911, one of the last he was to write to Rider.
As late as 10 November 1911 Rider had suggested to Lang an
idea for a collaboration on a novel about Old Kôr, Ayesha's
hidden city, but Lang declined and pointed out that when he

had collaborated with Rider on *The World's Desire* 'I brought you worse luck than you would have had alone.' In a letter of 3 November, Rider expounded his idea:

> I think Kôr was the mother of Egypt, which kept up a filial correspondence with her oracles. 'She' smashed the place in a rage because they tried her for the murder of Kallikrates. Foundation of history – papyrus records brought home by Holly and sent with 'Ayesha' MS. Entered up by that old priest Junis, or someone.

Although Lang declined to collaborate, Rider continued with the idea and turned it into *Wisdom's Daughter*, which Hutchinson published on 9 March 1923; this was to be the fourth and last book about his Ayesha creation. Previous to this, Rider was to write a romance coupling Allan Quatermain and Ayesha, *She and Allan*, which was published by Hutchinson on 17 February 1921.

Before he died, Lang had asked his wife to give Rider a ring for remembrance. It had belonged, it was said, to Queen Taia, the wife of Amenophis III or, again, to Nefertiti, his daughter-in-law who married Khu-en-aten, the fourth Amenophis. Rider wrote:

> And so to Andrew Lang, among men my best friend
> perhaps, and the one with whom I was most entirely in
> tune, farewell for a while. Of his character and gifts I have
> already written while he was still living, so I will say no more
> of them now. They are few such, and today the world is
> poorer and greyer for the loss of a pure and noble nature.
> For myself I am more lonely since of those men not my kin,
> whom I knew and loved while I still was young, now Charles
> Longman and Arthur Cochrane alone are left.

Lang had written to Rider on 20 February 1896: 'You have been more to me of what the dead friends of my youth were, than any other man, and I take the chance to say it, though not given to speaking of such matters.'

His affairs in order, Rider set sail for India on 29 November

1912. His first stop was to visit his daughter, Dorothy, now living with her husband, Major Cheyne, and their two sons, Archibald Rider and Reginald Comyn, then two and one years of age respectively. Rider spent the better part of January and February in India and Ceylon before continuing his journey to Melbourne in Australia. On his arrival there, Rider received a letter from Rudyard Kipling, on board SS *Prince Abbas*, dated 3 March 1913. The ship was stuck on a sand bar between Assouan and Luxor at the time Kipling was writing. He adds: 'Lord knows where this will catch you. Probably in Australia among the unchaste and idle democracy but whenever it fetches up it carries my best wishes for your happiness. I *am* glad you're seeing India, old man.'[13]

Lilias recalled that 'Rider was, however, greatly interested in Australia, in this wide, new country "with land for everybody" but without a past, or traditions, and in his opinion too little imagination as regards its future.'[14] Rider greatly enjoyed New Zealand and was extremely interested by the Maori civilization. The royal commission attracted a lot of attention in the press and Rider – as a world-renowned writer – was often employed as the spokesman for the group. By the mid-summer of 1913 he was back at Ditchingham House working once again and finishing some stories before setting forth on the next tour for the commission. This tour was to be different from the previous one, a tour which he looked forward to with growing excitement, for the commission was to visit South Africa, the country which he had left as a young man over thirty years before and which had always remained in his heart and imagination.

CHAPTER 12

SOUTH AFRICA REVISITED

Before leaving for South Africa, Rider let his house, Kessingland Grange, near Lowestoft, to the Kiplings. It was at Kessingland that he had first begun his experiments with coast erosion. The house had once been a coastguard station and was a strange structure, perched on top of a cliff and surrounded by nine acres of land. In keeping with the nautical tradition Rider had named each room after a British admiral and furnished it with various memorabilia including a bust of Nelson, said to have been carved from the timbers of HMS *Victory*. Kipling, writing to a friend on 4 August 1914, described it as 'for all practical purposes the side of a ship'. Rider and Kipling had been growing close in their friendship in recent years and found that each had a deep understanding of each other's work. They each acted as 'sounding boards' for ideas. In 1907 Kipling had helped Rider work out the plot for a new romance entitled *The Ghost Kings* (1908). They wrote their ideas down alternately on sheets of paper.

> Among my pleasantest recollections during the last few years are those of my visits to the Kiplings, and one that they paid me here, during which we discussed everything in heaven above and earth beneath. It is, I think, good for a man of rather solitary habits now and again to have the opportunity of familiar converse with a brilliant and creative mind. Also we do not fidget each other. Thus only last year (1911) Kipling informed me that he could work as well when I was sitting in the room as though he were alone, whereas generally the presence of another person while he was writing would drive him almost mad. He added that he

supposed the explanation to be that we were both of a trade, and I dare say he is right. I imagine, however, that sympathy has much to do with the matter.

On 24 January 1914 Rider and Louie, with 22-year-old Lilias, set out for South Africa. On the outward voyage they stopped at Madeira, a place of memories, where Rider, Louie, Jock and Gibbs the maid, had spent some weeks on their return from Africa thirty-two years ago. Rider, who was now being severely troubled by bronchitis, delicate chests being a general weakness of Squire Haggard's children, toyed with the idea of buying a place on the island to which he could escape from the harsh winter months of Norfolk. After a few weeks the *Kinfauns Castle* arrived with the other members of the royal commission and the Haggards joined the ship, arriving at Cape Town towards the end of February. As he watched Table Mountain in the early morning light, Rider recorded in his diary:

> I have passed from youth to age since then but it was with
> pleasure mingled with a certain sadness that I saw the
> cloud-cap hanging like poured water down the kloofs and
> steep sides of Table Mountain; the noble outline of the
> Lion's Head, and the long line of rounded hills they call the
> Twelve Apostles. Much has changed, but the sunshine is the
> same.[1]

There were official receptions and other functions to be attended by the commissioners and at a dinner party shortly after his arrival Rider found himself seated next to the Prime Minister of the new Union of South Africa, General Louis Botha. In 1899 Botha, then aged thirty-seven, had become one of the youngest Boer generals and a formidable military commander whose dogged generalship had defeated the British at Colenso. In 1910, with the southern African territories unified under the British flag, Botha was elected Prime Minister with Jan Smuts as his deputy. Rider, whose opinion of the Boers had mellowed through the years, was pleasantly surprised by Botha. 'There is no "down on" the Kaffir about Botha,' he

wrote in his diary, 'in every way he impresses me enormously.'[2]
Naturally, the talk turned to the recent war. Botha suggested
that it could have ended eighteen months before it did had it
not been for the stubborn intransigence of the British
commander Lord Milner. Botha was, by then, in supreme
command of the Boer forces. According to Rider:

> The point on which they split was that of granting an
> amnesty to all the rebel Boers who had fought against us.
> Botha pointed out that it was impossible for him to accept
> safety for himself and leave these out, but Milner would not
> yield, so the war went on. In the end these men were
> amnestied, so nothing was gained.[3]

A few days later Rider was invited to a dinner party at which
he met Sir Abe Bailey and other wealthy financiers, many of
whom had recently made their fortunes in diamonds and gold
in the former Boer territories. Here, for a moment, Rider came
face to face with the grim reality of imperialism. Empire was
made and ruled by financiers and was not created by the
'civilizing mission' of one nation. When Rider expressed his
ideals he was soon told 'You are old fashioned.'[4] In speaking
particularly about the Jameson Raid, Sir Abe disagreed with
Rider's estimate that it was a failure. 'On the contrary it was a
great success as it led to the war and all that has followed from
the war.' When Rider pointed out the cost to England in lives,
Bailey, with a frankness unusual for a financier, merely replied:
'What matters, lives are cheap.'[5] Rider was shocked. This was
not his empire, an empire beneficial, spreading peace
throughout the various warring nations of the world. But had
his empire ever existed, or was empire merely the sordid
business enterprise envisaged by the financiers? By the time he
entered the event in his diary he had sought to rationalize the
moral problem.

> Well, they have won the game, and the evil they did is now
> practically forgotten. Also, out of this evil, good has come,
> as there seems to be little doubt that the racial animosities

are beginning to die down. So at least Botha and everyone
else of weight to whom I have spoken declare with
emphasis, although it is true there is another side to this, as
all who know the Boers, know only too well.

Rider's pessimism was justified for, rather than racial animos-
ities dying, they were, on the contrary, increasing.

While in Cape Town Rider met several former friends, among
them Justice John Kotzé with whom he had a long talk about
their days administering the then primitive Transvaal courts. In
March, Rider, Louie and Lilias followed the commissioners to
Natal and on their arrival in Newcastle were besieged by
newspaper reporters. He had a lengthy interview with the *Natal
Witness*[6] before going out to see Hilldrop, his old farm. It was,
he wrote, 'the last place on earth I ever expected to see'.[7] He
spent the day wandering round the farm that he and Arthur
Cochrane had built, where Louie had given birth to his lost son
Jock. They returned to Newcastle and spent the night in a rather
primitive hotel where his daughter complained about the bugs
on the wall. 'Bugs won't give you malaria, and you have a
mosquito net which is all that matters', admonished her father.[8]
The next day they went to Pietermaritzberg where he met
another old friend, James Stuart, a former assistant secretary for
native affairs in Natal, and to whom he had dedicated *Child of
Storm* (1913). The old Government House, where he had lived
and worked in the early days, was now a girls' school.

> I saw where I used to sit at the end of the table – the room is
> unaltered except that folding doors have been built into the
> wall. My office in the Executive Council Chamber has been
> pulled down, and with it the little bedroom where I tossed
> Sir George Colley in his bath as to the price of a gun, and
> where I saved Cox's life when an artery broke out on his
> wounded leg. Every corner is full of memories, even the
> porch where the big yellow spider always spun her web.[9]

The most moving moment of Rider's return visit was an
episode that he had predicted in his autobiography, completed

nearly two years before, and now lying in Charles Longman's safe. Rider, writing of his departure from Africa, had said:

It was sad to part with the place, and also to bid goodbye to my Zulu servant Mazooku. The poor fellow was moved at this parting, and gave me what probably he valued more than anything he possessed, the kerry that he had carried ever since he was a man – that same heavy redwood instrument with which on more than one occasion I have seen him battering the head of some foe. It hangs in the hall of this house but where, I wonder, is Mazooku, who saved my life when I was lost upon the veld? Living, perhaps, in some kraal, and thinking from time to time of his old master Indanda, of whose subsequent doings some vague rumours may have reached him. If so, were I to revisit Africa today, I have not the faintest doubt but that he would reappear. I should go out of my hotel and see a grey headed man squatted on the roadside who would arise, lift his arm, salute me and say 'Inkoos Indanda, you are here: I am here, come back to serve you'.

I have seen the thing done. As a young man Sir William Sergeaunt was in South Africa – I forget how or when – and then had a Zulu servant, a Mazook. He departed and thirty years later returned. *His* Mazook appeared from some kraal, of which he was then the head, and was with him during all his stay. I saw him then.

Or if my Mazook should be dead, as well as he may be, and if there is any future for us mortals, and if Zulus and white men go to the same place – as why should they not? – then I am quite certain that when I reach that shore I shall see a square faced, dusky figure seated on it, and hear the words, 'Inkoos Indanda, here am I, Mazooku, who once was your man, waiting to serve you'. For such is the nature of the poor despised Zulu, at any rate towards him whom he may chance to love.

Incredibly enough, one morning after the Haggards had arrived at Pietermaritzberg, Rider did come out of his hotel to see an old man, though without a touch of grey in his hair. *'Inkoos pagate! Baba!* (Chief from of old! Father!) Here am I returned to serve you.'[10] It was Mazooku, indeed. The newspapers seized on the reunion and the *Natal Witness* published a picture of Mazooku, spelled Mazuku in the newspaper, in European clothes with an article headed 'Saved His Master's Life – Novelist and his Faithful Servant'.[11] The *Pictorial* in Durban also published a similar piece with a photograph of Mazooku and Rider together.[12] The two men spent many hours talking of old times and what had happened to each since last they met. Mazooku had fallen into a bad patch, he had recently lost all his cattle from east-coast fever and Rider promised to see that they were replaced. Rider also told him that he still had his knobkerrie and the Zulu was impressed, commenting that he had not thought it possible for so small a thing to have 'lived through the years'.

The day after the reunion Rider accompanied James Stuart to see Mr Addison, the Chief Magistrate of Zululand. There were several chieftains waiting outside his office to see him and to these Stuart introduced Rider as 'Sompseu's child'. The Zulus gave an enthusiastic volley of salutes. 'Such is the magic of that name', recorded Rider. He was also introduced to John Shepstone, his old chief's brother, and to Sir Theophilus' son, Henrique. Stuart then introduced him to an old Zulu named Socwatsha, who was noted for his good memory and store of history and folklore. As a warrior, Socwatsha had fought for Cetywayo and this man and Mazooku were to provide Rider with many details for his novel *Finished* (1917). *Finished*, with *Marie* and *Child of Storm*, were to comprise his trilogy on the fall of the Zulu nation.

> It was wonderful to watch old Socwatsha as he told his story of the battles, acting them as he spoke as only a Zulu can. Thus he gave Chaka's words when mourning for his mother in the same weeping voice, repeating his epithets, some of which were of the strangest, referring as they did to her amorous propensities. Both he and Mazooku declared that

it is universally believed amongst the Zulus that Chaka did kill his mother. Whether, as Socwatsha alleged, outright with a kerrie after he had destroyed his child whom she was hiding 'and hung its body on a post of the hut fence' or by wounding her in the abdomen with a little assegai, so that she subsequently died while he was away hunting, as Fynn thought, of dysentery. Of Umbelazi's death at the battle of the Tugela he had nothing certain to tell. One version with a curious authentic touch which he gave us, is that he was last seen after the rout by a younger brother of his own and whom he had hidden in a bush 'lifting the grass with his spear' when he had finished hiding him, so that it might not be seen that men had walked there. A little picture not likely to have been invented. The mystery of the end of the handsome and ill starred Umbelazi will never be solved I think. I thought I had invented the story of the hiding of the child of Chaka in *Nada the Lily* but perhaps I heard of it somewhere.[13]

At the end of March Rider, Louie and Lilias, accompanied by the faithful Mazooku, continued with the commissioners to Pretoria. The special train, which ran them to the old Transvaal capital, was stopped so that the commissioners could see Majuba Hill, the scene of the ignominious defeat of General Colley during the first Boer War in 1881.

There poor Colley rests with all the others. It is a high hill, very easy to attack as its flanks are filled with hollows. I noted the little bush clad kloof up which the ninety Boers crept on that fatal morning. At its foot is a nice farmhouse – but I should not care to live within the shadow of Majuba, but then as I said in a speech at 'Maritzberg my name should be Rip Van Winkle, for few remember the defeats and the tragedies of my generation in Africa.

We reached Pretoria that night. The Grand Hotel at which we stayed is in the Church Square where we outspanned when I came up by ox-wagon in 1877 – I think the Hotel is on the site of the old European which was kept

by poor Carter, the brother of the present Archbishop of
Cape Town – I remember that afterwards he was killed by
lightning. The whole aspect of the place had utterly
changed. Who would know it for the same that I described
in *The Witch's Head* where the Boers used to assemble in
their wagons at Naachtmaal? The Old Dutch Church 'The
House with the Horns' as the Kaffirs used to call it, had
been pulled down; in these Colonial towns they always seem
to pull down such historical monuments as they possess!
Oh, I hate this grandeur – give me the Pretoria of the
seventies – Rip Van Winkle, Rip Van Winkle – alas as well
might I ask for my lost youth.

The Union of South Africa has taken away its pride of
place from 'Maritzberg and has made Pretoria the official
capital of this dear and lovely land, and here the gold of the
Rand has been lavished in unnecessary splendour. Opposite
the Hotel where stand the Government offices was the low,
thatched building in which I had my office. All the time I
was sitting there on the Royal Commission I kept thinking
of it. From the low verandah of that building was read the
proclamation annexing the Transvaal to the Empire.[14]

Among the people to whom Rider was introduced was the
Administrator of the Transvaal, J. Rissik, a patriotic Boer who
recalled the annexation. He told Rider that at the moment the
English flag was being hoisted 'I would gladly have shot you.'[15]
Now Rider was fêted by Boers and Britons alike. On 30 March a
municipal luncheon was given in his honour at the Pretoria
Grand Hotel[16] and he was asked to speak at the Transvaal
Agricultural Conference[17] and attend a dinner at the Johannesburg Chamber of Commerce at which he had to respond to a
toast.[18] He managed to find time to visit The Palatial, the house
in Pretoria that he and Cochrane had built and which was now
widely known as Jess's Cottage. It had been put up for auction
in October 1907 and bought for £1600 by a Mr G. Rissik.[19] 'I
could not help thinking of it as it used to be with its pretty
English furniture and the engravings on the walls, and the

stable, now empty and tumbledown, where stood my two horses, Moresco and Black Billy.' Rider was distinctly morbid as he recalled the past:

> I felt as one returned from the dead. I seemed to forget all
> the intervening years and grow young again. I saw walls rise;
> I saw the sapling gums, the new planted roses and
> gardenias – I went away with a sad heart – Oh, where are
> the friends of my youth who used to pass in and out of that
> little gate?

Sadly, he adds: 'Everything is so changed I do not think I want to see it again.'

Louie and Lilias went down to Zululand to wait for Rider while he continued on a special commission via Johannesburg to Rhodesia to collect material. He went as far as Bulawayo, the Place of the Slaughter, the site of Lobengula's great kraal on which a new colonial town was rising. He also climbed to the granite slab on the crest of Matoppos which marked the grave of Cecil John Rhodes, who had died in 1902. Rider recalled 'The last time I was so near to this remarkable man was in a very different place – a sitting-room in the Burlington Hotel in London.' He added: 'I have good reason to believe that in his last years Rhodes regretted some of the avenues by which he mounted to success and fame.'[20]

While in Rhodesia Rider visited the Zimbabwe excavations and saw the landmarks which had been named from his novels – Allan Quatermain's Road, Sheba's Breasts and so on. Rider met the curator of the excavations, Richard Nicklin Hall, who accused him of giving false ideas about Zimbabwe. It was generally accepted that Rider had used the site of Zimbabwe in his books and Rider had some difficulty in convincing Hall that the ruins in *She* and *King Solomon's Mines* were inventions of his imagination and not based on Zimbabwe.

> When I wrote *She*, I had only heard in the vaguest way of
> the Zimbabwe ruins, and not at all of the famous caves in
> East Africa which are also reported to have been her

residence. Those early romances were entirely the product of
my imagination, stimulated in the case of *King Solomon's
Mines* by vague rumours I had heard when I lived in South
Africa. Mr Hall seemed somewhat aggrieved with me
because he said I was responsible for various false ideas
about Zimbabwe. . . .[21]

Eventually Rider returned to Durban, Natal, and there bade
farewell to Louie and Lilias who were returning to England by
an earlier boat while Rider journeyed to Zululand and then
went on with the commission to East Africa before departing for
England.

Rider, accompanied by James Stuart and Mazooku, went to
Eschowe where the British Resident's house was situated. It had
been built there by his old friend Sir Melmoth Osborn, who had
occupied the office for five years before handing over to Sir
Marshal Clarke. Zululand had been left virtually unscathed
from the Boer War but the Boers still occasionally carried out
commando raids on the Zulu kraals in search of cattle and easy
plunder. In 1902 one such commando raid into Zululand cost
the Boers dear for the Zulus retaliated and killed fifty-six out of
the fifty-nine Boers who comprised the commando; however,
200 Zulus were killed. 1902 was the year when the British
opened up Zululand to European settlement and taxes were
levied against the Zulu people. The King, Dinuzulu, found he
could not control the rising antagonism of his chieftains. Even if
he could, the British did not even recognize Dinuzulu as ruler
of the Zulu nation. As the Zulus staggered under the weight of
new taxes, as Europeans poured in to take their land, and as
they found themselves little more than serfs in their own
country, the Zulus were forced into one last attempt to retain
their diminishing freedom. In April 1906, the Zulus rose in an
ill-planned insurrection which was led by Sigananda Cube, who
was personally known to James Stuart. Sigananda Cube was
then ninety-six years old and had fought in Chaka's *impis* as an
uDibi boy. The result of the uprising was that 2300 Zulus were
killed, twenty-three Europeans and six native levies also died.

Some 5000 Zulus were brought to trial and received varying sentences from death to imprisonment. Sigananda Cube died in jail and Dinuzulu was sent into exile where he died in 1913 aged forty-five years. Dinuzulu's son, Maphumuzana, called Solomon by the British, was proclaimed king in exile but it was not until 1916 that he was allowed to return to Zululand. By that time the Zulu nation's hopes of retaining their lands and independence had been entirely smashed. As Rider toured Zululand he found great unrest and resentment directed especially against the British who were now regarded as 'betrayers'.

In fact, all Africans in southern Africa now regarded the British as the arch villains. From their viewpoint the situation was thus: before 1900 southern Africa was a territory divided up into various independent and semi-independent republics, kingdoms and territories. The Boers had been quite happy in the Orange Free State and the Transvaal. But the British had come with a greed for territory and, by forcing the Boers into a war, had succeeded in eventually uniting all the territories into the Union of South Africa. They had then declared this union as an independent dominion of the British Empire under a democratic government, such democracy, however, totally excluding all Africans. This was the ultimate betrayal in African eyes because the Boers constituted the largest white ethnic group in southern Africa which ensured that, under democratic elections, the Boers would dominate the entire union and not, as before, their small republics. The act of the union itself gave unlimited power over the millions of non-whites in the new dominion and this establishment of a racist constitution when, in 1909, South Africa became a dominion, laid the foundation-stone for the modern day South African state. From the very first election, the Boers dominated the government with Botha as Prime Minister, Smuts, his deputy, and including General J. M. B. Hertzog, who was eventually dropped from the government because of his flagrant anti-British attitudes. Hertzog was to eventually form the Afrikaner Nationalist Party which won the 1948 election, establish the modern South

African police state, taking the country out of the commonwealth and declaring it a republic.

From the start the Africans saw clearly how the political
situation would develop and they were already organizing in
their defence in 1910 when a Native National Congress was
established. It was led by three editors of African newspapers,
Reverend Walter Rubusana, John Tengo Jabavu and Reverend
John Dube who, while approving the Union in principle,
objected to Britain allowing a racist constitution with its colour
bar and voting rights for white men only. It is true that at the
Cape Colony this was amended so that Africans with
educational qualifications could vote, but they were only
allowed to vote for white men. The Africans pressed for 'full
and equal rights'. After the union and its racist constitution had
come into being an Indian lawyer named Gandhi started to
organize passive resistance to the laws in the Transvaal.

Rider was especially concerned about the effect of the new
political situation on the Zulus and at the end of May, after he
had returned from Zululand to Durban, he wrote a letter to
Lord Gladstone on the situation. He amplified his ideas in a
fuller report to the Rt Hon. Lewis Harcourt at the Colonial
Office which he wrote on the RMS *Gaika*, on the journey home
through the Red Sea, on 1 June 1914. Rider believed that if the
Africans were treated right they would 'play a worthy part in the
world'.

> The Zulu peoples are crushed and bewildered. Monarchical
> by instinct and practice they have no visible chief to whom
> to give their adherence. To their wonder and grief they
> found themselves handed over first to Natal and then to the
> Union. Commissions appear and disappear. Ministers come
> and go, there is no one permanent entity on whom they can
> fix their eyes as the shadow of their distant king, to whom at
> heart they are intensely loyal. They were defeated in war,
> and like a nation of warriors accepted the issue with
> resignation, hoping and believing they would be taken over
> and nursed by their victor the Queen and her successors,

and ruled as subjects like the Basutos. Instead of this they were made the bloody sport of a number of rival kinglets, while the Boers and others were allowed to rob them of their hereditary lands.

It is I am sure the greatest mistake to suppose that the native does not feel or forgets harsh treatment. On the contrary, I believe that at the bottom of that secret mind of his, which so few of alien race have the imagination and the sympathy to understand at all, he feels a great deal. Also his memory is very long. Listen to some old Zulu describing events which took place in the day of Chaka or Dingaan, when his nation was great and ruled the land. He quotes the very words that were said, the very deeds that were done. No syllable, no gesture is overlooked. It is all there written upon the book of the mind, and much else is there also, of which he does not speak to the white man – as yet. But a day may dawn when he, or his son, or his grandson will do so and then it will be found that no single blow or curse, or humiliation or act of robbery or injustice has been overlooked. Deaths in war he will take no account of, for he springs from a race of soldiers and is prepared to accept what he gives without complaint or malice. Death is, so to speak, the coin of his trade, as victory and defeat are its stakes but with the rest it is otherwise. For these in some shape probably one that is quite unforseen, an hour of reckoning will surely strike. It is not possible in this or any other human affair, continually and with intent, to sow the wind and always escape the reaping of the whirlwind.

I think that even now, at the eleventh hour, much might be done to give these people something to replace all that they have lost.

The reign of chiefs is finished, the pageant, the spoils, and the pomp of battle have gone with it to the limbo of the past. A new condition has appeared. The son of him who slew our soldiers by the fatal mound of Isandhlwana, or rushed through a storm of bullets until he fell pierced upon Ulundi's plain, often the man himself, walks along the hills

and valleys of Zululand, with greasy trousers for his kilted
uniform, holding a tattered parasol in the hand that once
grasped the shield or the stabbing spear. . . .

Their crimes and errors for the most part are those of
kings and chiefs, and of the witch doctors preying upon the
superstitions of a primitive race. Their virtues are their own,
and if encouraged with understanding these should in the
end give them no mean place among the coloured subjects
of the Crown. If, however, they are embittered by injustices
and ill treatment, if their proffered loyalty and trust are
scorned and rejected; if in the place of help, education and
good counsel, they receive from the white man, their
master, little save his dislike, his disease and his drink; if
their lands continue to be taken from them and the morality
of their women corrupted; ultimately they will add all his
vices to their own.

In the case of the Zulus, civilisation has one of its great
opportunities, for certainly in them there is a spirit which
can be led on to higher things. My earnest hope, like to that
of all who have given impartial and sympathetic
consideration to their case, is that this opporunity may not
continue to be neglected in years to come. If so it seems to
me that we shall incur a heavy responsibility towards a
bewildered people, that we have broken and never tried to
mend, and suffer evils to arise of which effects will not be
endured by them alone.

This letter was 'printed confidentially for the use of the
Colonial Office' in July 1914 but as history, alas, has shown,
Rider's passionate plea for the fate of the African in South
Africa was ignored. 'It is not possible in this or any other human
affair, continually and with intent, to sow the wind and always
escape the reaping of the whirlwind', wrote Rider. Today, the
whirlwind is poised over southern Africa.

Rider spent his time in Zululand to good advantage. With
Stuart and Mazooku he stayed at a kraal called Jazi (Finished)
which he used as the title of his last book on the fall of the

Zulus. It was the kraal where Cetywayo died. It had been on 8 February 1884 that a messenger had summoned Sir Melmoth Osborn to the Gqikazi kraal and, arriving with a medical officer, he found the Zulu king dead. The doctor had tried to perform an autopsy but the attendants stopped him. Officially, under the circumstances, the doctor ascribed the death to 'fatty disease of the heart' but privately confessed he thought that Cetywayo had been poisoned. Osborn had written to Rider at the time:

> You will have learnt ere this of Cetywayo's fate. It could not have been otherwise; he was bound to come to grief, as from the day he returned and set foot in Zululand after his restoration he has never ceased in doing that which he ought not to have done.

Now Rider inspected the hut in which the Zulu king died, making notes for future reference.

From Eshowe, the Resident's seat, Rider, with Stuart, Mazooku and a British official named Gibson, continued the journey in a motor car which was driven by a man named Edwards whose grandfather, by coincidence, came from Bungay a short distance from Ditchingham. At Hlabiau Rider attended an *indaba*, a meeting held by several Zulu chieftains to discuss the state of affairs in Zululand. Gibson introduced Rider as 'Sompseu's child' but they did not seem very impressed and asked for his given name. When Gibson replied 'Sir Rider Haggard', a chieftain smiled and said 'Their tongues could not go round such words.' Gibson then told them 'in this land years ago he had been called Lundanda u Ndandokalweni'. 'Ah,' answered the Zulus, 'now we hear, now we understand – now we shall never forget.'[22] Rider was allowed to address the chieftains but had to choose his words carefully and he only made indirect allusions to the terrible conditions prevailing in the country. One chieftain rose, however, and said that Rider did well to allude to their sorrows 'which were as countless as the leaves and endless as the sky'. Cetywayo's son, Manzowandhle, attending the *indaba*, told the chieftain to be silent. In this

Rider saw an example of old Zulu courtesy which would not allow a guest to be questioned or criticized.

Continuing his journey, Rider toured Mahalabatini and the Imbegamuzi valley, and visited the battlefield of Ulundi where, in July 1879, Chelmsford's avenging army, seeking to exonerate themselves after the fiasco of Isandhlwana, had mown down thousands of Zulu warriors at a cost of ten of their own dead and sixty-nine wounded. Regiment after regiment of Zulu warriors had perished under the sustained fire of British artillery, machine guns and rifles. At Ulundi stood the only memorial ever erected to the honour of the Zulu nation: 'In memory of the brave warriors who fell here in 1879 in defence of the old Zulu order.' Mazooku managed to find for Rider an old warrior who was able to recount that frightful massacre, for it could hardly be called a battle.

Rider continued visiting historical sites, such as Dingaan's kraal, and Kwa Matiwane, the Hill of Slaughter, where Piet Retief and his men were massacred and which Rider so vividly described in *Marie*. Scattered over the nearby hills were little piles of stones, supposedly placed over the remains of Retief and his men by a Boer commando who came later. Rider, in fact, uncovered a cairn and found in it not one skeleton but several. The Boers, it seems, had made mass graves for their fallen compatriots.

> So it came about, after a lapse of seventy-six years, we stood and actually looked upon the mortal remains of Retief and his murdered company. It was a strange scene upon this ill-omened Golgotha, now the home of silence and old memories; memories as Osborn had said, of dark deeds, of evil and violence.
>
> As we turned our horses and rode down the wandering paths to the veld, I pictured the poor folk who had trodden those very paths at the dreaded summons of the King – yet unmurmuring they went – 'The King has spoken – are we not the King's kine – bred to be butchered?'[23]

They spent a night at Empandhleni where Sigananda Cube,

the 96-year-old chieftain, had led his *impis* in one more futile effort to shake free from the imperial yoke. Sigananda Cube had known Stuart and had taught him a great deal of Zulu history. He had even declared that much of what Rider had written in *Nada the Lily* was true. Now the old chieftain had taken his place in the tragic history of Zululand. The party then continued on to Isandhlwana and Rider saw the site of the famous battle where Cetywayo's *impis* had defeated a modern, well-equipped British army. Rider wrote:

> It was sad for me to stand by the piles of stone that cover all that is left of so many whom I once knew; Durnford and Pulleine and many other officers of the 24th, George Shepstone and the rest. Coghill I knew also very well, but he died with Melville by the river bank. It makes me feel too how old I have become, for few others whom I meet today can remember them, not even Gibson.
>
> When I had gone some way I turned and looked back at this lonesome formidable hill. The swift tropical night was falling, the stark mount had become very black and solemn, a trembling star had vanished and of the falling crescent of the young moon but one horn appeared above the hill. It looked like a plume of faint unearthly fire burning upon Isandhlwana's rocky brow. A quiet place for man's eternal sleep – but the scene that went before that sleep!
>
> Even today I can scarcely bear to think of the last incidents of that tragedy of which I heard so much when I was young. They are forgotten among men – overlaid by worse things.[24]

The journey eventually had to come to an end and Rider bade farewell to his friends and travelling companions. Mazooku accompanied him back to Pietermaritzberg.

> At 'Maritzburg I said goodbye to Mazooku whom I suppose I shall never see again. Poor Mazooku! His last salute to me 'Inkoos Baba' was given in a quavering voice, for the old man loved me. I felt very sad as I watched him disappear

with his bundle in the crowded station. He served me
faithfully for many years, he saved my life, and by good
fortune I have been able at the expenditure of only a few
pounds to set his affairs in order. Stuart is going to try and
find a new home for him away from the white man, where I
trust he will grow old and die in peace. Good fortune go
with him! Whoever forgets me I am sure Mazooku never
will, in whatever land memory remains to him.[25]

So the time had come to leave his beloved South Africa but
Rider was sad about the conditions he had found.

I have been very grateful for this chance to have made this
journey. To 99 out of 100 a native is just a native, a person
from whom land may be filched upon one pretext or
another, or labour and taxes extracted, and who, if he resists
the process, or makes himself a nuisance, must be
suppressed. 'Make haste boy, bring my horse – go hoe my
corn – pay your taxes in malt or meal – or see, here are
whips and rifles.'
   It is the dominant note of the tune to which we white
people have made them dance. Fortunately not all men
think thus.[26]

But those who did not think thus were very, very few indeed.
   It was on that depressing and sombre note that Rider
embarked on the RMS *Gaika* at Durban. As the ship steamed
northwards, past the hazy coast of Zululand, Rider felt himself
falling into a melancholia and went into his cabin to write his
diary.

So ends my visit to South Africa – on the whole it has been
successful, if sad in some ways. I am truly and deeply
grateful for the extreme kindness with which I have been
welcomed everywhere, in fact, I have experienced quite a
little triumph. Affectionate as was my greeting I think really
it was more to do with the fact I am a sort of curiosity, a
survival from a past generation, than to my own
individuality. Also my subsequent career has interested

those among whom I spent the first years of my manhood, when I was concerned with great men and great events.

So to South Africa, farewell, which is the dominant word in my life. It is a fair land of which the charm still holds my heart and whose problems interest me more than ever. How will they work out their fate, I wonder? When I have gone to sleep or may be to dream elsewhere. My name will perhaps always be connected with Africa if it remains a white man's 'house' and even if it does not – perhaps. It is impossible for me avoid contrasting the feelings with which I leave it now that I have grown old, with those with which I bade goodbye to its shores in 1881 when I was young. Then life was before me, I had hopes and ambitions. Now life is practically behind me, with its many failures and its few successes.[27]

After a short visit to East Africa, Rider continued to Suez and utilized his journey to write out his reports 'setting down, often under difficult circumstances, a faithful account of the things which I have seen in many thousands of miles of travelling. I dare say I shall never read it through and whether anyone else will who can say? Still it is done – but in truth I grow weary of journeying by land and sea!'[28]

He arrived back in England on 6 June 1914 and spent some time in London reporting to the colonial secretary who asked him to sit as a member of a Royal Commission on Imperial Communications. The commission sat for only a few days during which Rider asked the manager of the Marconi Company whether the day would come 'when a subscriber can have a telephone in his house by which he can telephone all over the world?'[29] The Marconi manager did not want to commit himself that far in his predictions. Rider, back at Ditchingham, also paid a visit to the Kiplings at Kessingland and, it would seem from a letter Kipling wrote to him at the time, that Rider had written 'an Irish drama'. The drama was sent to W. B. Yeats at the Abbey Theatre in Dublin but Yeats politely declined it.[30] The manuscript seems to have been lost. By the end of July 1914

Rider was once more off on his travels with the Dominions Royal Commission – this time to Canada.

CHAPTER 13

THE GREAT WAR

On 25 July 1914 Rider began to keep a detailed diary which he was to continue until 22 April 1925, three weeks before his death. The twenty-two volumes of diaries, written either in Rider's own hand or dictated to Ida Hector, are now in the Norfolk Record Office, although a typescript of the entire set of diaries was made by Ida Hector and is now in the hands of Rider's grandson, Commander Mark Cheyne RN. The murder of Archduke Franz Ferdinand of Austria had taken place at Serajevo on 28 June that year and on 23 July Austria had sent her ultimatum to Serbia. Five days later Austria was at war and Rider, then on board ship bound for Canada, sat down on 25 July and wrote 'Something, I know not what, makes me apprehensive.' The following day he had landed in Canada and within a week learnt that Germany and Britain were at war and the nations of the world were taking sides. Rider, realizing the commencement of a world catastrophe, decided to record his activities and reaction to the war, clearly intending them to be edited and published after his death.[1]

The Dominions Royal Commission were now uncertain as to how they should proceed and decided to press on with their work until they heard word from the British government clarifying their position. It was agreed that they should not make any public speeches on the war until the situation was made clear but on 12 August at a dinner given for them by the Mayor of St John, a cry arose from the audience for Rider to speak. Rider rose to his feet and made a rousing appeal for imperial solidarity in a time of crisis. The audience applauded him heartily. An eyewitness said it was a speech that cut into the flesh of all who heard it. In a few words of intense earnestness and conviction the speaker pierced all present with a sudden realisation of the world tragedy upon which the curtain had risen – of their part in it, their personal part. [2]

Rider asked his audience:

Do you understand that if Germany and her allies become masters of England they become masters of the world: and that in two or three years there will be no British Empire? If you realise that, every man of you must go as we must go, must play his part with us to the end. For today we stand at desperate straits with Fate.

The commission was soon recalled and Rider was back in England by 31 August. A few days later, on 4 September, he was addressing a recruiting meeting in the Drill Hall, Bungay, urging the local young men to join the services. His speech was published in the *Eastern Daily Press* on the following day and then used in the *Surrey Herald*. [3] Rider ordered 10,000 copies of the speech to be privately printed and distributed under the title *A Call to Arms*. But Ditchingham that autumn was a peaceful place, the harvest had been a good one and the idea of war seemed far away. It was an illusion which was soon shattered and the war came home to Rider with a personal loss. His favourite nephew, Captain Mark Haggard of the Welsh Regiment, his brother Bazett's third son, was killed in France. He was thirty-five years old. Rider recorded in his pocket book: 'Well, he said he would never live to be taken prisoner and he has not lived. All honour to him who has died the best and greatest of deaths – the first of the family to go – this time.' Rider wrote a letter to *The Times*, which was published on 10 October, on the significance of Mark Haggard's death.

That October a play based on *Child of Storm*, called *Mameena*, opened at the Globe Theatre in London. While Rider had been in Brisbane, Australia, in the previous year, he had met the actor Oscar Asche who wanted to dramatize the book. The production was pushed through in spite of protests from Rider who noted 'The scenes are beautiful and the incidents interesting, but the drama as he conceives it is nowhere. However, it is no use arguing with Actor-Managers. I should imagine its career will be short lived.' In this Rider was correct. Asche had gone in for a lavish production. Forty oxen were slaughtered to make the Zulu accoutrements and three Zulu kraals were hired for three months for authentic Zulu costumes to be made. Two Zulu chieftains were brought to London for the songs and dances and James Stuart, Rider's friend, was engaged as 'technical adviser'. A first night critic wrote: 'The book does not lend itself well to dramatic treatment, in fact, the play would have been as effective if acted in a dumb show.'[4] It ran for 133 performances and lost £8000.

Rider and Louie now moved into a flat in London. There were two reasons for this: first, because Rider could work more easily, attending the meetings of the royal commission in London and, second, the cost of heating Ditchingham House through the winter, especially with the greenhouses, was proving prohibitive. Many of his hothouse plants, the orchids and ferns, had to be sacrificed through lack of heating. In January 1915, Rider had a bout of bronchitis and influenza and, on his doctor's advice, he and Louie took a house in St Leonards-on-Sea, in Sussex, where the sea air helped him recover. They liked the seaside town very much. But once recovered, Rider returned to London and threw himself into the war effort, speaking on war savings, recruiting and national food shortages. On the latter subject he found himself out of favour with the government and his daughter says that his letters to *The Times*, pressing for the appointment of a Minister of Food, were censored because the government did not want to suggest at this stage of the war that serious food shortages would occur from the German U-boat menace to merchant shipping.[5] Several times Rider offered to serve the country in whatever capacity the government saw fit and on more than one occasion his services were politely but firmly declined. In June he wrote somewhat bitterly in his diary:

It would appear that men like myself who have lifelong experience and accumulated knowledge are of no value to the country. Well, there is nothing more to be said except that the conclusion is, I think, wrong. Or perhaps it is right and nobody is of value now save those who can shoulder a rifle or wield a hammer. Yet foolishly enough, perhaps, I feel sore.

On 22 March Rudyard Kipling and his wife paid a visit to the Haggards and Rider noted the next day:

The Kiplings, neither of them, look so well as they did at Kessingland. He is greyer than I am now and he says his stomach has shrunk, making him seem smaller I expect that anxiety about the war is responsible. Their boy John, who is not yet 18, is an officer in the Irish Guards and one can see that they are terrified lest he should be sent to the Front and killed, as has happened to nearly all the young men they knew.

Kipling's only son, John, had enlisted in the Irish Guards in September 1914. Tragically, the anxieties of the Kiplings were to be fulfilled for on 22 October 1915 John Kipling was reported wounded and missing in action in France. Rider's diaries chart the anxiety of the Kiplings as they wavered between hope and despair, each day waiting for some news. On 16 October Rider wrote:

Still he may be captured and alive. It is terribly anxious work for his family. If perchance he is dead, it would be better to know the worst at once. Yet he is only one of hundreds of similar cases which excites my particular interest because I happen to know his parents.

On 22 December that year, Rider saw Kipling and reported 'he has heard nothing of John and evidently has practically lost hope'.

Lilias was now a nurse, doing war work in a Surrey hospital and among the wounded soldiers she was nursing she found

Guardsman Michael Bowe of the Irish Guards who was with John Kipling on the day he was reported 'missing in action'. On 27 December Lilias invited the soldier to lunch and introduced him to her father. Bowe recalled being with John Kipling when the regiment entered a wood near Givenchy. He was of the opinion that the young officer was 'blown absolutely to bits by a large shell'. On 28 December, noting the information in his diary, Rider added: 'I shall not send this on to RK: it is too painful, but, I fear, true.'

Rider, his services turned down by the government, returned to writing and on 31 March 1915 another Quatermain adventure was published under the title *The Holy Flower* by Ward Lock. This had been serialized in the *Windsor Magazine* from December 1913, to November 1914. He followed it with *The Ivory Child* which was published as an eighteen-part weekly serial in various newspapers from 4 January 1915 and then published on 6 January 1916, in book form by Cassell. But in a letter dated 5 May 1915, he confessed that he was growing weary of storytelling and could he manage it, he would rather 'devote the days that remain to me to the problems of the Land, that greatest of all Causes, and to the service of my Country'.[6] When he did write he preferred to write about ancient Egypt or on historical subjects; but editors demanded new Allan Quatermain adventures.

> But what happens? My name, as you remark, is connected in the public idea with a certain stamp of African story and especially with one famous character. Therefore editors and publishers clamour for that kind of story reintroducing that famous character. If I write other things I am told they are 'not so good' though I well know them to be much better. At the bottom of all this are the fashion-following critics themselves who absolutely resent any new departure, although often enough they also blame the author for sticking in his old cliché.[7]

In spite of the war, the Dominions Royal Commission stuck doggedly at its task and from 1912 to 1917 it produced no less than twenty-four volumes of reports and statistics about life in the dominion countries. Rider was now lobbying for a plan which he considered would decrease the high unemployment which would surely be created by demobbed soldiers returning home after the war. Not only that, but it would also improve the state of English agriculture. His plan was to have Britain and the various dominion governments set aside allotments of land for returning veterans to enable them to take up farming as a profitable way of life. The government was not interested. There was a war to be fought and won first. However, the Royal Colonial Institute, which represented powerful factions in colonial politics, were sympathetic to the idea and suggested that Rider should go, as their representative, to the dominion governments to sound out their interest in the scheme.

On 1 February 1916, the institute held a luncheon in Rider's honour, which was also attended by Louie and Rider's brother, Sir William Haggard, among a host of distinguished guests. Rider's health was proposed by Lord Curzon who said the luncheon was 'to give a send off to our friend Sir Rider Haggard who is about to add another chapter of public beneficience to a singularly useful and patriotic career'. The toast was seconded by Lord D'Abernon. In replying, Rider told the institute:

> You cannot live on trade alone. The land breeds people which in the end the cities eat. Without the land everything will die. Therefore the land is the most vital of all the problems with which we have to deal. So convinced was I of that, that once I wrote a book to prove it. It is half a million words long, and I don't expect it to be widely read by my generation. It is for the benefit of future generations, and I hope you will not think me vain when I say that I believe these will read it to learn what happened in our time upon and concerning English land.[8]

Before leaving for his tour Rider discussed the subject with the high commissioners of various dominions in London and on 3 February, with Sir Henry Wilson, the Secretary of the Royal Colonial Institute, he visited the Board of the British South

Africa Company. The same day he attended a dinner in his honour at the Author's Club. A week later, during which a controversy raged in *The Times* as to the benefits of his trip, Rider bade farewell to his family at Paddington station. On 11 February with A. R. Uvedale Corbett acting as his secretary, Rider sailed for South Africa on the RMS *Kenilworth Castle*. Lord Grey, the chairman of the Empire Land Settlement Committee of the Royal Colonial Institute, sent him a telegram:

> Regret illness prevents my seeing you off and personally wishing you bon voyage, a successful mission and a safe return. I am very sorry to notice that your mission is objected to by critics who apparently have not realised that if the Empire is to continue they must regard it as their country, of which England is only a province, and that inter-migration between England and the Dominions should now be regarded in the same way as migration from one part of England to another in the past. Gratitude to our overseas kinsmen for their heroic sacrifices, as well as recognition of the fact that settlement of the vacant Dominion lands with Britons will contribute strength and safety to the Empire, should obtain for your mission the universal goodwill of all sane and patriotic Imperialists.[9]

Rider's own comment on his trip was made in his diary: 'Here is my war offering.' He sat down to write to Louie:

> My dearest, dearest wife, I feel parting from you and the children very much indeed. I am under no delusions as to the risks of this journey, but I felt it my duty to go, hoping and indeed, believing that I shall emerge safe out of it at the end – so there is nothing more to be said. You know whatever comes I shall always be thinking of you my dear – also of them – the worst of it is that though I shall (all being well) be able to write to you frequently, I cannot often expect to have letters from my home, or anything but cables.[10]

The journey to Cape Town was not without 'anxieties usual in these times'[11] with marauding U-boats and German surface raiders prowling the seas. However, Rider arrived at Cape Town on 28 February but was 'careful to avoid all interviewers and speech making during my visit to Cape Town and indeed, although with much difficulty, to keep my name and business quite out of the papers'. Lord Buxon, the Governor-General, provided Rider with an office in Government House and from here he sounded out various politicians, including Prime Minister Louis Botha. Rider was able to report that the South African Government was not willing to undertake to officially start any such migration policy but 'there exists a general desire for more white population in the Union'.[12] The problem from the Boer viewpoint was, while they wanted an increase in white population, they did not want British migrants to swamp Boer superiority of numbers. Rider recalled that a politician came up to him at one function and said: 'I was watching you hob-nobbing with Botha – and last night I was looking at your book *Cetywayo and his White Neighbours* again. You say some straight things in that book – I wonder if Botha ever read it!' If he had, Botha was obviously too polite to recall Rider's anti-Boer attitude. Rider spent a while in Cape Town also learning about migration prospects in Rhodesia, East Africa and German South-West Africa. He also spent some time with his old friends like John Kotzé. Finally, he sailed for Australia and reached Hobart on 3 April 'after a long tedious voyage'. He was seized with acute depression on this voyage and confined himself to his cabin for most of the time. He wrote to Louie:

This kind of solitary confinement is not gay. All one's failures and failings rise before one in a melancholy procession till one is sick of contemplating them. In short it is a lonesome job and there is another fortnight of it ahead. No wonder everyone on this boat makes love furiously. . . . However, it is supposed to be very healthy and one eats and sleeps a lot, which with novel reading and reflections on one's latter end makes up the day! I am wearing my famous bright blue suit – also a thick jersey, a wool waistcoat, and the camel hair dressing jacket in which you packed the camphor, topped up with a long ulster.

Today (Sunday) has been much better, though the actual temperature is colder the sun has shone and, wrapped in a multitude of garments, I have been able to sit on deck. Here four or five people arrived to photograph me – a nice bundle I shall appear, will try to send you one if I can get it. On looking back I see I have been writing some melancholy stuff which I would not have set down tonight. The truth is, my dear, that I have as many moods as a woman – as She herself. I have half a mind to tear it up, but there – skip it and don't laugh at me, there's a good girl.[13]

On landing in Hobart, Rider discussed his brief with J. Earle, the Premier of the Tasmanian state with whom, he had been told, he stood no chance at all as his was a Labor government. However, he was surprised when Earle told him he was interested in providing land for at least 300 British soldiers who wanted to take up farming. On 9 April Rider arrived in Melbourne and met Mr Hagelthorn, Minister of Lands and Agriculture for Victoria, at his private house, and went on to meet Sir Alexander Peacock, the Victoria Premier on 11 April. On 12 April he saw G. F. Pearce, the acting Prime Minister of the Commonwealth of Australia. He was wined and dined and allowed to attend government meetings and make speeches supporting his cause before leaving for Sydney on 17 April. He reached Sydney the next day and was received by more local dignitaries and lunched by W. R. Holman, the Premier of New South Wales. On 21 April he dined with the Governor-General, Sir Ronald Munro Ferguson, and then went on to Brisbane to meet the acting-Premier of Queensland, Edward G. Theodore. His last stops were to see J. Scadden, the Premier of Western Australia, and Crawford Vaughan, the Premier of South Australia. On 22 May Rider was invited as a guest at the formal opening of the Australian Premiers' Conference at which he was allowed to read his proposals for a migration scheme. Then W. R. Holman, of New South Wales, moved:

That we give Sir Rider Haggard an assurance that this
Conference will give its best consideration during the
forthcoming Conference to the new important points which
he has raised in connection with this scheme of the
settlement of Empire ex-servicemen. [14]

Somewhat exhausted, Rider embarked on 25 May on the SS
Manuka at Sydney, bound for Wellington, New Zealand. He
recorded:

Our crossing was of an order that may without exaggeration
be called terrible, one of the worst indeed, I believe, that
any ship on this line has ever experienced. After a gale we
ran into a cyclone and for many hours were obliged to lie to
as the ship could not face the seas, the passengers not being
allowed on deck.

He reached Wellington two days later than expected, on 31
May. Again there was the usual round of receptions and talks
and during this time he stayed with the Governor, Lord
Liverpool. The Prime Minister, W. F. Massey, seemed quite
friendly and sympathetic to the scheme. Rider's opinion was
that:

The country as a whole is uncommonly comfortable as it is
and does not bother to take 'long views'. The fact that a day
may come ere the world is fifty years older when before
some unforeseen combination of enemies – say a
resuscitated Germany and a powerful Eastern nation, it
might vanish like a puff of smoke before the gale, has no
terrors for it. And yet – who knows? [15]

On 13 June Rider embarked on the RMS *Niagara* sailing for
Canada. He was still plagued by melancholia and on 22 June he
passed

a very lonesome birthday among all this crowd of strangers,
and to-day I have entered upon old age, for at sixty a man is
old, especially when he begins as young as I did. Of my
early friends but two remain . . . for me the world is largely

peopled with the dead; I walk among ghosts, especially at
night. Well ere long I must join their company. Ten years
more the Psalmists would give me, but with my weakened
health I cannot expect as much. My work for the most part
lies behind me, poor stuff it may be but I will say this, I
have worked.

The same day he had been reading a copy of Andrew Lang's
Adventures Among Books and found that Lang had included a
passage from *Eric Brighteyes* as one of the five most moving
passages he had ever read:

Dear, dear Andrew, how I wish you were here, how you
would argue about what I have been writing and turn
everything topsy turvy after your aggravating way, making
out you meant something quite different to what you did
etc. But that quiet voice is still and that kind eye shines no
more.

That evening he sat down and wrote to his daughter Lilias
and included a description of the plot of a new book he was
working on. He had already shown the idea to Kipling – a story
entitled *Oro*, a tale of a highly developed civilization on a South
Sea Atlantis. It was a new departure for Rider, his only true
science fiction tale. Kipling had written to him on 7 January of
that year 'Oro promises well. Gad what an undefeated and
joyous imagination you have! I want fuller details please, of
what Oro did when he re-entered life on the earth.'[16] The tale
included many characters that Lilias knew including her black
spaniel, Jeekie. Rider told her:

It may sound a little unusual but I assure you it will make an
excellent romance – wait and see. But don't give the
gyroscope idea away, it is really priceless and there must be
something of the sort otherwise why did Atlantis go down
and Europe appear?[17]

The tale of Oro was eventually to be published by Cassell in
1919 under the title of *When the World Shook*.

The *Niagara* put into Honolulu where Rider had declined an invitation from the authorities to stay some weeks as an official guest. The ship arrived at Victoria, British Columbia, on Thursday, 29 June, and Rider was delighted to find his brother Andrew waiting on the quayside to greet him. Rider found he (himself) was an extremely popular figure in Canada, so popular, in fact, that he was rather staggered to learn that the Geographical Board of Canada proposed to name a 10,000 feet high mountain and adjacent glacier after him. The mountain lay at the end of the Grand Trunk Pacific Railway, in the Rockies near Calgary. Before the largest gathering ever held in Calgary, Rider was informed the peak would be called Mount Sir Rider and the glacier would be Haggard Glacier. He wrote in his diary that night: 'Here they give my name to a towering Alp – in Norfolk they would not bestow it upon the smallest pightle.'

Through early July he worked his way through Canada, interviewing provincial premiers and officials and speaking at various functions. On 17 July he met the Canadian Premier, Sir Robert Borden, who assured Rider that legislation would soon be introduced in the Ottawa parliament to aid immigration. 'You may be assured that this policy will be satisfactory to all those who have at heart the great purpose to which, during the past months, you have directed your energies in the overseas Dominions.'[18] In late July Rider spent a day in New York where he visited his old friend, the ex-president, Theodore Roosevelt. Roosevelt had completely retired from politics earlier that year.

> He had grown older and stouter since last we met six years ago, and at times his burning manner of speech is nervous in its intensity – and heaven, how we talked! Of all sorts of things; of the world and its affairs, of religion, of heaven and hell, of the fundamental truths, and the spirit of man; for when Roosevelt and myself meet – men who are in deep and almost spiritual sympathy with one another, there are many vital matters on which we need to know each other's mind.

That night Rider added to his diary:

> I wonder if we shall ever meet gain? No, I do not wonder,
> for I am sure we shall somewhere for we have too much in
> common not to do. . . . A great man indeed but oh! how
> misunderstood by millions. It was well worth coming to
> America just for those few hours of comradeship.

Rider arrived at Liverpool on 30 July and was home at
Ditchingham within a few days, busy compiling his report to
the Royal Colonial Institute. He finished the report on 7 August
and sent it to the institute's secretary, Sir Henry Wilson KCMG.
By the end of the month the report was published as *The After
War Settlement and Employment of Ex-Servicemen*. Although
he had been interviewed by the newspapers on his return, Rider
found that his report did not provoke a great deal of comment.
The institute gratefully elected him an honorary life member in
October and Rider addressed the opening meeting of a new
session of the institute on 14 November at the Cecil Hotel,
London, choosing as his subject 'Empire Land Settlement in the
Overseas Dominions'.[19] A few days later, on 17 November, he
was guest of honour at a luncheon given by the Liberal War
Committee.

Rider was finding that the now popular medium of the
cinema was promoting the sales of his books. That year the
Barker Motion Photography Company of Great Britain
produced a version of *She* starring the screen idol Alice Delysia
as Ayesha. And in America Pathé had produced a film called
Hidden Valley starring Valkyrien which was based on *She*.
These, of course, were not the first film adaptations, for as early
as 1899 George Melies, a French filmmaker, had produced a
65-foot short called *La Danse du Feu* or *La Colonne de Feu*
based on the book's final scene. There was also a 1908 version
produced by the Edison Company of London[20] and a 1911
version produced by Thanhouser Productions starring Marguerite Snow and James Cruze. As well as *She*, Bluebird Universal
Productions were issuing a film called *Grasp of Greed*, based on
Mr Meeson's Will, starring Lon Chaney.[21]

That autumn the war came to Ditchingham causing some excitement in the Haggard household. On 3 September Rider recorded in his diary that a little after eleven o'clock the previous evening his daughter Lilias called to him from the top floor of Ditchingham House. 'Dad, I hear a Zeppelin!' Rider called her to come down to the cellar but she was too fascinated, watching the approach of the great German flying machine as it came towards the house from the direction of Earsham. Louie was also a fascinated spectator from a bathroom window.

> A bomb exploded quite near, about 200 yards from the house and 60 or so feet from the stockyard pond, where it has made a large hole, but by some miracle did not kill the horses. . . . Then followed a veritable rain (of bombs), the idea being that the guns at the Pulham sheds had hit this machine and it was lightening itself. . . . By the goodness of God, they missed both this house and the cottages etc. near the gate. It was hellish, the whine of the machine above the fearful boom of bombs and the cracking glass in the greenhouse.

Christmas Day, 1916, was spent at Ditchingham House. All Louie and Rider's children had managed to get home – Angela, Dorothy and Lilias and Dorothy had her two small sons, Archibald, aged five years, and Reginald, aged four years, with her. But Angela and Dorothy's husbands, Tom Haggard and Reggie Cheyne, were 'somewhere in France'. It was an unusually sombre Christmas and Lilias recalled that her father seemed to have no heart for the usual drinking of healths after the Christmas dinner. Indeed, 1916 had been a black year for the empire. Conscription had been introduced to fill the diminishing ranks of the army and people were already talking of 'a lost generation'. Britain had finally evacuated Gallipoli after a disastrous and ill-advised campaign. The devastating battle across the Somme had been fought. Ireland had risen in insurrection. Prime Minister Asquith had given way to a more dynamic Lloyd George. It was a long and bitter winter with the weather to suit the mood, the snows were to last until April. In the evening of that Christmas Day, after the household had gone to bed, Rider was left in the drawing-room writing up his diary. Suddenly there was a peal at the front door bell. On the doorstep was Reggie Cheyne, unexpectedly home on leave.

It was one of those small incidents that are apt to remain for always a picture in one's mind when far more important and moving events are forgotten. That impressive and war-worn figure, laden with heavy equipment, his uniform covered with trench mud, haggard, exhausted, almost speechless with laryngitis, coming suddenly in out of the winter night and standing in the warm firelit room asking for his wife. So might the ghosts of thousands of his generation come in from the shadows, and with outstretched hands demand of us the things that for our sakes they had surrendered in the days of their youth. Truly there are many men alive today who have reason to fear that accusing company.

I have been to a children's party at Dolly's, it was happy yet sad to an old man; one remembers so many Christmas parties, and where are the children who played at them? There is a tall clock ticking away at the end of the room, the man who cleaned it the other day said it was the oldest he had ever handled. Remorselessly it ticks on, counting the tale of the fleeting years. In front of me stands the statue of one Roy, prince and priest of Egypt – like me 'An excellent scribe in very truth' who died between three and four thousand years ago. There he sits, staring with calm eyes and fixed, sweet countenance at the centuries as they flow past him. One can almost envy Roy in his repose with the flowers of offering set in front of him, as doubtless in the far past they were offered at whatever feast corresponded to Christmas in his faith, probably that of the rising of Osiris. Osiris, who also rests in marble on my desk, who died that men might live, like another Saviour whom in those days men did not know.

The clock and Roy, and Osiris, even the old table at which I write, into whose massive oak the feet and swelling

paunches of full fed monks have eaten hollows, suggests
many thoughts – but what is the use of setting them down.
Yes, Christmas is a sad feast for the old, and yet one that is
full of hope, as perchance Roy of the calm eyes knows today.

That winter Rider finally completed *Finished* which was first
published as 'The Marble Temple' in the December issue of
Cassell's *Storyteller*. He continued to suffer from acute
melancholia and began to visit the scenes of his youth, paying a
special trip to 69 Gunterstone Road, where he had written *She*.
He did not enter the house but stood outside in the gloom with
his memories. He did not seem able to shake loose from the idea
that he had reached the end of his career. He and Kipling saw a
great deal of each other that year and Rider visited Kipling's
house, Batemans, in March in order to show him the manuscript
of *When the World Shook*. The same month Rider found
himself elected Vice-President of the Royal Colonial Institute.
The influential members of the institute had finally convinced
the government to create an Empire Settlement Committee to
consider Rider's proposals and Rider was invited to sit as a
member. The sittings were to begin in April. In the meantime
Rider continued speaking in public on subjects ranging from
the conservation of the empire's resources to the care of young
girls.[22] At the end of March Kipling, who was staying at Brown's
Hotel, returned the manuscript of *When the World Shook*. In a
note dated 31 March he said: 'As I told you yesterday it's as
fresh and as convincing as the work of a boy of 25 and it held me
like a drug. That's your d-d gift!' Lilias, who had been nursing
in Exmouth, was staying with her parents at the time and had
contracted German measles. Kipling jocularly adds: 'All our
sympathy to poor Lilias who could justly be reported as
"wounded in action". Let us know how she is coming on.'
During the first week in April 1917, the United States
declared war on Germany. Rider believed it to be a stupendous
event in world history. He saw it as 'an alliance between the
English-speaking peoples – a league to enforce peace upon the
world'.

If Germany is not absolutely crushed and a peace declared
on any reasonable terms, even if these should happen to
leave her defeated, she will shut down the war as soon as she
can for about a generation. Then, unless vision fails me or
God intervenes in some strange way, she will employ this
period in exploiting her vast annexed territories filled with
her slaves, and in extracting therefrom enormous wealth as
she knows well how to do. She will recruit their endless
manpower into her armies; also during this time she will
breed up her own on stud farm principles, choosing the
finest fighting stock. Then at the end of thirty years from
the end of the forthcoming peace she will attack and lay all
Europe beneath her feet, since a number of disunited
nations, soaked, under the guidance of Democracy, with
disintegrating revolutionary principles, can never resist her
concentrated and instructed might, whatever they have
suffered from the burden of armaments in the intervening
years, which will be much, I believe that in this event
Britain will go with the rest. Then there will be but one
hope for the inhabitants – to flee to America – if they
can – to make new homes in Canada or the States; since in
such a case America alone will be able to hold her own
against the Germans, and this only by ceaseless watching
and the creation of vast armed forces on sea and land. Such
are some of the dangers and mischiefs that this talk of peace
with Germany may breed. People do not like to believe in
the possibility still less in the probability of another war. I
shall never forget how angry I made a considerable section
of Canadian opinion by inculcating this very truth, namely
that unless Germany was crushed, Germany would most
certainly re-arise and crush us, who from our nature, our
party political system, and the power of labour in the
community, cannot long remain prepared for war. Another
war, they declared, was impossible. Germany would change
her heart. But what says Germany – 'There is no
International Law – treaties are but scraps of paper'. These
are some of the things which would result unless God

intervenes as He alone can do. I pray, too, that I may be mistaken. But I do not feel as though I were. The rise of the British Empire in the teeth of the hamperings and opposition of British Statesmen and the elephantine obstinacy and stupidity of permanent officials, is and always must remain one of the marvels of the world. Truly the Anglo-Saxon race is great. The folly and self-seeking of such creatures lost us America, but the genius of our blood, even when mixed, is going to bring it back into a closer and more enduring union.

In spite of his interest in public affairs and his continuing literary output, Rider could not shake the feeling that he was at the end of his career. True, sales of his books were dropping. But how much was due to the war? It was with this feeling, however, that he decided to present a collection of his original manuscripts, letters and other memorabilia to the Corporation of Norwich to be placed in Norwich Castle Museum. In his diary he notes 'since Norfolk has been the home of my family for several generations and I am Norfolk born, I have given them to the Castle Collection – the gift of a Norfolk man to Norfolk. All the same it made me rather sad to part with them.' The presentation was made on 9 September and formally accepted at a meeting of the Town Council in the Guildhall on 18 September. In a letter to the Lord Mayor, Rider stipulated:

1 That they should be kept in a place of safety during the present and any subsequent troubles; 2 That as soon as it is safe to do so, the MSS are to be exhibited in a suitable glass case with a selection of them open (for example, *She* with the original sherd and ring, *King Solomon's Mines* with Da Silvestra's map and pen, etc.); 3 That I and my family and representatives shall always have access to the MSS if this is required.

Accepting, the Lord Mayor, Alderman G. M. Chamberlain, moved a vote of thanks to Rider. The *Eastern Daily Press* commented:

The permanence of literary fame is proverbially uncertain; men with an immense vogue in their own day often pass into forgetfulness within a very brief period, and not infrequently the men whose fame is ultimately greatest walked the world unguessed at in their own day. But we confess that there are few names indeed in contemporary literature for which we would more confidently predict an abiding fame than that of Sir Rider Haggard. If everything else went, we cannot imagine a time when such a book as *A Farmer's Year* will cease to be read with admiration and delight. It will be a matter of pride to the City that these MSS should be placed in our keeping, and the citizens generally will join in the thanks with which the Norwich Town Council yesterday accepted the gift.[23]

It was in September, too, that Rider decided to sell most of his farming interests and his livestock. It was a hard decision but the cost of running the Ditchingham estate was growing prohibitive. He noted in his diary that 'I have made nothing if return on capital is taken into account, but I have gained a vast amount of experience – and perhaps I am well out of the business.' His chest was still troubling him and because the war precluded his wintering abroad and escaping the harsh Norfolk winters, he decided to buy a place on the south coast. He had already spent some time in St Leonards-on-Sea and liked the town. Using the money from the auctions at Ditchingham he bought a house called North Lodge, part of the original Toll Gate house, at the top of Maze Hill. His study was a room above an archway which spanned the road. Rider found that he could work here during the winters while, in summer, he could return to Ditchingham. St Leonards, being only sixty-two miles from London and connected with a good train service, was ideal for when he had to travel to London on business.

The winter of 1917–18 was spent at the new house and in December 1917, Rider looked with anxious eyes as Germany began negotiations with the new revolutionary government of Russia which were to culminate in the Treaty of Brest–Litovsk.

Russia, who had suffered much through the incompetence of the Tsarist generals and, indeed, suffered much through the centuries from the autocratic misrule of the Tsars, had finally been seized by a successful revolution in March which led to the abdication of Tsar Nicholas. A moderate government had tried to continue the war but in October, the war-sickened Russian people brought the Bolshevik party to power. Now Britain had one ally less. This did not deter Rider from a feeling that, with America in the war, it was already won. He wrote on 14 February 1918:

> I, too, feel that the war will end this year, one way or another. My views about America I have often expressed in these pages. Their appearence on the field will win the war – and the Germans know it, or at any rate their leaders do. Hence their anxiety for Peace before the American strength develops, especially their strength. My fear, as I have also written to Rudyard, is that our food position may be profoundly unsatisfactory and that our people may refuse to bear the privation and discomfort which it will entail. By the way it appears from an official statement that we are compelled to rely on the US and Canada for no less than 65 per cent of our essential foodstuffs.

He spent 22 May with the Kiplings at Batemans.

> Rudyard is not well, I thought him looking better when I arrived but when he came to see me off at the gate I noticed how thin and aged and worn he is. Elsie says that he varies much. He suffers from fits of pain in his inside but he told me that although there is 'something' funny there, X-ray examinations show that there is no cancer or tumour or anything of that sort. I hope and pray that this is so. Seated together in his study in the old house at Batemans we had a most interesting few hours together while he fiddled about the fishing tackle with which he tries to catch trout in the brook. There are two men left living in the world with whom I am in supreme sympathy. Theodore Roosevelt and

Rudyard Kipling. The rest, such as Theophilus Shepstone
and Andrew Lang, have gone.

Early on 23 May Rider rose from his bed at St Leonards and
commenced to write his diary before the family started out on
their journey to Ditchingham for the summer months.

> I've slept well and it has been a blessing for a night to go by
> without the sounds of bursting bombs or mines or other
> hellish explosions. Last night there were only thunder and
> lightning which seemed quite innocent by comparison.
> Wherever one goes – St Leonards, or London, or
> Ditchingham where the distant guns growl continually, one
> is pursued by these voices of war and death. What then
> must it be at the Front!

Ditchingham that summer seemed a safe haven to return to
with the orchard in blossom and the bloom on the front lawn.
No sooner had Rider arrived there than he had to go to
Bradenham.

> It is odd at the end of life coming back to houses at which
> one has spent its beginnings, for then such become one vast
> living memory. Every bit of furniture, every picture on the
> walls, every stone and tree bring forgotten scenes before the
> eyes, or find tongues and talk. Scenes in which dead actors
> played, voices that can stir the air no more. Where are they
> all? Where do they hide from the searchlights of our love?
> Well, ere long the play of our generation will be finished
> and we too shall learn. Bradenham . . . where I first saw the
> light, you are a sad spot for me, the echoes from your old
> walls are many and dear.

Bradenham, the house where he had been born, took up much
of his thoughts that summer. His brother, Sir William, was
running into difficulty as, indeed, Rider had run into
difficulties in managing Ditchingham. William eventually had
to consider selling the property for he was in poor health and
could not stand the Norfolk winters. His remaining son had no

interest or love for the old house and its land. Rider understood his brother's position but the sale of Bradenham was not without a certain amount of friction and recrimination from the family. Rider bought several items and intended to buy Wood Farm, where he had been born, and another small farm house called Verderer's, but eventually Bradenham was purchased outright by a speculating timber merchant who cut down the great oaks of Bradenham Wood for which the estate was famous. All that is left of the generations of Haggards at Bradenham is some graves in the little churchyard.

The literary work continued and two new books came out in 1918. One was *Love Eternal*, a novel, published by Cassell on 4 April, the other was a romance about the Exodus entitled *Moon of Israel* which John Murray published on 31 October after it had been serialized in the *Cornhill Magazine* between January and October. As early as May of the previous year, Rider's agent, A. P. Watt, had been trying to get Murray to publish the book with advances of £500 against British serial rights and £750 against British and colonial book rights, as well as returning to Rider a half-share of Murray's interest in *Jess*, which had passed to Murray via Smith & Elder. On 23 May 1917, John Murray had replied:

> I have given most careful consideration to the proposal of Sir Rider Haggard but I must warn you and him at the outset that in these days pre-War prices for novels are out of the question, as it takes twice as many copies sold to pay for the original outlay. As a serial for the *Cornhill* the utmost limit which we could possibly offer is £250. For the novel we are prepared to give a royalty of 25 p.c. on a 5s net book and advance £500 on the day of publication. . . . I cannot in prudence make a proposal which might involve me in a heavy loss.[24]

A. P. Watt pointed out on 6 July that Smith & Elder had offered to pay £1000 for British serial rights and advances against royalties. In the end Watt compromised and accepted Murray's terms plus the half-share in the copyright of *Jess*, which Murray also republished. Longman were to publish *Moon of Israel* in America and wanted to use Murray's illustrations but, on 23 January 1918, L. Huxley, the editor of *Cornhill Magazine* informed Rider that the book was not going to be illustrated. The jacket cover was submitted to Rider for comment and he was not enthusiastic. From Ditchingham on 25 May 1918, he wrote:

> The pyramid is all right but I can't say much about the lady. For one thing the face is so painfully thin – suggestive of a prolonged course of war bread! However, I daresay I am no judge and of course one doesn't want her blowsey.

The American edition was illustrated by Enos B. Comstock. Kipling was enthusiastic about the book and wrote to Rider from Brown's Hotel on 6 November 1918:

> Meanwhile I've been reading *The Moon of Israel*. – E[lsie[bagged it first tho' I got it for myself. What is your secret, old man? It goes, and it grips and it moves with all the first freshness of youth and – I got into a row with the wife because I had to finish it in bed with the electrics turned on. It's ripping and I'm d-d jealous. You've got a new type in Ana – which you know as well as I do. Also, you've developed (that) which Scripture makes plain but no one else dwells on – the essential turbulence and unaccommodativeness of the Israelites in their captivity.[25]

Rider was delighted by Kipling's praise and sent the relevant paragraph to John Murray on 8 November with the comment: 'It's some unsolicited testimonial, isn't it?' Murray replied on 9 November: 'Unfortunately it is difficult to give such praise to the world, as neither you nor I would care to make use of a letter of this kind but if it could be used it would make great ammunition.' Rider replied: 'No, of course no use can be made of it but I thought you would like to see the opinion.'

Moon of Israel turned out to be one of Rider's most popular romances. D. Lipsheits, then the news editor of the *Jewish Times*, translated the book into Yiddish and ran it serially in the newspaper in 1919. In 1921 permission was given for a braille edition and all royalties were donated by Rider to the National Institute for the Blind. Esperanto, German, Czech and Swedish translation rights were sold in a short space of time. Film rights were also sold and in 1924 Sascha Films made *Die Sklavenkönigin* based on the book with the screenplay by Ladislau Vajda and direction by Michael Curtiz. The stars were Maria Corda and Adelphi Miller. The film, as *Moon of Israel*, was distributed in Britain by Stoll Pictures and Rider's agent, Watt, lost no time in suggesting 'whether it would be worth Murray's while to make a push with some special edition of *Moon of Israel* now that this book is in the world's mouth'.[26] Murray, in fact, produced a special two-shilling film-tie-in edition on 16 January 1925. At the same time George Newnes had produced the first film tie-in edition of *She* which went with the G. B. Samuelson and Lisle Productions version starring Betty Blythe as Ayesha.

In spite of such success Rider continued to be discouraged by the declining volume of sales of his books. In his diary for 8 November he wrote:

> But as I wrote to Rudyard today it makes me laugh to hear him say that he is jealous of me who am written down as the deadest of dead letters. Also I wish that I could rise to his high opinion of my work.

CHAPTER 14

THE HUMBLE HEART

On 11 November an armistice was signed with Germany and the Great War came to an end. In the evening of that day Rider sat down and wrote his diary, an entry that was not jubilant and in many ways was a prophetic one.

> I dare say that in these pages I have made some bad prophecies, but one I recall, namely that the tramp of the first American battalions upon the soil of France was the premonitory rumblings of the earthquake in which Prussia and her bloody doctrines were to go down living to the Pit. Without America I believe we should have fallen, but some madness made the Germans stake their all upon a policy of sea murder, and bring in the great Republic on our trembling line. Now it must be the task of the Allies to make sure it is never built again to span the river of human destinies.
>
> So it comes about that our nation emerged from the struggle more potent, more splendid than ever she has shone before, laughing at all disloyalties, with mighty opportunities open to her grasp. How she will use them in the years to come, I shall never see. The Germans will neither forgive nor forget; neither money nor comfort will tell with them henceforth. They have been beaten by England and they will live and die to smash England – she will never have a more deadly enemy than the new Germany. My dread is that in future years the easy-going, self-centered English will forget that just across the sea is a mighty, cold-hearted and remorseless people waiting to

strike her through her heart. For strike they will one day, or so I believe.

A few months later Adolf Hitler was organizing the National Socialist German Workers' Party.

In December, Rider, who was wintering in St Leonards, received a letter from Theodore Roosevelt agreeing with his pessimistic view of the peace. 'Like you, I am not at all sure about the future. I hope that Germany will suffer a change of heart, but I am anything but certain. I don't put much faith in the League of Nations, or any corresponding universal cure-all.'[1] A few weeks later Roosevelt was dead. He died on 6 January 1919 and his death was a shock both to Rider and to Kipling. Entering his diary for 10 January Rider records Roosevelt's last letter to him 'because I know that great and good man, in whom the world lost one of its purest and most intrepid spirits, would wish that his views should be put on record at this time of crisis'. On the same day Kipling wrote to Rider: 'Like you, I am awfully heavy hearted about Roosevelt. He was the best friend we had out there and I can't see who takes his place.'

The sad news was also linked with good news. Rider's name once more appeared in the New Year's Honours List and this time he was created a Knight of the British Empire for his services during the war on the Dominions Royal Commission and on the Empire Settlement Committee. Congratulating him, Kipling wrote: 'Dear old man, I am glad to see you took it because if ever there was a Knight of the Empire – by land, and sea and shipwreck – you are it.' Kipling jocularly refers to Rider's shipwreck on his return from Iceland in 1888.

Although his decline in popularity as a writer continued to worry Rider and initial print runs on new editions sank from 15,000 before the war to as low as 3000 in the case of *Smith and the Pharaohs* (1920) Rider began to increase his activities once again. He continued to engage in public life, speaking on a diversity of topics. Speaking in March on 'Population and Housing' he urged the wider use of electricity.

I think that electric power should be introduced into every parish so that it can be used for all household purposes; also, there should be a bath house where men coming in tired from work can have their clothes dried while they wash, with which a wash house and perhaps a public kitchen might be combined.[2]

In April he accepted an appointment on the British Rate Commission and his concern with the birth rate, poor housing conditions and related matters caused him to give evidence before the National Birth Rate Commission. In May he was supporting the idea of establishing a day of National Celebration for Empire Day and on 13 May he was heatedly debating the problems of waifs and strays at the anniversary festival of the Church of England's Waifs and Strays Society, at the Caxton Hall, London. The next day he was sharing the same platform with George Bernard Shaw, to oppose the establishment of a Ministry of Fine Arts, at the annual meeting of the Incorporated Society of Authors, Playwrights and Composers at the Central Hall, Westminster.

Rider also decided to throw his weight against the growing communist movement. The revolution in Russia and its empire and the establishment of a Marxist (Bolshevik) government there had caused widespread repercussions throughout Europe. The success of the Bolsheviks or Marxists served as an inspiration to working-class movements throughout war-weary Europe. The very armistice itself was a direct result of this for Germany became riddled with strikes by people sick of the years of slaughter. The German Fleet mutinied at its bases in Kiel, Cuxhaven and Bremen and established Workers' Councils to run their affairs. The Kaiser was forced to abdicate and on 8 November 1918 Germany was declared a republic and moved to make peace. The British Government was terrified at the mobilization of the working classes against the war. Sir Henry Wilson described a cabinet meeting on 10 November at which messages from the Allied Commander-in-Chief, Field Marshal Ferdinand Foch, confessed he was afraid Germany would become communist unless an armistice was signed with the moderate republican government. Lloyd George asked his cabinet whether they should risk this and continue the war or agree to an armistice. 'All the Cabinet agreed', wrote Wilson. 'Our real danger now is not the Boches but Bolshevism.' The disengagement of troops allowed Britain and America to send armies to Russia in a vain attempt to overthrow the communist government there.

By early 1919 the British workers, who had suffered deprivation and hardship during the war years, began to campaign for a betterment of their lot. The most active group were the Clydeside workers led by John MacLean, a fiery Scottish Marxist theoretician and revolutionary, who was twice condemned to penal servitude for his anti-war utterances and twice released under popular pressure. He was to die in 1923, aged forty-four, from the ill treatment he had received in prison. Ship builders were joined by miners and engineers and the government, fearing revolution, brought in the army. In major industrial cities such as Liverpool, Manchester and Glasgow, tanks were positioned on street corners and machine-gun posts dominated cross-roads. A battleship steamed up the Mersey and trained its guns on the slum areas of the city as even the police force of Liverpool had come out on strike in an effort to improve their conditions. Winston Churchill, most active in the cabinet for the move to send a British army into Russia, also wanted to call out the Royal Air Force to bomb the workers' strongholds. The British crisis was eventually overcome but in Ireland matters were not so easily solved. In the general election of 1918 the people of Ireland had voted to break away from England and establish an independent republic. Of the 105 Irish seats in Westminster, the Republican party, Sinn Fein, won 73, the Irish Nationalist Party won 6 and the Unionists won 26. The British Government's somewhat emotional answer to this was to try to arrest all the elected Sinn Fein representatives and to send in troops. By the end of the year the Irish War of Independence had broken out.

Thus revolution and war and the new communist 'bogey'

were uppermost in the minds of people of property. Rider himself thought revolution was just around the corner and wrote to Kipling on 25 August 1919 that 'meanwhile, I have insured this place and contents against "Riot"'. Kipling, airing his prejudice, believed that all the troubles of the world, especially bolshevism, could be blamed on the Jewish people. Rider gently rebuked him: 'For my own part I should be inclined to read Trade Unions instead of Jews, for surely they are the root of most of our embarrassments and perplexities.'[3] Rider, in fact, went further and suggested to Kipling that a mutual friend of theirs, The Very Reverend William Ralph Inge (1860–1954), should send a letter to *The Times* 'setting out this Bolshevist business clearly and trying to arouse the country to a sense of all its horror'. So strongly did Rider believe that communism, or bolshevism as he called it, was a menace that he went to see the editor of *The Times*, H. Wickham Steed, on 22 January 1920. He recorded: 'Mr Steed unfolded to me a mighty plan for fighting Bolshevism in this country by means of elaborate propaganda.' Steed's idea was to form a council, with the blessing of the government, and financial and moral aid from various churches, to issue propaganda against communism. He suggested that Rider become its president.

On 3 March a letter drafted by Rider and signed by seven signatories, led by Rider and Kipling, appeared in *The Times* announcing the formation of a Liberty League to 'combat the advance of Bolshevism in the United Kingdom and throughout the empire'. The same day *The Times* ran a story congratulating the league on its formation and following it up on the next day with an article headed 'The Bolshevist Peril' which outlined the aims of the league in detail. The *Daily Herald* was among the newspapers who also noted the emergence of the league. Its tone was somewhat ironic.

Sir Rider and the rest have discovered that Bolshevism is 'the sermon on the Mount read backwards; that it leads to bloodshed and to death and destruction; that it repudiates God, and would build its own throne upon the basest

passions of mankind'. 'Sawful, aint it? But all is well. The
Leaguers will fight the plague – 'in a clean and open
fashion'. Lenin and Trotsky shall never see the day when, as
the poet put it,

> The Rudyards cease from Kipling,
> And the Haggards Ride no more.

'Light is to be let in on dark places.' 'The Truth is great
and shall prevail'. And lots more to the same effect.
Meanwhile money is needed and they ask you to help. You
won't? 'Then sir, I perceive you are a vile Bolshevik!'

The account also included a poem entitled 'Two Hearts that
Beat as One – The Way of the World' and signed 'G.C.'

> Every Bolshe is a blackguard
> Said Kipling to Haggard
>   – And given to tippling
> Said Haggard to Kipling.

> And a blooming outsider
> Said Rudyard to Rider.
>   – Their domain is a blood yard
> Said Rider to Rudyard.

> That's just what I say,
> Said the author of *They*
>   – I agree; I agree,
> Said the author of *She*[4]

Rider became President of the Liberty League and spent a
considerable time devoted to turning out its propaganda and
making speeches and writing letters propounding its cause.
Alas, Rider the idealist soon found that his fellow patriots were
not the honest men he took them for. By 21 April the League
was in financial difficulties and it was discovered that one of the
founders had mishandled the funds. According to Rider: 'One's
natural impulse would be to return the subscriptions and wash

one's hands of the whole affair, but that would be almost a national catastrophe and cause Bolsheviks everywhere to rejoice.' Rider had, perhaps, a rather exaggerated idea of the importance of the league.

On the evening of 23 April Rider went to the Festival Dinner of the Royal Society of St George at which Kipling was the main speaker. Rider had become a life member of the society. After the meal and the speeches, Rider went back to Brown's Hotel with Kipling to discuss the affairs of the league. He had spent two hours that afternoon trying to sort out the financial mess with a lawyer. Kipling agreed to attend the next meeting of the league which was on Thursday, 29 April, with Rider in the chair. A Finance Committee was set up but on 7 May Rider wrote:

> The Liberty League worries are overpowering. I spend most of my days trying to deal with them, but without much result. We seem plunged in an atmosphere of deception or worse. Today I have been talking to Mr Wickham Steed on the telephone and told him straight that if Lord Northcliffe makes up his mind he will not help, we must wind up the League.

An appeal for finance had been made to the press baron. Northcliffe did not solve the league's financial problems and, on 14 May, the members agreed to end its existence.

As a prominent personality Rider was invited to many functions, usually public-speaking engagements but on 21 July 1921 he received an invitation to a royal garden party at Buckingham Palace which was, he recorded, 'on the whole an agreeable function'. He met the Kiplings there and Kipling

> held forth about this diary, saying that he wished that I would make him my literary executor with discretion to publish such portions of it as he wished (I expect that rightly he expects to live much longer than I shall). There is something in the idea. The work edited by Kipling would be a formidable document.

Rider's literary output did not slacken. *When the World*

Shook had finally been published on 20 March 1919, after a serialization in the *Quiver*. In February 1920, Cassell published *The Ancient Allan*, in which Allan Quatermain lives a previous existence in ancient Egypt. The seal in this story (the little white seal of the King of the East) used to hang from Rider's watch chain. One day, while at the house of a friend, a box full of antiquities arrived and this seal was amongst them. He was so attracted by it that the friend gave it to him. In November 1920 a collection of short stories appeared from Arrowsmith under the title *Smith and the Pharaohs*. Throughout July 1919 to March 1920, *Hutchinson's Story Magazine* serialized a new *She* adventure entitled *She and Allan* in which Rider brought together his two most famous characters. Between March 1922 and March 1923 *Hutchinson's Story Magazine* also serialized Rider's last attempt to explain the phenomenon of Ayesha, a story called *Wisdom's Daughter* which is Ayesha's own account of how she came to slay Kallikrates. It was published in volume form in March 1923. Rider's restless imagination ranged from the Aztec theme in *The Virgin and the Sun* (1922) to further Allan Quatermain tales with *Heu Heu or The Monster* (1924) and back to his beloved theme of ancient Egypt with *Queen of the Dawn* (1925).

In his friendship with Kipling, Rider had found he was able to bounce ideas against Kipling. Kipling had already helped Rider devise the plot of *The Ghost Kings* (1908) and on 30 January 1922, Rider recorded that he had spent a most interesting day at Batemans and had returned with a plot for a new Allan Quatermain tale.

Incidentally, too, we hammered out the skeleton plot for a romance I propose to write under some such title as *Allan and the Ice Gods* which is to deal with the terrible advance of one of the Ice Ages upon a little handful of the primitive inhabitants of the earth. He has a marvellously fertile mind and I never knew anyone quite so quick at seizing and developing an idea. We spent a most amusing two hours over this plot and I have brought home the results in several sheets of manuscript written by him and myself.[5]

Allan and the Ice Gods was published posthumously on 29 May 1927 by Hutchinson in an edition of 6000 copies. It was a very low edition for an Allan Quatermain tale but indicative of the slackening of interest in his works.

Rider was back at Batemans on 23 March 1923. Kipling had been in a nursing home during the end of 1922 and was still not in good health. 'It struck me that we were a pretty pair of old crocks,' wrote Rider, who had a touch of gout which worsened in his last years, 'I lying with my leg up on the couch in his study and he bending over the fire.' Rider read Kipling extracts from *Wisdom's Daughter* and Kipling described it as 'good prose' asking Rider to reread certain passages that he might hear the fall of the cadences. According to Rider, Kipling described *Wisdom's Daughter* 'as a philosophy of life and an epitome of all the deeper part of my work'. About July, Kipling wrote to Rider more fully on his opinions of the book.

> The more I went through it the more I was convinced that it represented the whole sum and substance of your convictions along certain lines. That being so, it occurred to me that you might later on, take the whole book up again for your personal satisfaction – and go through it from that point of view. I am not suggesting this from the literary side – that is a matter of no importance – but as a means of restating and amplifying your ideas and convictions through the mouth of your chief character. All this is on the assumption that I never hid from you, that the book is miles above the head of the reader at large. It will not come into its own for a long time, but to those to whom it is a message or confirmation it will mean more than the rest of your work. . . . Damn it man – you have got the whole tragedy of the mystery of life under your hand, why not frame it in a wider setting? (This comes from a chap who could not write a novel to save himself.) That's what I suggest for *Wisdom's Daughter* because I know that as you did it, you'd take a

woman in hand and through her mouth speak more of what
is in her heart. You are a whale at parables and allegories
and one thing reflecting another. Don't cuss me. You
wanted to know what I thought and so I send it to you.[6]

On 1 August Rider noted in his diary the reply he had sent to
Kipling: 'As usual – you see the truth which few others do – few
indeed. In that book is my philosophy – or rather some of it.
The Eternal War between Flesh and Spirit, the Eternal
Loneliness and Search for Unity. . . .' Kipling answered that
Rider should use *Wisdom's Daughter* as the first book of a
trilogy, suggesting ways of developing it into a Wandering Jew
saga through the Crusades, the Black Death and Inquisition.
But, he chided,

> you won't do one little bit of this, but it will help stir you to
> block out the first rough scenario, and in the intervals of
> answering the demands of idle idiots and helpless imbeciles
> to which cheerful task I am now about to address myself for
> the next hour.[7]

Kipling was right, of course, Rider did not expand *Wisdom's
Daughter* or revise it.

By 1924 Rider's financial situation was much better and he
found he was able to let the house at St Leonards and enjoy a
holiday abroad for the first time in many years. He took his
daughter Lilias with him and the two set off for Egypt, meeting
a group of friends and relatives along the way. Going by the sea
route around Spain they ran into a gale in the Bay of Biscay but
eventually arrived at the mouth of the Nile. They spent long,
enjoyable days visiting the tombs at Sakkara and Assuit and as
far as Luxor. Lilias recounted a strange experience of an Arab, in
a green turban denoting he had been on a pilgrimage to Mecca,
who was telling people's fortunes. A nephew of Rider's wanted
to have his fortune told but Rider warned the boy against fakes.

> The Arab caught the tone if not the sense of the words, and
> suddenly swept his hand across the sand, wiping out the
> little maze of lines he had been tracing. Then he looked up

at Rider – the evening sun pouring in across the covered deck, lighting the harsh, dark face which reflected a sudden malignancy – and said in a low voice: 'You call me a common cheat – is it not so? – then what of the son of whom you always think?'[8]

Rider was visibly dumbfounded.

A week was spent in Cairo and Rider, who had planned to go on to Palestine, changed his mind and returned to Luxor to spend some quiet weeks with a friend. He recorded in his diary:

Sometimes it is possible to sit alone in some hall of the great temples as I did today. I looked about me in the silence which was broken only by the hum of bees who hive upon the walls, and the twitter of building birds. Everywhere sacred great columns as firmly set as when they were built; upon sculptured walls where Kings made offerings to painted gods, or goddesses led them by the hand into some holy presence. Here was the place where for tens of centuries priests marched from Sanctuary to Sanctuary following the order of their ritual; where proud Pharaoh, himself a god, bent the knee before other gods, whose company he soon must join, and receive from them all blessings and the gift of life for thousands and thousands of years. Surely such a spot should be holy if there is aught so on earth? Yet see – there the early Christians have hacked out the sacred effigies, forgetting how much of their own faith came straight from that which, to their heated imaginations, was peopled with devils and inspired by hell.

It is terrific to think that all these hordes were deluded by a faith which we know to be false, as are the multitudes of India and China, by other faiths that we know to be false. That the glorious temples were in vain, the gifts to the gods were meaningless offerings, benefiting none except the priests who received them: the worshippers pursued an empty life, and lay down to sleep at last leaning upon a broken reed. If this inference were true, their lot was terrible indeed. But I for one do not believe it to be true. I look

upon religion (from that of the lowest savage up to that of
the most advanced Christian) as a ladder stretching from
earth to heaven – a Jacob's ladder if you will, whereby
stretching with many slips and backward fallings, mankind
climbs towards the skies. In that ladder the faith of the old
Egyptians was a single rung, that which we follow is another
rung, and perhaps there are many more, out of our sight
and knowledge, for God's skies are far away.

From Luxor Rider and Lilias went to the Great Pyramids and
spent some time with some archaeologists before returning to
England about April. Rider was in better health and flung
himself back into public life with a new zest. He hardly ever
refused to lend his name to a cause he thought was worthwhile
and during this period he became Vice-President of the Council
for Public Morals, President of the Hastings and District Boy
Scouts' Association, President of the Vegetable, Fur and Feather
Society, and was appointed to serve on the East African
Committee. He spoke at numerous meetings from Rotary clubs,
the London Society of East Anglians, to the National Council
for Promotion of Physical and Moral Race Regeneration and
countless other groups. He attended another Buckingham
Palace garden party and a party given by the Prime Minister,
Stanley Baldwin, at Hampton Court. 'Much of his zest for life,'
wrote Lilias, 'his ever present sense of fun, his pleasure in
meeting people and in small things, came back to him.'[9] Rider
even took up fishing which he found an excellent pastime and
he went on frequent fishing trips with Charles Longman and Sir
Ronald Ross who had won the Nobel Prize in 1897 for
identifying the cause of malaria.

On 5 November Charles Longman asked Rider if he would be
the main speaker at the bicentenary celebration of Longmans,
Green, which was held at the Stationers' Hall. Rider shared the
top table with Mrs Andrew Lang, Sir Arthur Conan Doyle, Sir
Edmund Gosse, G. M. Trevelyan and the Dean of St Paul's. In
his speech Rider said he had often wondered when the
publishing trade began. Authors came before publishers and he

supposed that Homer was his own publisher, collecting his royalties in a hat. 'Publishers and authors were supposed to be deadly enemies. It was not true. They would be uncommonly great fools if they were, because they were united in bonds of matrimony from which there was no possibility of divorce.'[10]

Leaving this congenial dinner Rider set off for his club. The next day he was to record in his diary:

> While I was hurrying to find a taxi in order to catch a train at Charing Cross (which didn't exist) I was seized with a most fearful attack of indigestion that almost seemed to stop my heart from beating. How I managed to get down to St Leonards and into this room really I do not know, it was a great struggle. Luckily Scarlyn Wilson, the doctor, was in the club and came to help me undress, sent for remedies etc. Today I am better but still have wind etc. The immediate cause of this attack was, I believe, eating some oysters and then a sort of lobster stew, after which I drank a glass of champagne and a liqueur brandy. Also the heat of the room followed by the cold of the street and the excitement of speaking may have had something to do with it. The fact is, however, that I am no longer robust, and I do not know how long I shall be able to undertake London enjoyments in winter.

By 25 November Rider was sufficiently recovered to speak at the Delphian Coterie, debating with his friend Sir Ronald Ross on 'The Good and Bad of Imagination'.[11] On the way home Rider fell ill again. The family was at Ditchingham and Rider lay bedridden there throughout December. Christmas Day was a mild day on which the sun shone weakly and Rider recorded on 27 December that he was able to get to a motor car and attend the second service at Ditchingham Church. 'I suppose it is the first time I had been able to enter a church for about six weeks.' He was pessimistic. 'I begin to think that my active career is at an end. I wish to begin a new romance but I cannot face it.'

The new year started on a sad note. Arthur Cochrane, the

friend of his youthful days in Africa, died. Cochrane had written in the summer of 1923 to Rider:

> I always remember your age because you are just two months my senior – I shall be at the hitch of 66 directly, a milestone well on the way of the Road of Life. I wonder how long the road is for you and I, and who shall see the end of it first?

So it was that Macumazahn was to die first. Then came news that Rider's younger brother Arthur was also dead and, within a few days, another friend, William Carr of Ditchingham Hall, also lay dead. Rider's spirits and strength began to fail.

Kipling continued to write regularly, his bantering chatty letters seemed designed to keep up Rider's spirits although Kipling could not help repeating his plea that he be allowed to edit Rider's diaries.

> What of your War and Post War diaries? A good deal of what you foresaw (as you told me) six or eight years ago ought to have ripened by now. Are you going to make any use of it; or are you going to have it locked up in the B[ritish] M[useum] with instructions to open it next Armageddon?[12]

He warns Rider not to bother to reply 'but tell Miss Hector to send a secretarial line at your good leisure'. On 28 February Rider was well enough to dictate to Miss Hector a letter for Kipling. It ran to fourteen pages and in it he tried to assess his life's work. Kipling, fortunately, valued it so much that he stopped his practice of burning all incoming letters so the document survived. Rider displays his old sense of humour in recounting:

> I am glad to say that I am somewhat better. I got up yesterday and sat in the old study next door for a little while, but of course my limbs are like sticks and the sight of meat is abhorrent to me. You would laugh to see me being fed by the nurse with milk pudding from a spoon just like a

baby. Also my rings fall off my hands and there was a deuce of a hunt for one of them the other night – finally retrieved from the seat of my pyjamas.

Lying in bed, Rider says, he has dissected himself and found 'a somewhat miserable anatomy appears'.

> Lack of sufficient principle, or so it seems to me, rashness, want of steady aim (except where the country was concerned of which at heart I have always been the servant) and of character, liability to be swept away by primary impulses, which you will observe never trouble heroes in really first-class novels, for these turn them on and off with a tap of which the spout is directed only towards the heroine – all these bones and others equally unseemly, such as little secret jealousies, are large and prominent. But the Powers that made me thus, perhaps to excite strength of repentance and opposition, did give me one great gift which probably I don't deserve – that of attracting the affection of which you speak – though this has sometimes been of a kind that leads to disaster.[13]

In early March the Kiplings set out on RMS *Normania* from Southampton to Chartres from where, in the Hôtel du Grand Monarque, Kipling wrote to Rider of his impressions of the town. He kept up the correspondence from Perigueux, Biarritz and Paris. By this time the doctors attending Rider had diagnosed a perforating ulcer and decided to move him to London for an extensive examination and a probable operation. 'More likely 'twill be some kind of treatment – of infinite length and boredom', wrote Kipling cheerfully. 'But you've got the year with you and the love of your friends round you.' Lilias recalled:

> Looking back on those days, it is obvious that Rider knew the end had come. So in her heart did Louie. On the grey spring morning that the ambulance was coming to fetch him, she was in his room helping with the last minute preparations. The nurse had dressed him and left him in a

chair, but he looked down at his overcoat as if something was missing, then got up, walked to the table where there was a bowl of daffodils and taking one out pulled it through his buttonhole – then turned with a rather sad smile to his wife. How many hundred times had she seen him do that. The last little action of the morning ritual in his dressing room; for every day the gardener brought in a buttonhole, a rose or carnation in summer, an orchid in winter. Rider was never without a flower. The little incident broke her self-control –

'Rider,' she said, 'do you really want to go, dear? You have only got to say if you don't and we will send the ambulance back – are you quite sure, quite sure . . .?'[14]

Rider did go and the doctors decided, after an examination, to operate. They reported that the operation was 'entirely successful'. The Kiplings were now back in England and anxiously Kipling contacted Ida Hector who informed him of the latest developments. On 13 May he wrote thanking her. 'Seeing that the operation was last Saturday morning and he is reported as reading and smoking on Tuesday, there seems to be a chance of the luck turning', he wrote optimistically. 'I'm off tonight for Brussels where I shall be staying at the Hotel Astoria till Sunday in case there should be anything to tell or wire in a hurry. I expect to be back in London on the 19th or 20th. I shan't trouble him with a letter unless you tell me to.'[15]

On the following day Rider was dead. Another abscess had formed after the operation. Rider had lain in pain for some time before lapsing into unconsciousness. His nephew Godfrey Haggard was to recall in May 1950:

His son-in-law Major Cheyne, the most prosaic of men, was with him the night before. He tells the story always in the same words. The window blind was up, and the blaze from a large building on fire was visible in the distance. Rider rose up in bed, and pointed to the conflagration with arm outstretched, the red glow upon his dying face. My God! said Cheyne to himself, an old Pharaoh.[16]

About midday on 14 May 1925 Rider died without saying anything. His wife Louie (who was to survive him until 4 September 1943) had been watching by his bedside. With her usual calmness and efficiency she met the demands of an indifferent matron who ran the private nursing home for the removal of Rider's body that evening. This same matron took Lilias to see her father's body. She recalled:

> No flowers, no beauty, no dignity or reverence had served that death-bed – there was only a sheeted figure looking strangely small . . . something lay there, wrapped in a dignity and peace which defeated the careless arrangement of the slack hands and crumpled clothes.[17]

The remains were taken to Ditchingham and his ashes were eventually interred under a slab of black marble in the chancel of the parish church, not far away from the family pew and not far away from the spot where his beloved Jock was buried. On the stone was cut a simple sentence which Rider had chosen himself:

Here lie the ashes of Henry Rider Haggard
Knight Bachelor
Knight of the British Empire
Who with a Humble Heart Strove to Serve his Country

It could also be added 'who created a revolution in popular literature and stirred the imagination of generations throughout the world'. For *She* was indeed a turning point in presenting a new brand of fantasy literature to the world. If the test of time and endurance supplies the qualification of a classic then many of Rider's tales demand, today, admittance to the Valhalla of literature. There may have been many greater literary figures than Henry Rider Haggard, but there have been few finer storytellers.

NOTES

In the Introduction and chapters 1 to 12 all quotations by Haggard and correspondence to and from Haggard which have not been given a note are taken from *The Days of My Life*.

In chapters 13 and 14 all quotations by and correspondence from Haggard which have not been given a note are taken from his Diaries, MS 4694 1/22, Norfolk Record Office.

INTRODUCTION

1 *Die Anima als Schicksalsproblem des Mannes*, Cornelia Brunner.
2 *Croidhe na Cruinne (Heart of the World)* translated by Niall Ó Domhnaill, Ofig Díolta Foillseacháin Rialtas, Baile Átha Cliath, 1937.
   There are three other Haggard titles which have been translated into Irish; *Ise (She)* translated by Niall Ó Domhnaill, Ofig Díolta Foillseacháin Rialtas, Baile Átha Cliath, 1933; *Márie (Marie)* translated by Niall Ó Domhnaill, Ofig Díolta Foillseacháin Rialtas, Baile Átha Cliath, 1935; and *Cineadh an Cheo (The People of the Mist)* translated by Aodh Mac Seághain, Ofig an tSolathais, Baile Átha Cliath, 1939.
3 Kipling to Haggard, 3 March 1913, Norfolk Record Office, MS 4694 1/42. Also published in *Rudyard Kipling to Rider Haggard: The Record of A Friendship*, Morton Cohen.
4 *The Cloak That I Left*, Lilias Rider Haggard.
5 *Allan Quatermain*, H. Rider Haggard.
6 *The Wheel of Empire*.
7 Ibid.
8 Ibid.
9 *Rider Haggard: His Life and Works*.
10 *The Wheel of Empire*.
11 *The Times*, 26 November 1924.

Notes

CHAPTER 1 NORFOLK CHILDHOOD

1 *History of the Haggard Family in England and America*, David D. Haggard.
2 *Life and Its Author*, Ella Haggard.
3 *Myra, or the Rose of the East: A Tale of the Afghan War*, Ella Haggard.
4 These words were penned on 5 February 1890.
5 *Life and Its Author*.
6 Foreword to *The Cloak That I Left*, Lilias Rider Haggard.
7 *The Days of My Life*.
8 Ibid.
9 'On Going Back', *Longmans Magazine*, November 1887.
10 Ibid.
11 Ibid.
12 The full poem was:

To My Son Rider
(On leaving home July 1875)

And thus, my son, adown Life's vernal tide
   Light drifting, hast thou reached her troublous sea,
Where never more thy bark may idly glide,
   But shape her course to gain the far To be!

Rise to thy destiny! Awake thy powers!
   Mid throng of men enact the man's full part!
No more with mists of doubt dim golden hours,
   But with strong Being fill thine eager heart!

Nineteen short summers o'er thy youthful head
   Have shone and ripened as they flitted by:
May their rich fruit o'er coming years be shed,
   And make God's gift of life a treasury.

That Life is granted, not in Pleasure's round,
   Or even Love's sweet dream, to lapse content:
Duty and Faith are words of solemn sound,
   And to their echoes must thy soul be bent.

Conscience shall hallow all; grant noble aim,
   And firm resolve the paths of vice to shun;
And haply, in reward, Love's lambent flame
   Through storms of life shall shine, like Earth's fair sun!

But a few days: and far across the flood,
   To stranger lands with strangers wilt thou roam;

Yet shall not absence loose the bonds of blood,
  Or still the voices of thy distant home.

So, go thy way, my child! I love thee well:
  How well, no heart but mother's heart may know –
Yet One loves better, – more than words can tell, –
  Then trust Him, now and evermore; – and go!

16 July 1875   Ella Haggard

CHAPTER 2 AFRICA

1 *The Outlanders*, R. Crisp and P. Davies.

CHAPTER 3 THE ANNEXATION

1 *The Cloak That I Left*, Lilias Rider Haggard.
2 *Cetywayo and His White Neighbours*, H. Rider Haggard.
3 Diary quoted in *The Cloak That I Left*, Lilias Rider Haggard.
4 Ibid.
5 *Cetywayo and His White Neighbours*.
6 *The First Boer War*, J. Lehmann.
7 *Cetywayo and His White Neighbours*.
8 Ibid.
9 *Bibliographical Memoirs and Reminiscence*, John Kotzé.
10 Ibid.
11 Ibid.

CHAPTER 4 AFRICA AT WAR

1 *The Cloak That I Left*, Lilias Rider Haggard.
2 Ibid.
3 *The First Boer War*, J. Lehmann.
4 Ibid.
5 *The Cloak That I Left*.
6 *The Cloak That I Left*.
7 Ibid.
8 *The First Boer War*.
9 Ibid.
10 Ibid.
11 *The Cloak That I Left*.

12 *The Cloak That I Left.*
13 *The First Boer War.*

CHAPTER 5 LAW AND LITERATURE

1 *The Cloak That I Left*, Lilias Rider Haggard.
2 *Daily News*, 23 August 1882.
3 *Saturday Review*, 7 April 1888.
4 *South African*, 28 September to 9 November 1882.
5 *My First Book*, introduced by Jerome J. Jerome.
6 Ibid.
7 *My First Book.*
8 Ibid.
9 Quoted in *The Days of My Life.*
10 22 March 1884.
11 4 April 1884.
12 22 March 1884.
13 *My First Book.*
14 Ibid.
15 17 June 1885.
16 6 February 1885.
17 2 May 1885.
18 *My First Book.*
19 *The Cloak That I Left.*
20 Ibid.
21 *Cornhill Magazine*, vol. VII, no. 39, 1886.
22 Lockwood Collection, Lockwood Memorial Library, University of Buffalo.
23 MS 4694 (10), Norfolk Record Office, copy of agreement signed on 29 May 1885.
24 *My First Book.*
25 *Sixty Years Ago and After*, Max Pemberton.
26 31 October 1885.
27 7 November 1885.
28 6 November 1885.
29 7 November 1885.
30 30 October 1885.
31 10 October 1885.
32 December 1885.
33 Vols IX and X.
34 Vols VI, VII and VIII. Nos 35–46.

CHAPTER 6 'KING ROMANCE HAS COME INDEED!'

1 Lang to Haggard, Lockwood Collection, Lockwood Memorial Library, University of Buffalo.
2 *Ayesha: The Return of She*, Ward Lock, 1904.
3 Lang to Haggard, Lockwood Collection.
4 Christos Pittas, the Greek composer, talking to author.
5 Lang to Haggard, Lockwood Collection.
6 *Graphic*, vols XXXIV and XXXV, nos 879–93.
7 *Academy*, 15 January 1887.
8 *Athenaeum*, 15 January 1887.
9 *Saturday Review*, 8 January 1887.
10 *Spectator*, 15 January 1887.
11 *Pall Mall Budget*, 22 January 1887.
12 *Public Opinion*, 4 January 1887.
13 *Murray's Magazine*, 1 February 1887.
14 *Blackwood's Edinburgh Magazine*, February 1887.
15 *The Critic*, 12 February 1887.
16 *Queen*, 15 January 1887.
17 *Vanity Fair*, 22 January 1887.
18 Corelli to Haggard, Columbia Collection, 29 October 1906.
19 'Can Rider Haggard Write?', *Court and Society*, 30 March 1887.
20 *Some Harwarden Letters 1878–1913*, Lisle March-Phillips and Bertram Christian.
21 *Bookman* (*New York*) November, 1895.
22 First published in *He*, 23 February 1887.
23 *Andrew Lang*, Roger Lancelyn Green, 1946.
24 *The Checklist of Fantastic Literature*, Everett F. Bleiler.
25 First published in *Misfits*, Oxford, 1905; later collected in *At The Mountains of Murkiness*, Ferret Fantasy, London, 1973.
26 First published in *Hood's Comic Annual*, 1888, and then in *Tinkletops Crime*, George R. Sims, Chatto & Windus, 1891.
27 *The Story of JMB*, Denis Mackail.
28 *The Vengeance of She*, Peter Tremayne.
29 *Sonnets and Love Poems*, Countess de Bremont.
30 *The Integration of Personality and Psychology of the Unconscious* by Carl G. Jung. See also *Die Anima als Schicksalsproblem des Mannes*, Cornelia Brunner.
31 *New Approaches to Dream Interpretation*; *The Search for the Beloved*, by Nándor Fodor.
32 *Rider Haggard: His Life and Works*, Morton Cohen.
33 *Athenaeum*, 15 January 1887.

34 'Modern Men', *Scots Observer*, 27 April 1889.
35 *The Poetical Works of Andrew Lang*, edited by Mrs Lang.

CHAPTER 7 THE LURE OF EGYPT

1 *The Cloak That I Left*, Lilias Rider Haggard.
2 Ibid.
3 Ibid.
4 *Contemporary Review*, February 1887.
5 *Athenaeum*, 10 July 1886 (letter by Haggard on 'Fact and Fiction').
6 *Pall Mall Gazette*, 11 March 1887.
7 *Church Quarterly Review*, January 1887.
8 *Fortnightly Review*, January 1887.
9 *Pall Mall Gazette*, 19 April 1887.
10 24 March 1887.
11 26 March 1887.
12 *Pall Mall Gazette*.
13 Lang to Haggard, Lockwood Collection: also quoted in *The Days of My Life*.
14 Lang to Haggard, Lockwood Collection: also quoted by Morton Cohen in *Rider Haggard: His Life and Works*.
15 *The Cloak That I Left*.
16 Ibid.
17 Ibid.
18 *Life and Its Author*, Ella Haggard.

CHAPTER 8 ICELANDIC SAGA AND MEXICAN GOLD

1 Diary, quoted in *The Cloak That I Left*, Lilias Rider Haggard.
2 Lang to Haggard, 11 October 1888, quoted in *The Days of My Life*.
3 *The Cloak That I Left*.
4 *National Observer*, 13 December 1890.
5 *Spectator*, 14 February 1891.
6 *Athenaeum*, 6 December 1890.
7 *Andrew Lang*, Roger Lancelyn Green.
8 *The Days of My Life*, also MS 4692/18, Norfolk Record Office.
9 *Rudyard Kipling to Rider Haggard: The Record of a Friendship*, Morton Cohen.
10 *Something of Myself*, Rudyard Kipling.
11 *Cambridge Review*, February 1891.
12 'Rider Haggard Here', *New York Times*, 11 January 1891.

13 Ibid.
14 Quoted in *The Cloak That I Left*.
15 Foreword to *The Cloak That I Left*.
16 *The Cloak That I Left*.
17 *Pall Mall Gazette*, 17, 31 January, 19 April and 14 May 1894.
18 *A Strange Career*, Mrs B. Jebb.
19 *Christian Commonwealth*, 1 November 1906.
20 *The Times*, 19 December 1892.

CHAPTER 9 THE AGRICULTURAL REFORMER

1 *The Times*, 31 July 1895.
2 *Standard*, 31 July 1895.
3 *New York Times*, 28 July 1895.
4 *The Times*, 6 March 1896, and *African Review*, 7 March 1896.
5 *African Review*, 25 July 1896.
6 *The Red True Story Book*, 7 October 1895.
7 *The Times*, 2, 8, 25 January 1895.
8 *A Farmer's Year*, H. Rider Haggard.
9 *Literary World*, 23 March 1900.
10 *New York Times*, 19 August 1899.
11 *Daily Telegraph*, 7 May 1899. *The Times*, 8 May 1899.
12 *The Times*, 31 May 1899.
13 *Rudyard Kipling to Rider Haggard: The Record of a Friendship*, Morton Cohen.
14 *African Review*, 21 May 1898.
15 Ibid.
16 *African Review*, 25 June 1898.
17 Author's Note in *Doctor Therne*.
18 Quoted in *The Days of My Life*.
19 *The Cloak That I Left*, Lilias Rider Haggard.
20 Ibid.
21 *Rider Haggard: His Life and Work*, Morton Cohen.
22 *Rudyard Kipling to Rider Haggard: The Record of a Friendship*, Morton Cohen.
23 *Quarterly Review*, April 1903.
24 *Literary World*, 15 March 1906.
25 *The Cloak That I Left*.
26 *Rudyard Kipling to Rider Haggard: The Record of a Friendship*, Morton Cohen.

CHAPTER 10 ROYAL COMMISSIONER

1 'Egypt Today'; 'The Land of Cleopatra' (I, II and III) in *Daily Mail*, 23 April, 30 April, 7 May, 1904; also 'The Giant Dam: A Miracle in the Land of the Pharaohs', 21 May 1904; 'The Debris of Majesty: Plundering of the Graves of Kings', 4 June 1904; and 'The Trade in the Dead', 22 July 1904.
2 Quoted in *The Cloak That I Left*, Lilias Rider Haggard.
3 *Journal of the Society for Psychical Research*, October 1904.
4 *The Times*, 1 July 1904.
5 Ibid.
6 *New York Herald*, 19 March 1905.
7 Diary quoted in *The Cloak That I Left*.
8 Ibid.
9 *The Cloak That I Left*.
10 Dated 23 April 1905; quoted in *The Days of My Life*.
11 *The Cloak That I Left*.
12 Ibid.
13 Ibid.
14 Ibid.
15 Reviews of the Blue Book were contained in *The Poor and the Land*.
16 *The Cloak That I Left*.
17 Ibid.

CHAPTER 11 PUBLIC SERVANT

1 MS 4694/3 Norfolk Record Office.
2 Ibid.
3 *The Cloak That I Left*, Lilias Rider Haggard.
4 Ibid.
5 MS 4694/8, Norfolk Record Office.
6 Ibid.
7 Ibid.
8 MS 4694/8. Norfolk Record Office.
9 *The Times*, 27 November 1910.
10 Quoted in *Rider Haggard: His Life and Work*, Morton Cohen.
11 *The Times*, 3 February 1906.
12 *Cassell's Magazine*, June 1908.
13 MS 4694/21 and /22, Norfolk Record Office; these also quoted in *Rudyard Kipling to Rider Haggard: The Record of a Friendship*, Morton Cohen.
14 *The Cloak That I Left*.

CHAPTER 12 SOUTH AFRICA REVISITED

1 *The Cloak That I Left*, Lilias Rider Haggard.
2 Ibid.
3 Ibid.
4 Ibid.
5 Ibid.
6 *Natal Witness*, 26 March 1914.
7 *The Cloak That I Left*.
8 Ibid.
9 Ibid.
10 *Natal Witness*, 30 March 1914.
11 Ibid.
12 *Pictorial*, Durban, 3 April 1914.
13 Diary quoted in *The Cloak That I Left*.
14 Ibid.
15 Ibid.
16 *Rand Daily Mail*, 31 March 1914.
17 *Pretoria News*, 1 April 1914.
18 *Transvaal Leader*, 3 April 1914.
19 *Transvaal Leader*, 28 October 1907.
20 *The Cloak That I Left*.
21 Ibid.
22 Ibid.
23 Ibid.
24 Ibid. See also 'A Journey Through Zululand', *Windsor Magazine*, December 1916.
25 Ibid.
26 Ibid.
27 Ibid.
28 Ibid.
29 *New York Times*, 2 July 1914.
30 *Rider Haggard: His Life and Works*, Morton Cohen.

CHAPTER 13 THE GREAT WAR

1 Haggard's Diaries; MS 4694 1/22, Norfolk Record Office. The twenty-two volumes were presented by Miss Lilias Rider Haggard, 24 August 1956. Typescript copies are retained by Commander Mark Cheyne, Haggard's grandson. Kipling several times expressed his wish to edit the diaries and Haggard clearly intended they should be published after his death. In a note to his executors dated 7 September 1915: 'the diaries of my journey

and of the war might be published, perhaps as a separate volume, though I daresay that these will require editing.' Recently Peter Dennis (of the Department of History of the Royal Military College of Canada) and Adrian Preston have compiled an edited version of the Great War Diaries which is currently awaiting publication.

2 *The Cloak That I Left*, Lilias Rider Haggard.

3 *Eastern Daily Press*, 5 September 1914, and the *Surrey Herald*, October 1914.

4 *Athenaeum*, 10 October 1914.

5 *The Cloak That I Left*, Lilias Rider Haggard.

6 Quoted in *Rider Haggard: His Life and Works*, Morton Cohen.

7 Ibid.

8 *The After War Settlement and Employment of Ex-Service Men in the Oversea Dominions*, H. Rider Haggard.

9 Ibid.

10 *The Cloak That I Left*.

11 *The After War Settlement etc.*

12 Ibid.

13 *The Cloak That I Left*.

14 *The After War Settlement etc.*

15 Ibid.

16 Kipling letters, MS4694 21/1–42. Norfolk Record Office. Also quoted in *Rudyard Kipling to Rider Haggard: The Record of a Friendship*, Morton Cohen.

17 *The Cloak That I Left*.

18 *The After War Settlement etc.*

19 *Daily Telegraph*, 18 November 1916.

20 *Bioscope*, 3 December 1908.

21 Haggard's bibliographer J. E. Scott says this was the year when the first film version of *King Solomon's Mines* was made for African Film Productions, South Africa. This production was directed by H. Lisle Lucoque and the cast included Albert Lawrence as Allan Quatermain, H. J. Hamlin as Sir Henry Curtis, Ray Brown as Commander Good, Vivien Talleur as Gagool and Bertie Gordon as Foulata. Morton Cohen follows Scott. However, the *Bioscope* of 15 May 1919, says the film was released in 1919. Scott does say 'a private view of *another* film version of the story was held at St Leonard's in March 1919' and so it would seem that he confused this version, thinking there were, in fact, both a 1916 *and* a 1919 version.

22 *Daily Telegraph*, 27 May 1917, and *News Chronicle*, 27 June 1917.

23 *Eastern Daily Press*, 19 September 1917.

24 John Murray Manuscripts.

25 Kipling Letters, MS 4694 1/42, Norfolk Record Office; also quoted in John Murray Manuscripts.
26 John Murray Manuscripts.

CHAPTER 14 THE HUMBLE HEART

 1 Diaries; also quoted in *Rudyard Kipling to Rider Haggard: The Record of a Friendship*, Morton Cohen.
 2 *The Times*, 25 March 1919.
 3 4 December 1919, MS 4694 21/1–42, Norfolk Record Office.
 4 *Daily Herald*, 4 March 1920.
 5 Diaries: MS 4694 1/22, Norfolk Record Office.
 6 Kipling letters, MS 4694 21/1–42, Norfolk Record Office.
 7 Ibid.
 8 *The Cloak That I Left*.
 9 Ibid.
10 *The Times*, 6 November 1924.
11 *The Times*, 26 November 1926.
12 Kipling letters, MS 4694/ 21/1–42, Norfolk Record Office.
13 *Rudyard Kipling to Rider Haggard: The Record of a Friendship*, Morton Cohen.
14 *The Cloak That I Left*.
15 Kipling letters, MS 4694 21/1–42, Norfolk Record Office.
16 Foreword to *The Cloak That I Left*.
17 *The Cloak That I Left*.

BIBLIOGRAPHY

THE WORKS OF H. RIDER HAGGARD

Bibliographies

The most complete and excellent bibliographical study, listing all Haggard's
writings from his letters to *The Times*, his articles, the reports of his speeches
to his books, remains the superb 1947 volume by J. E. Scott. Bibliographical
works on Haggard are:

Mackay, George L., 'A Bibliography of the Writings of Sir Rider Haggard',
    The Bookman's Journal, London, 1930. (Limited edition of 475 copies,
    originally published as separately paged supplements in *The Bookman's
    Journal*, vol. XVII, no. 12 and vol. XVIII, no. 13.)

Bibliography

Mackay, George L. and Scott, J. E., *Additions and Corrections to the Haggard Bibliography*, Mitre Press, London, 1939. (Limited edition of 100 copies.)

Scott, J. E., *A Bibliography of the Works of Sir Henry Rider Haggard 1856–1925*, Elkin Mathews Ltd, Takeley, Bishops' Stortford, Herts, 1947. (Limited edition of 500 copies.)

The following makes no attempt to emulate Mackay or Scott but gives a list of the first British and American editions of the books of Haggard plus their first serialization forms in those countries. This is indicated in the following manner:

(a) first British book edition
(b) first British serialization
(c) first American book edition
(d) first American serialization

Fiction (*contemporary novels*)

1 *Dawn*
   (a) Hurst & Blackett, London, 21 February 1884.
2 *The Witch's Head*
   (a) Hurst & Blackett, London, 18 December 1884.
3 *Jess*
   (a) Smith, Elder, London, March 1887.
   (c) Munro's Library, New York, 2 March 1887.
4 *Mr Meeson's Will*
   (a) Spencer Blackett, London, October 1888.
   (c) Harper, New York, 1888.
5 *Colonel Quaritch VC*
   (a) Longmans, Green, London, 3 December 1888.
   (b) Serialized in Tillotsons newspaper, *Newcastle Chronicle*, *Yorkshire Post*, *Liverpool Daily Post*, *England Magazine* and others.
   (c) John W. Lovell, New York, 27 November 1888.
6 *Beatrice*
   (a) Longmans, Green, London, 12 May 1890.
   (b) Serialized in *Yorkshire Post*, *Ipswich Journal*, *Cardiff Times*, *Liverpool Daily Post*, *Nottingham Guardian*, *Pictorial World* and others, January to May.
   (c) George Munro, New York, 12 May 1890.
7 *Joan Haste*
   (a) Longmans, Green, London, 12 August 1895.
   (b) *Pall Mall Magazine*, vols 4, 5 and 6, September 1894 to July 1895.
   (c) Longmans, Green, New York, October 1895.

8   *Doctor Therne*
    (a) Longmans, Green, London, 28 November 1898.
    (c) Longmans, Green, New York, 28 November 1898.
9   *Stella Fregelius*
    (a) Longmans, Green, London, 3 February 1904.
    (b) *T.P.'s Weekly* vol. 1, nos 1–21, 14 November 1902 to 3 April 1903.
    (c) Longmans, Green, New York, 27 October 1903.
10 *The Way of the Spirit*
    (a) Hutchinson, London, March, 1906.
11 *Love Eternal*
    (a) Cassell, London, 4 April 1918.
    (c) Longmans, Green, New York, 1 June 1918.
12 *Mary of Marion Isle*
    (a) Hutchinson, London, 4 January 1929.
    (c) USA editions as *Marion Isle*, Doubleday, Doran, New York, 17 May
         1929.

                          Fiction (romances)

13 *King Solomon's Mines*
    (a) Cassell, London, 30 September 1885.
    (c) 500 sheets bound for Cassell, New York, November 1885.
14 *She*
    (a) Longmans, Green, London, 1 January 1887.
    (b) *Graphic*, vols 34–5, nos 879–93, 2 October 1886, to 8 January 1887.
    (c) Harper's Franklin Square Library, New York, 24 December 1886.
15 *Allan Quatermain*
    (a) Longmans, Green, London, 1 July 1887.
    (b) *Longman's Magazine*, vols IX–X, January to August 1887.
    (c) Harper, New York, 1 July 1887.
16 *A Tale of Three Lions*
    (c) John W. Lovell, New York, 28 November 1887.
         See also *Allan's Wife*, no. 19 below.
17 *Maiwa's Revenge*
    (a) Longmans, Green, London, 3 August 1888.
    (c) Harper, New York, 28 July 1888.
    (d) *Harper's New Monthly Magazine*, vol. LXXVII, July to August 1888.
18 *Cleopatra*
    (a) Longmans, Green, London, 24 June 1889.
    (b) *Illustrated London News*, vol. XCIV, nos 2594–2619, 5 January to
         29 June 1889.
    (c) George Munro, New York, 18 June 1889.

19   *Allan's Wife*
 (a) Spencer Blackett, London, December 1889.
 (b) Consists of four short stories:
        'Allan's Wife' (first publication);
        'Hunter Quatermain's Story from "In a Good Cause"',' 1885;
        'A Tale of Three Lions', *Atalanta*, vol. 1, nos 1–3, October to
        December 1887;
        'Long Odds', *Macmillan's Magazine*, vol. LIII, February 1886.
 (c) Frank F. Lovell, New York, 7 October 1889.
20   *The World's Desire*
 (a) Longmans, Green, London, October 1890.
 (b) *New Review*, vols II–III, nos 11–19, April to December 1890.
 (c) Harper, New York, 8 November 1890.
21   *Eric Brighteyes*
 (a) Longmans, Green, London, 13 May 1891.
 (b) *People*, April/May 1891.
 (c) John W. Lovell, New York, May 1891.
22   *Nada the Lily*
 (a) Longmans, Green, London, 9 May 1892.
 (b) *Illustrated London News*, vol. C, nos 2750–2768, 2 January to 7 May
        1892.
 (c) Longmans, Green, New York, 30 April 1892.
 (d) *New York Herald*, 3 January to 1 May 1892.
23   *Montezuma's Daughter*
 (a) Longmans, Green, London, 13 November 1893.
 (b) *Graphic*, vol. 48, nos 1231–1250, 1 July to 11 November 1893.
 (c) Longmans, Green, New York, 1894.
24   *The People of the Mist*
 (a) Longmans, Green, London, 15 October 1894.
 (b) *Tit-Bits Weekly*, vols XXV–XXVI, nos 636–70, between 23
        December 1893 and 18 August 1894.
 (c) Longmans, Green, New York, November 1894.
25   *Heart of the World*
 (a) Longmans, Green, London, 27 March 1896.
 (b) *Pearson's Weekly*, vol. 5, nos 212–36, 11 August 1894 to 26 January
        1895.
 (c) Longmans, Green, New York, May 1895.
26   *The Wizard*
 (a) J. W. Arrowsmith, London, 29 October 1896.
 (b) *African Review*, vols VIII–IX, 27 July to 24 October 1896.
 (c) Longmans, Green, New York, 8 December 1896. See also
        Black Heart and White Heart and Other Stories, no. 28, below.

27 *Swallow*
   (a) Longmans, Green, London, 1 March 1899.
   (b) *Graphic*, vol. 58, nos 1492–1509, 2 July to 29 October 1898.
   (c) Longmans, Green, New York, 24 February 1899.
   (d) *Munsey's Magazine*, vols XIX–XX, June 1898 to March 1899.

28 *Black Heart and White Heart and Other Stories*
   (a) Longmans, Green, London, 29 May 1900.
   (b) Consists three long stories:
       Black Heart and White Heart, *Africa Review*, January 1896;
       Elissa, *The Long Bow*, vols I–II, nos 1–19, 2 February to
       8 June 1898;
       The Wizard (see no. 26 above).
   (c) USA edition as *Elissa*, Longmans, Green, New York, 15 June 1900.
   (Containing 'Elissa' and 'Black Heart and White Heart' only.)

29 *Lysbeth*
   (a) Longmans, Green, London, 11 April 1901.
   (b) *Graphic*, vols 62–3, nos 1605–1631, 1 September 1900 to 2
   March 1901.
   (c) Longmans, Green, New York, 9 April 1901.

30 *Pearl-Maiden*
   (a) Longmans, Green, London, 2 March 1903.
   (b) *Graphic*, vol. 66, nos 1701–1726, 5 July to 27 December 1902.
   (c) Longmans, Green, New York, 13 March 1903.

31 *The Brethren*
   (a) Cassell, London, 30 September 1904.
   (b) *Cassell's Magazine*, December 1903 to November 1904.
   (c) McClure, Phillips, New York, 2 October 1904.

32 *Ayesha*
   (a) Ward Lock, London, 6 October 1905.
   (b) *Windsor Magazine*, vols. 21–2, nos. 120–30, December 1904 to
   October 1905.
   (c) Doubleday, Page, New York, 6 October 1905.
   (d) *Popular Magazine*, vols III–IV, January to August 1905.

33 *Benita*
   (a) Cassell, London, 7 September 1906.
   (b) *Cassell's Magazine*, December 1905 to May 1906.
   (c) USA edition as *The Spirit of Bambatse*, Longmans, Green, New
   York, 7 September 1906.

34 *Fair Margaret*
   (a) Hutchinson, London, 9 September 1907.
   (b) *The Lady's Realm*, vols 21–2, November 1906 to October 1907.
   (c) USA edition as *Margaret*, Longmans, Green, New York, 11 October
   1907.

35 *The Ghost Kings*
    (a) Cassell, London, 25 September 1908.
    (b) *Pearson's Magazine*, vols XXIV–XXV, nos 142–50, October 1907 to
        June 1908.
    (c) USA edition as *The Lady of the Heavens*, Frank F. Lovell, New York,
        15 May 1909.
36 *The Yellow God*
    (a) Cassell, London, 5 March 1909.
    (c) Cupples & Leon, New York, 25 November 1908.
37 *The Lady of Blossholme*
    (a) Hodder & Stoughton, London, 15 December 1909.
    (b) *British Weekly*, vols XLVI–XLVII, nos 1182–1203, 24 June to
        18 November 1909.
38 *Morning Star*
    (a) Cassell, London, 11 March 1910.
    (b) *Christian World News of the Week*, vols LIII–LIV, nos 2742–2762,
        21 October 1909 to 10 March 1910.
    (c) Longmans, Green, New York, 27 May 1910.
39 *Queen Sheba's Ring*
    (a) Everleigh Nash, London, September 1910.
    (b) *Nash's Magazine*, vol. 1, nos 1–8, April to November 1909.
    (c) Doubleday, Page, New York, 8 September 1910.
40 *Red Eve*
    (a) Hodder & Stoughton, London, 28 August 1911.
    (b) *Red Magazine*, from December 1910.
    (c) Doubleday, Page, New York, 27 October 1911.
    (d) *New York Herald*, 2 October to 18 December 1910.
41 *The Mahatma and the Hare*
    (a) Longmans, Green, London, 16 October 1911.
    (c) Henry Holt, New York, 16 October 1911.
42 *Marie*
    (a) Cassell, London, 25 January 1912.
    (b) *Cassell's Magazine*, vol. LIII, nos 1–6, September 1911 to February
        1912.
    (c) Longmans, Green, New York, 18 March 1912.
43 *Child of Storm*
    (a) Cassell, London, 23 January 1913.
    (c) Longmans, Green, New York, 6 February 1913.
44 *The Wanderer's Necklace*
    (a) Cassell, London, 29 January 1914.
    (c) Longmans, Green, New York, 11 February 1914.
45 *The Holy Flower*
    (a) Ward Lock, London, 31 March 1915.

(b) *The Windsor Magazine*, vols XXXIX–XL, nos 228–39, December 1913 to November 1914.

(c) Longmans, Green, New York, 1915.

46 *The Ivory Child*

(a) Cassell, London, 6 January 1916.

(b) Serialized in various newspapers over eighteen weeks from 4 January 1915.

(c) Longmans, Green, New York, 1 April 1916.

47 *Finished*

(a) Ward Lock, London, 10 August 1917.

(b) *Storyteller*, London, December 1916 as 'The Marble Temple' (novelette).

(c) Longmans, Green, New York, 28 August 1917.

(d) *Adventure*, New York, January to May 1917.

48 *Moon of Israel*

(a) John Murray, London, 31 October 1918.

(b) *Cornhill Magazine*, vols XLIV–XLV, nos 259–68, January to October 1918.

(c) Longmans, Green, New York, 14 November 1918.

49 *When the World Shook*

(a) Cassell, London, 20 March 1919.

(b) *The Quiver*, vol. 54, nos 1–6, November 1918 to April 1919.

(c) Longmans, Green, New York, 22 May 1919.

50 *The Ancient Allan*

(a) Cassell, London, 12 February 1920.

(b) *Cassell's Magazine*, nos 84–91, March to October 1919.

(c) Longmans, Green, New York, 25 March 1920.

51 *Smith and the Pharoahs*

(a) J. W. Arrowsmith, Bristol, 4 November 1920.

(b) six short stories:

Smith and the Pharaohs, *The Strand Magazine*, vols XLIV–XLV, nos 264–6, December 1912 to February 1913;

Magepa the Buck, *Pears' Christmas Annual*, 1912;

The Blue Curtains, *Cornhill Magazine*, vol. VII, 1886;

Little Flower, *Pall Mall Magazine* (no details);

Only a Dream, *Harry Furniss's Christmas Annual*, 1905;

Barbara Who Came Back, *Pall Mall Magazines*, vol. LI, March to April 1913.

(c) Longmans, Green, New York, 5 August 1921.

52 *She and Allan*

(a) Hutchinson, London, 17 February 1921.

(b) As 'She meets Allan' in *Story Magazine*, vols I–II, July 1919, to March 1920.

(c) Longmans, Green, New York, 5 January 1921.

53 *The Virgin of the Sun*

(a) Cassell, London, 26 January 1922.

(c) Doubleday, Page, New York, 26 May 1922.

54 *Wisdom's Daughter*

(a) Hutchinson, London, 9 March 1923.

(b) *Hutchinson's Story Magazine*, vols 6–8, March 1922 to March 1923.

(c) Doubleday, Page, New York, 9 March 1923.

55 *Heu-Heu*

(a) Hutchinson, London, 29 January 1924.

(b) *Hutchinson's Story Magazine*, vol. 10, nos 55–7, January to March 1924.

(c) Doubleday, Page, New York, 4 April 1924.

56 *Queen of the Dawn*

(a) Hutchinson, London, 21 April 1925.

(c) Doubleday, Page, New York, 27 March 1925.

57 *The Treasure of the Lake*

(a) Hutchinson, London, September 1926.

(b) *Adventure Story Magazine*, February to May 1926.

(c) Doubleday, Page, New York, 7 May 1926.

58 *Allan and the Ice-Gods*

(a) Hutchinson, London, 20 May 1927.

(c) Doubleday, Page, New York, 20 May 1927.

59 *Belshazzar*

(a) Stanley Paul, London, 26 September 1930.

(c) Doubleday, Doran, New York, 31 October 1930.

Non-fiction

60 *Cetywayo and His White Neighbours*

(a) Trübner, London, 22 June 1882 (edition with new material printed in 1888).

Section on 'The Transvaal' published separately as

(a) *The Last Boer War*, Kegan Paul, Trench & Trübner, London, 20 October 1889.

(c) USA edition as *A History of the Transvaal*, Kegan Paul, Trench & Trübner, New York, 1899.

61 *My Fellow Labourer and The Wreck of the Copeland*

(b) 'The Wreck of the Copeland' appeared in *Illustrated London News*, vol. XCIII, no. 2574, 18 August 1888.

    (c) George Munro, New York, 30 November 1888.
    No British publication of this work.

62 *A Farmer's Year, Being His Commonplace Book for 1898*
    (a) Longmans, Green, London, 2 October 1899.
    (b) *Longman's Magazine*, vols 32–4, nos CXCI–CCIV, September 1898 to October 1899.

63 *A Winter Pilgrimage*
    (a) Longmans, Green, London, 7 October 1901.
    (b) *Queen*, vols CIX–CXI, nos 2819, 2844, 5 January to 29 June 1901, and nos 2847 to 2885, 20 July 1901 to 12 April 1902.
    (c) Longmans, Green, New York, 9 October 1901.

64 *Rural England*
    (a) Longmans, Green, London, 28 November 1902.
    (b) A quarter of the book was serialized in fifty articles in *Daily Express* and the *Yorkshire Post*, 17 April to 3 October 1901.
    (c) Longmans, Green, New York, 20 December 1902.

65 *The Poor and the Land*
    (a) Longmans, Green, London, 18 August 1905.
    (c) Longmans, Green, New York, 12 September 1905.
    A popular version of the 'Report on the Salvation Army Colonies', published as an HMSO Blue Book, June 1905.

66 *A Gardener's Year*
    (a) Longmans, Green, London, 13 January 1905.
    (b) The *Queen*, vols CXV–CXVI, nos 2976–3027, 9 January to 31 December 1904.
    (c) Longmans, Green, New York, 25 January 1905.

67 *Regeneration: Being an account of the social work of the Salvation Army in Great Britain*
    (a) Longmans, Green, London, 16 December 1910.
    (c) Longmans, Green, New York, 3 January 1911.

68 *Rural Denmark*
    (a) Longmans, Green, London, 6 April 1911.
    (b) Four articles from the book in *The Times*, 22 and 27 February, 6 and 13 March 1911.

69 *The Days of My Life*
    (a) Longmans, Green, London, 7 October 1926.
    (b) Abridged version in *Strand Magazine*, vols 71–2, nos 424–30, April to October 1926.
    (c) Longmans, Green, New York, October 1926.

Royal commission reports and pamphlets

An Heroic Effort, pamphlet, 26 April 1893.

Church and State, pamphlet, March 1895.

East Norfolk Representation, pamphlet, 23 March 1895.

Speeches of the Earl of Iddesleigh and Mr Rider Haggard, pamphlet, 1895.

A Visit to the Victoria Hospital, pamphlet, 19 October 1897.

The New South Africa, pamphlet, 1900.

Royal Institution of Great Britain, pamphlet, 8 May 1903.

Report on the Salvation Army Colonies (Royal Commission), HMSO, June 1905.

The Real Wealth of England, pamphlet, January 1908.

Royal Commission on Coast Erosion, 3 vols, HMSO, 1907, 1909 and 1911.

Letter to the Rt Hon. Lewis Harcourt, pamphlet, July 1914.

A Call to Arms, pamphlet, September 1914.

The After-War Settlement and Employment of Ex-Servicemen, pamphlet, August 1916.

Dominions Royal Commission, 24 vols, HMSO, 1912 to 1917.

The Salvation Army, pamphlet, January 1920.

Works with an introduction by H. Rider Haggard

Haggard, Ella, *Life and Its Author*, Longmans, Green, London, 1890.

Jebb, B., *A Strange Career: Life and Adventures of John Gladwyn Jebb*, Blackwoods, 1894.

Wilmot, Hon. A., *In Monomopata* (Rhodesia): *Monuments and History*, 1896.

Dutt, William A., *The King's Homeland; Sandringham and North-West Norfolk*, 1904.

Adams, Thomas, *Garden City and Agriculture*, Simpkin Marshall, 1905.

Robertson-Scott, J. W., *The Case for the Goat by 'Home Counties'*, 1908.

Wills, W. A. and Collinbridge, L. T., *The Downfall of Lobengula: The Cause, History and Effect of the Matabele War* (chapter XVI by Haggard), 1894.

A SHORT FILMOGRAPHY

King Solomon's Mines

1 1919. African Film Productions, South Africa. Director, H. Lisle Lucoque. Starring Albert Lawrence as Allan Quatermain, H. J. Hamlin as Sir Henry Curtis and Ray Brown as Commander Good.

2 1936. Gaumont, Great Britain. Director, Robert Stevenson. Starring Sir Cedric Hardwicke as Allan Quatermain, John Loder as Sir Henry Curtis, Roland Young as Commander Good with Paul Robeson as Umbopa. First talking version.

3 1950. Metro Goldwyn Mayer, USA. Directors, Compton Bennett and Andrew Morton. Starring Stewart Granger as Allan Quatermain, Deborah Kerr as Elizabeth Curtis and Richard Carlson as John Goode. Technicolour version.

4 'Maciste in King Solomon's Mine', late 1950s. Italian version. Starring Reg Park, Wandisa Guida and Dan Harrison.

5 'Watusi' 1959. Metro Goldwyn Mayer, USA. Sequel to 'King Solomon's Mines'. Director, Kurt Neuman. Starring George Montgomery.

She

1 'La Danse du Feu/La Colonne de Feu', 1899. French silent by George Melies.

2 1908. Edison Manufacturing Co., London.

3 1911. Thanhouser Production, USA. Starring Marguerite Snow.

4 1916. Barker Motion Photography, Great Britain. Director, Will Barker. Starring Alice Delysia as Ayesha.

5 'Hidden Valley', 1916. Pathé, USA. Starring Valkyrien.

6 1917. Fox Films, USA. Director, Kenean Buel. Starring Valeska Suratt as Ayesha.

7 1925. G.B. Samuelson/Lisle Productions, Great Britain. Director, Leander de Cordova. Starring Betty Blythe as Ayesha.

8 1935. RKO, USA. Directors, Irving Pichel and Lansing G. Holden. Starring Helen Gahagan, with Randolph Scott in the cast. First talking version.

9 'Malika Salomi', 1953. Indian version. Director, Mohamed Hussein. Starring Krishna Rumari and Rupa Varman.

10 1965. Hammer-Seven Arts, Great Britain. Director, Robert Day. Starring Ursula Andress as Ayesha with Christopher Lee, Peter Cushing and John Richardson in support.

11 'The Vengeance of She' (sequel), 1967. Director Cliff Owen. Starring Olinka Berova as Ayesha supported by John Richardson.

Moon of Israel

'Die *Sklavenkönigin*' 1924. Sascha Films. Relesed in Britain as 'Moon of Israel' by Stoll Pictures. Director, Michael Curtiz. Starring Maria Corda and Adelphi Miller.

Jess

1 American silent made in 1905 but not shown in Britain.

2 'Heart and Soul', 1917. Fox Films, USA. Director, J. Gordon Edwards. Starring Theda Bara and Harry Hillard.

Beatrice

1920. Unione Cinematografica Italiana. Starring Marie Doro as Beatrice.

Swallow

A scenario of story was approved by Haggard in 1920 but no data is available on its production.

Stella Fregelius
> Not on general release but was shown privately in London on 12 April 1921, under the title of 'Stella'.

Joan Haste
> Produced about 1920 but no other details available.

Allan Quatermain
> 1918. African Film Productions Ltd, South Africa.

Mr Meeson's Will
> 'Grasp of Greed', 1916. Bluebird Universal Production. Director, Joseph de Grasse. Starring Lon Chaney.

Cleopatra
> 1921. Fox Films, USA. Haggard took out a successful action against the company for 'pirating' the story. He won heavy damages.

PARODIES AND SEQUELS TO H. RIDER HAGGARD'S BOOKS

Books

Biron, Sir Henry Chartres, *King Solomon's Wives: or the Phantom Mines by Hyder Ragged*, Vizetelly, London, 1887.

De Morgan, John, *Bess*, N. L. Munro, New York, 1887.

De Morgan, John, *He*, N. L. Munro, New York, 1887. (Not to be confused with Lang and Pollock's *He* published in London 1887 which is an entirely different book.)

De Morgan, John, *It*, N. L. Munro, New York, 1887.

De Morgan, John, *King Solomon's Treasures*, N. L. Munro, New York, 1887.

Lang, Andrew and Pollock, W. H. *He*, Longmans, Green, London, 1887.

Marshall, Sidney J., *The King of Kôr: or She's Promise Kept, A Continuation of the Great Story of She*, S. J. Marshall, Washington, 1903.

Tremayne, Peter, *The Vengeance of She*, Sphere, London, 1978.

Williams, J. X., *Her*, Corinth Publications, 1967.

Articles, poems and other shorter parodies (in chronological order)

1887 *St James's Gazette*, 16 February, 'An Interview with She'.
> *Punch*, 2 April, 'A Proposition and a Rider'.
> *Punch*, 27 August, 'Adam Slaughterman by Walker Weird, author of Hee-Hee and Solomon's Ewers'.

1888 *Punch*, 31 March, 'The Doom of She – Fragment of a Romance of Political Adventure'.
> *Punch*, 22 September, 'She-That-Ought-Not-To-Be-Played'.
> *Hood's Comic Annual*, Christmas, 'The Lost Author' by George R. Sims. (Also collected in *Tinkletop's Crime*, Chatto & Windus, 1891.)

Punch's Almanack for 1890, 5 December, 'A Haggard Annual – specially written by Walker Weird, author of Hee-Hee and Solomon's Ewers'.

1890 *Punch*, 24 May, The Pick of the Pictures – Royal Academy no. 551. 'Two Tales of a Tiger – advertisement for a new Romance by Rider Laggard and Andrew Hang'.

1891 *Punch*, 3 January, 'Literary Stars'.
   Punch, 17 January, Mr Punch's Prize Novels no. XI. *'The Book of Kookarie* by Reader Faghard, author of *Queen Bathshedba's Ewers, Yawn, Guess, My Ma's at Penge, Smallum Halfboy, Gen. Porridge D.T., Me a Kiss, The Hemisphere's Wish* & etc'.

1895 *Punch*, 30 March, 'An Election Address (Mr Rider Haggard has become accepted Conservative candidate for a Norfolk Constituency. The following is understood to be an advance copy of his address. . . .'

1899 *Punch*, 15 November, 'Allan Quatermain's Farm'. (A parody of *A Farmer's Year*.)

1902 *Punch*, 12 March, 'The Song of a Fireside Range'.
   Punch, 19 March, 'Authors at Bow Street' (Henry Rider Haggard, yeoman was prosecuted by the Aboriginees Protective Society for deserting one Ohm Slumpingas, a Zulu chieftain). A skit on the fact that Haggard had not written a romance for some time.

1905 *Misfits*, George Forrest, Frank Harvey, Oxford, 1905. This volume contains 'The Deathless Queen – She-Who-Must-Be-Decayed'. (Also collected in *At The Mountains of Murkiness*, edited by George Locke, Ferret Fantasy, London, 1973.)

1910 *Punch*, 5 October. A poetic parody on the publication of *Queen Sheba's Ring*.

UNPUBLISHED SOURCES

There are several unpublished sources of material relating to H. Rider Haggard such as the Lockwood Collection which contains letters from Andrew Lang, Thomas Hardy and W. B. Yeats to Haggard and which is contained in the Lockwood Memorial Library, University of Buffalo, USA. There is also a collection of Haggard correspondence in the Columbia University Library, USA.

The main unpublished sources used in this work have been the following:

1 Letters and other material in the keeping of John Murray (Publishers), Ltd, London.

2 Roger Lancelyn Green's unpublished biographical manuscripts for younger readers, entitled 'The Adventures of Rider Haggard', which he wrote in the late 1950s.

3 The still growing collection of Haggardiana in the Norfolk Record Office, Norwich. Among the items there, the following material may be found:

MS 4692/3 Catalogue of the Haggard Manuscripts, Norwich Public Libraries, and Addenda.

The original manuscripts of *Dawn, The Witch's Head, King Solomon's Mines, She, Jess, Maiwa's Revenge, Allan's Wife, Colonel Quaritch VC, Cleopatra, Beatrice, Eric Brighteyes, Nada the Lily, Montezuma's Daughter, The World's Desire*; notebooks for *Rural England, A Farmer's Year, A Gardener's Year, Rural Denmark* and related material.

Additional items such as the original of Da Silvestra's map (*King Solomon's Mines*) and the Sherd of Amenartes (*She*).

Bibliographical notes by J. E. Scott.

MS 4694 Covers the twenty-two diaries kept from July 1914, to April 1925, plus twenty-nine engagement and jotting notebooks *c.* 1880 to 1925.

Biographical sketch and notes by J. E. Scott, corrected by Lilias Rider Haggard.

Manuscripts of the play *Mameena* (for Oscar Asche production).

H. Rider Haggard's will.

Notes of conversation with Lloyd George, May 1909.

Notes for *The Virgin of the Sun*.

Letters from Rudyard Kipling to Rider Haggard (containing the bulk of extant correspondence, used in Morton Cohen's book *Rudyard Kipling to Rider Haggard: The Record of a Friendship* 1965).

Letters from Andrew Lang to Rider Haggard.

Sundry correspondence from Stanley Weyman, Theodore Roosevelt, M. W. Robins, W. H. Pollock and others.

The Norfolk Record Office also contains a selection of photographs, cartoons and other related material including the original twelve drawings for the *Graphic*'s serialization of *She* by E. K. Johnson.

PUBLISHED SOURCES

Major works on H. Rider Haggard

Cohen, Morton, *Rider Haggard: His Life and Works*, Hutchinson, London, 1960.

Cohen, Morton, *Rudyard Kipling to Rider Haggard: The Record of a Friendship*, Hutchinson, London, 1965.

Bibliography

Haggard, H. Rider, *The Days of My Life* (autobiography), Longmans, Green, London, 1926.

Haggard, Lilias Rider, *The Cloak That I Left* (biography), Hodder & Stoughton, London, 1951.

In German

Brunner, Cornelia, *Die Anima als Schicksalsproblem des Mannes* (Die Anima bei Rider Haggard), foreword by Carl G. Jung, Rascher Verlag, Zurich and Stuttgart, 1963.

Autobiographical articles and sketches by H. Rider Haggard
(in chronological order)

1887 *Contemporary Review*, February, 'About Fiction'.
British Weekly, May, 'Books Which Have Influenced Me'.
Longman's Magazine, July, 'On Going Back'.

1888 *Illustrated London News*, 18 August, 'The Wreck of the Copeland'.

1893 *Idler*, April. 'My First Book – *Dawn*'.

1897 *Pearson's Magazine*, April, 'The Output of Authors'.
Golden Penny, April 24–May 1, 'In the Transvaal of 1877'.

1903 *Windsor Magazine*, 'Lost on the Veld' (reprinted from *Youth's Companion*, New York, 25 September 1902).

1904 *Journal of the Society for Psychical Research*, October, Case L. 1139, 'Dream'.
London Magazine, November, 'Have We Lived on Earth Before? Shall We Live on Earth Again?'

1907 *Bookman*, London, January, 'The book of 1906 which has interested me the most'.
Cassell's Magazine, July, 'The Real King Solomon's Mines'.

1908 *Bookman*, London, November, 'Authors at Work – The Disadvantage of Working in London – and out of it'.

1911 *Bystander*, 18 January, 'Sex and the Short Story'.

1915 *Sheffield Independent*, November, 'The Solace of Books'.

1916 *Windsor Magazine*, December, 'A Journey Through Zululand'.

1922 *Daily Despatch*, 15 August, 'My Favourite Holiday'.

Biographical articles, sketches and criticism of H. Rider Haggard
(in chronological order)

1882 Reviews of *Cetywayo and his White Neighbours*
Vanity Fair, 29 July; *Saturday Review*, 12 August; *Spectator*, 19 August; *British Quarterly Review*, October.

1884 Reviews of *Dawn*
    Academy, 22 March; *Athenaeum*, 22 March; *Pall Mall Budget*, 4 April;
    Vanity Fair, 12 April.

1885 Reviews of *The Witch's Head*
    Athenaeum, 10 January; *Pall Mall Budget*, 16 January; *Academy*, 17
    January; *Saturday Review*, 17 January; *Literary World*, 6 February;
    Literary World (Boston) 2 May.
    Reviews of *King Solomon's Mines*
    Saturday Review, 10 October; *Public Opinion*, 30 October;
   Athenaeum, 31 October; *Vanity Fair*, 6 November; *Academy*, 7
    November; *Queen*, 7 November; *Spectator*, 7 November,;
    Independent, 3 December.

1886 *Critic*, USA. 3 April. 'London Letter' by W. E. Henley.

1887 Reviews of *She*
    Public Opinion, 4 January; *Pall Mall Budget*, 6 January; *Literary World*,
    7 January; *Saturday Review*, 8 January; *Academy*, *Queen*, *Spectator*,
    and *Athenaeum*, 15 January; *Vanity Fair*, 22 January; *Murray's*
    Magazine, February; *Critic*, 12 February.
    Review of *Allan Quatermain*
    British Weekly, 5 August.
    Review of *Devil Caresfoot* (dramatization of *Dawn*)
    Theatre, 1 August.
    Literary World (Boston), 5 March, 'A letter from London'.
    Pall Mall Gazette, 11 March, 'Who is *She* and where did *She* come
    from?'; 24 March, 'The Song of *Jess* and Who Wrote it'; 26 March,
    'The Strange Case of *She* and *Jess*'; 30 March–April 5. 'The Ethics of
    Plagiarism'; 19 April, 'The Song of *Jess* and How She Came by It – H.
    Rider Haggard's Explanation';
    Whitehall Review, 31 March, 'Mr Rider Haggard and the Song Of *Jess*'.
    Time, May, 'Rider Haggard and The New School of Romance' by
    Augustus Moore.
    Dial, May 'Mr Haggard's Romance'.
    Contemporary Review, June, 'Literary Plagiarism', by Andrew Lang.

1888 Reviews of *She* dramatization
    Illustrated London News, 15 September, and *Athenaeum*, 29
    September.
    Review of *Colonel Quaritch VC*
    Scots Observer, 22 December.
    Review of *Cetywayo* (new edition)
    Literary World, 27 July and *Westminster Review*, July.
    Church Quarterly Review, January, 'The Culture of the Horrible: Mr
    Rider Haggard's Stories'.
    Fortnightly Review, 1 September, 'The Fall of Fiction'.

Month, September, 'To the Author of 'She' by 'Theophilus' '.
Literary World (Boston), 10 November, 'Squire Haggard at Home'.
Illustrated London News, 15 December, 'Mr H. Rider Haggard'.
1889 Review of *Cleopatra*
Scots Observer, 27 July.
Scots Observer, 27 April, 'Modern Men: H. Rider Haggard' by W. E.
Henley.
1890 Reviews of *The World's Desire*
British Weekly, 20 November; *Literary World*, 28 November;
Athenaeum, 6 December; *National Observer*, 13 December; *Spectator*,
14 February, 1891.
Fortnightly Review, March, 'King Plagiarism and his Court' by James
Runciman.
Book News, June, 'H. Rider Haggard'.
1891 *Strand Magazine*, January, 'Portraits of Celebrities – H. Rider
Haggard'.
New York Times, 11 January, 'Rider Haggard Here'.
1892 *Strand Magazine*, January, 'Illustrated Interviews no. VII – Mr H. Rider
Haggard'.
Winter's Weekly, 19 March, 'Interesting People – H. Rider Haggard'.
Critic, 9 July, 'Rider the Ripper'.
1893 *East Anglian Daily Press*, October, 'Interview with H. Rider Haggard'.
1894 *The Month*, January, 'Mr Rider Haggard and the Immuring of Nuns',
by Herbert Thurston on *Montezuma's Daughter*.
Review of Reviews, January, 'How Mr Haggard Works' by Fred Dolman.
Black and White, 11 August, 'Mr Rider Haggard at Home'.
The Young Man, 'How I Write My Books' (interview by Fred Dolman).
1895 *The Cable*, 11 May, 'Agriculturalists at Home – Mr H. Rider Haggard at
Ditchingham'.
Answers, 15 June, 'Life Stories of Successful Men no. XXI – Mr H.
Rider Haggard'.
Pall Mall Gazette, 25 July, 'Rioting in East Norfolk. Interview with Mr
Rider Haggard'.
Saturday Review, 24 March, 'Mr Rider Haggard as a Politician'.
Pall Mall Gazette, 24 March, 'Rider Haggard in Parliament'.
New York Times, 24 March, 'Rider Haggard in Parliament'.
Bookman Chronicle and Comment, November. Sketch by Walter
Besant.
1898 *The African Review*, 19 February, 'The Transvaal Judicial Crisis – a chat
with H. Rider Haggard'.
1899 *Bookman*, New York, June. 'The Evolution of an Artist' by Katherine
Pearson Woods.
Gardener, 23 September, 'Mr Rider Haggard and His Orchids'.

East Anglian Daily Times, 9 October, 'Mr Rider Haggard on the Crisis'.
Amateur Gardening, 16 December, 'My Favourite Flowers. Mr Rider Haggard as an Orchid grower'.

1900 Reviews of *A Farmer's Year*
Bookman, December, 1899; *Athenaeum*, 6 January; *Literary World*, 23 March; and *New York Times*, 19 August.
New York Daily Tribune, 21 February, 'The Passing Throng'.

1901 *Longman's Magazine*, June. 'The Mission of Mr Rider Haggard and Rural Education' by R. R. C. Gregory.
New York Times, 1 June. 'Rider Haggard. His Achievements as a Farmer'.
Daily Mail, 7 December, 'After the War – Mr Rider Haggard's Prophecies'.

1902 *Commonwealth*, 'Living Talks with men who are Alive no. III – H. Rider Haggard' by H. A. Wilkinson.
Great Thoughts, 'Mr Rider Haggard's Reminiscences'.
East Anglian Daily Times, December 29–30, 'Mr Rider Haggard on Agriculture'.

1903 *Black and White Illustrated Budget*, 19 December, 'Real Places and Faces in Fiction. 1. Mr Rider Haggard's Umslopogaas'.
Reviews of *Rural England*
Contemporary Review, January; *Spectator*, 14 February; *Quarterly Review*, April; *Edinburgh Review*, April.

1905 *East Anglian Daily Times*, 29 April, 'Through America – Mr Rider Haggard's Tour'.
Daily Mirror, 21 June, 'A Man of the Moment – Mr Rider Haggard'.
Daily News, 23 June, 'Poverty and the Land' – an interview.
Review of Reviews, July. 'Character Sketch – Commissioner H. Rider Haggard'.
Graphic, 29 July, 'A Chat with Mr Rider Haggard'.
New York Herald, 19 May, 'H. Rider Haggard Turns Colonizer'.

1906 *Review of Reviews*, January, 'Where is Mr Haggard?'
Morning Post, 10 January, 'Land Settlement' – an interview.
Literary World, 15 March, 'H. Rider Haggard' – biographical sketch.
Tribune, 5 September, '"Triangle Camp" Canard. Mr Haggard denies the story of his "promise"'.
Christian Commonwealth, 1 November, 'H. Rider Haggard' – interview.

1908 *Cassell's Magazine*, 'H. Rider Haggard – Story Writer and Psychologist'.
Bibliophile, September, Bookplates of Celebrities.

1909 *Social Gazette*, 15 October, 'Mr Rider Haggard' – an interview.

1910 *Captain*, June, 'Literary Men of the Month' – biographical sketch.
      New Zealand Times, 5 November, 'Writers of the Day. No. 46 – H.
      Rider Haggard'.
1911 Review of *Regeneration*
      Outlook, USA, 1 July, by Theodore Roosevelt.
1912 *Churchwarden*, 15 July, 'Our Portrait Gallery. Prominent Wardens.
      LXII – Sir Henry Rider Haggard'.
1913 *Statesman*, 18 January, 'Sir Rider Haggard in Calcutta'.
      Commerce (Ceylon) 22 January, 'Empire Trade
      Commission' – interview.
      Amiens Illustrated Weekly, 25 January, 'Sir H. Rider Haggard in
      Colombo'.
      Evening Post and Advocate of Ceylon, 1 February, 'The Visit of
      Sir H. Rider Haggard'.
      Age (Melbourne), 18 February, 'Sir Rider Haggard – Fiction Writing
      and Agriculture'.
      Lyttelton Times, 1 March, 'Sir Rider Haggard. The Author of *King
      Solomon's Mines* not interested in Romance'.
      Sydney Evening News, 30 March, 'Sir Rider Haggard – Story Writer and
      Farmer'.
      Daily Mail (Brisbane) 18 April, 'Resources of the North, – interview.
      The Advertiser (Adelaide), 12 May. 'Sir Rider Haggard' – interview.
1914 *Cape Argus*, 2 March, 'After 30 Years – Sir Rider Haggard Again in
      South Africa'.
      Natal Witness, 26 March, 'Old Scents – Sir Rider Haggard's return to
      Natal'.
      Natal Witness, 30 March, 'Saved His Master's life. Novelist and his
      faithful servant'.
      Pictorial (Durban) 3 April, 'Sir Rider Haggard and Masuku'.
      Transvaal Leader, 31 March, 'Sir Rider Haggard's Return'.
      Natal Mercury, 18 April, 'Sir Rider Haggard – Talks of Old Durban'.
      Athenaeum, 10 October, 'Mameena' – review.
1915 *Eastern Daily Press*, 28 August, 'Lord Selborne's Speech' – interview.
1916 *Morning Post*, 10 January, 'Land Settlement after the War' – interview.
      Mercury (Hobart) 4 April, 'Land for soldiers' – interview.
      Sydney Morning Herald, 25 May, 'After the War' – interview.
      The Dominion (Wellington) 1 June, 'To Save the Race' – interview.
      Victoria Daily Times, 30 June, 'Seeking Avocations for Ex-Servicemen'
      – interview.
      New York Tribune, 22 July, ' "Britain's Superfluous Women Driving
      Men Out", says Haggard' – interview.
      East Anglian Daily Times, 9 August, 'Sir Rider Haggard's Colonial
      Tour'.

Lloyd's Weekly News, 26 November, 'Land Settlement and the Empire' – interview.

1917 *Daily Chronicle*, 2 January, 'Sir Rider Haggard's Plea of ''More from the Land'' ' – interview.

1920 *St Leonards' Chronicle*, 9 January, 'The Man of the Week – Sir H. Rider Haggard'.
John O'London's Weekly, 1 May, 'A Rider Haggard Boom in France? – Has *She* been plagiarised?'
Daily Sketch, 28 June, 'Parentage is far too costly' – interview.

1921 *Bookman*, London, March, '*She* and Allan' – a biographical sketch.
John O'London's Weekly, 5 March, 'The Romances of Rider Haggard' by M. Joseph.

1922 *Bookman*, London, August, 'Sir H. Rider Haggard and his work' by Wilfred L. Randell.

1923 *Westminster Gazette*, 14 February, 'Opening of the Inner Tomb (of Tutankhamen) on Sunday' – interview.
Sunday Express, 18 February, 'Descrating the Dead. A Protest by Sir H. Rider Haggard' – interview.
John O'London's Weekly, 17 November, 'Ride On, Sir Knight, Ride On! Sir Rider Haggard and His Art'.

1924 *London Mercury*, November, 'Sir Rider Haggard and the Novel of Adventure' by Edward Shanks.

1925 *New York Post*, 14 May. 'H. Rider Haggard'.
The Times, 15 May, 'H. Rider Haggard' – obituary notice.
The Times, 25 May, 'Sir H. Rider Haggard. His Life and Career'.
John O'London's Weekly, 30 May, 'A Master of Romance. Sir H. Rider Haggard and his many novels'.
John O'London's Weekly, 27 June, 'A Memory of Sir Rider Haggard'.
The Times, 1 August, 'Report of the Legacies in Haggard's will'.

1926 Reviews of *The Days of My Life*
Edinburgh Review, October; *Bookman*, London, November.

1928 *The Times*, 18 November, 'The sale of Kessingland Grange'.

1935 *Pearson's Magazine*, January, 'The Real Rider Haggard' by Lilias Rider Haggard.

1936 *The Farmer's Weekly*, 11 September, 'Champion of the British Farmer' by Wilfred Partington.

1937 *Dictionary of National Bibliography*, 'Sir H. Rider Haggard' by Hugh Walpole.

1944 *The Papers of the Bibliographical Society of America*, first quarter, 'The New South Africa', by J. E. Scott (proving that Haggard did not write this pamphlet but one William Adolf Baillie-Groham).
Times Literary Supplement, 27 May, 'He, She and It' by Roger Lancelyn Green.

Times Literary Supplement, 1 July, 'King Solomon's Wives' by Roger
Lancelyn Green.

1945 *Everybody's Weekly*, 12 May, 'Africa's Writer of Romance' by Norman
Colgan.
John O'London's Weekly, 18 May, 'The Two Rider Haggards' by Peter
Gamble.
English, Summer issue 'The Romances of Rider Haggard' by Roger
Lancelyn Green.

1946 Elikin Mathews Ltd, Catalogue 102, May. *Books from the library of
Sir H. Rider Haggard.*

1951 *Illustrated London News*, 26 May, 'The Adventurous Life of a Great
Storyteller'.
Spectator, 15 June. Arthur Ransome reviews *The Cloak That I Left.*
New Statesman, 14 July, Graham Greene reviews '*The Cloak That I
Left*' (later collected in Greene's *Collected Essays*, Bodley Head, 1969).

1956 *Kipling Journal*, April, 'Rudyard Kipling and Rider Haggard' by Mrs G.
Broughton.
Times Literary Supplement, 11 April. 'The Wheat and the Chaff'.
Radio Times, 29 June. 'The Most Amazing Book Ever Written' by
Newman Flower.
Library World, July. 'H. Rider Haggard' by Roger Lancelyn Green.
Eastern Daily Press, 22 June, 'H. Rider Haggard' by Roger Lancelyn
Green.
Junior Bookshelf, October, 'H. Rider Haggard' by Roger Lancelyn
Green.

1971 *Classic Film Collector*, Fall issue, 'A Penetrating Look at a Famous
Novel and Movie' by Charles E. Carley.

1974 *Classic Film Collector*, Winter issue, 'Haggard a Biography and a
Filmography' by Charles E. Carley.
Riverside Quarterly, vol. 6 nos 1 and 2 (January and April), 'The
Prudish Prudence of H. Rider Haggard and Edgar Rice Burroughs' by
Richard Dale Mullen (Indiana State University).

1976 *Country Life*, 9 December, 'Rider Haggard As a Rural Reformer' by
Peter Berresford Ellis.

Two interesting articles on the chronology of the Allan Quatermain novels can
be found as follows:

1 'A Note Concerning the late Mr Allan Quatermain' by J. E. Scott
introducing his *A Bibliography of the Works of Sir Henry Rider Haggard
1856–1925*, Elkin Mathews Ltd, Takeley, Bishop's Stortford, Herts, 1947.

2 'An Interview with the late Mr Allan Quatermain' by Roger Lancelyn
Green was written in 1947, in reply to Scott, but not published until

1975 in his book *Holmes, this is amazing – essays in unorthodox research*, privately printed, London, 1975.

General works

Allen, Ralph Bergen, *Old Icelandic Sources in the English Novel. A Thesis*, Pennsylvania Press, University of Philadelphia, 1933.

Asche, Oscar, *Oscar Asche, His Life*, Hurst & Blackett, London, 1929.

Barker, Ernest, *History of the English Novel*, H. F. and G. Witherby, London, 1938.

Bleiler, E. F., *The Checklist of Fantastic Literature*, Shasta, Chicago, 1948.

Bensusan, S. L., *Latter Day Rural England*, Ernest Been, London, 1928.

Bremont, Anna, Comtesse de, *Sonnets and Love Poems*, J. J. Little, New York, 1892.

Buckley, Jerome Hamilton, *William Ernest Henley: A Study in Counter Decadence of the 'Nineties*, Princeton University Press, 1945.

Carrington, Charles Edmund, *The Life of Rudyard Kipling*, Macmillan, 1955.

Colvin, Sir Sidney (ed.), *The Letters of Robert Louis Stevenson to his Family and Friends*, 4 vols Methuen, London, 1899.

Connell, John, *W. E. Henley*, Constable, London, 1949.

Crisp, R. and Davies, P., *The Outlanders*, Historical Assocation, London, 1964.

Darton, F. J. Harvey, *Children's Books in England*, Cambridge University Press, 1932.

Ernle, Lord, *English Farming Past and Present*, Longmans, Green, London, 1932.

Fodor, Nándor, *New Approaches to Dream Interpretation*, Citadel Press, New York, 1951.

Fodor, Nándor, *The Search for the Beloved. A clinical investigation of the trauma of birth and the pre-natal condition*, Hermitage Press, New York, 1949 (based on a piece in the *Psychiatric Quarterly*, State Hospital Press, Utica, New York, 1946).

French, Gerald, Lord Chelmsford and the Zulu War, John Lane, London, 1939.

Fussell, G. E. and K. R., *The English Countryman*, Andrew Melrose, London, 1955.

Gosse, Sir Edmund William, *Critical Kit-Kats*, Heinemann, London, 1896.

Green, Roger Lancelyn, *Andrew Lang: A Critical Biography*, Edmund Ward, Leicester, 1946. Revised edition, Bodley Head, London, 1962.

Green, Roger Lancelyn, *A. E. W. Mason*, Max Parrish, London, 1952.

Green, Roger Lancelyn, *Teller of Tales*, Edmund Ward, Leicester, 1946. Revised edition, 1965.

Greene, Graham, *Collected Essays*, Bodley Head, London, 1969.

Bibliography

Haggard, David, *A History of the Haggard family in England and America 1433 to 1899*, Bloomington, Illinois, 1899.

Haggard, Lilias Rider, *Too Late for Tears* (about the Margitson family), Waveney Publications, Ditchingham Lodge, Bungay, Suffolk.

Hofmeyer, Jan H., *South Africa*, Ernest Benn, London, 1921.

Hopkins, G. M., *The Letters of Gerard Manley Hopkins to Robert Bridges*, Oxford University Press, London, 1935.

Howe, Susanne, *Novels of Empire*, Columbia University Press, New York, 1949.

Jeaffreson, John Cordy, *A Book of Recollection*, 2 vols, Hurst & Blackett, London, 1894.

Jerome, K. Jerome, *My First Book*, Chatto & Windus, London, 1897.

Jung, Carl G., *The Integration of Personality*, translated by Stanley M. Dell, Kegan Paul, London, 1940.

Jung, Carl G., *Psychology of the Unconscious* etc., translated by Beatrice M. Hinkle, Kegan Paul, London, 1916.

Kipling, Rudyard, *Something of Myself*, Macmillan, London, 1937.

Kotzé, John, *Biographical Memoirs and Reminiscences*, Maskew Miller, Cape Town (undated).

Kotzé, John, *Cases Decided in the High Court of the Transvaal Province July 1877 to 1881*, Stevens & Haynes, London, 1912.

Lang, Andrew, *The Poetical Works of Andrew Lang*, edited by Mrs Andrew Lang, 4 vols, Longmans, Green, London, 1923.

Lawrence, David Herbert, *The Letters of D. H. Lawrence*, edited and introduced by Aldous Huxley, Heinemann, London, 1932.

Lewis, C. S., *Rehabilitation and Other Essays*, Oxford University Press, London, 1939.

Leyds, W. J., *The First Annexation of the Transvaal*, Unwin, London, 1906.

Lehmann, Joseph, *The First Boer War*, Cape, London, 1972.

Longman, Charles J., *The House of Longman (1724–1800)*, Longmans, Green, London, 1936.

Mackail, Denis, *The Story of JMB*, Peter Davies, London, 1941.

March–Phillips, L. and Christian, B., *Some Harwarden Letters 1878–1913*, London, 1918.

Martineau, John, *The Life and Correspondence of Sir Bartle Frere*, 2 vols, John Murray, London, 1894.

Miller, Henry, *The Books in My Life*, Peter Owen, London, 1952.

Morris, Donald R., *The Washing of the Spears*, Cape, London, 1965.

Nathan, Manfred, *Paul Kruger. His Life and Times*, Knox Publishing, Durban, 1942.

Norris-Newman, Charles L., *In Zululand with the British Throughout the War of 1879*, W. H. Allen, 1880.

Nowell-Smith, Simon, *The House of Cassell 1848–1958*, Cassell, London, 1958.

Orwin, C. S., *History of English Farming*, Thomas Nelson, London, 1949.

Pemberton, Max, *Sixty Years and After*, Hutchinson, London, 1936.

Pemberton, W. Baring, *Battles of the Boer War*, Batsford, London, 1964.

Sandison, Alan, *The Wheel of Empire*, Macmillan, London and St Martin's Press, New York, 1967.

Scarborough, Dorothy, *The Supernatural in Modern English Fiction*, G. P. Putnam, New York and London, 1917.

Stevenson, Fanny (van de Grift) and Robert Louis, *Our Samoan Adventure*, edited and introduced by Charles Neider, Weidenfeld & Nicolson, London, 1956.

Stevenson, Fanny (van de Grift) and Robert Louis, *An Object of Pity: or the Man Haggard. A Romance by Many Competent Hands*, Constable, Edinburgh, 1898. (A burlesque in prose and verse by R. L. Stevenson, the Hon. Rupert Leigh, Lady Jersey, Fanny Stevenson, Isobel Strong, Sir Graham Balfour.)

Theal, G. M., *History of South Africa 1873–1884*, Allen & Unwin, London, 1919.

Tindall, William York, *Forces in Modern British Literature 1881–1946*, Knopf, New York, 1947.

Ulys, Cornelius Janse, *In The Era of Shepstone. Being a study of British expansion in South Africa 1842–1877*, Lovedale Press, Lovedale, 1933.

Walker, Eric A., *A History of South Africa*, Longmans, Green, London, 1928.